Ethiopian Amharic

lonely planet

phrasebooks
and
Tilahun Kebede

Ethiopian Amharic phrasebook
3rd edition – September 2008

Published by
Lonely Planet Publications Pty Ltd ABN 36 005 607 983
90 Maribyrnong St, Footscray, Victoria 3011, Australia

Lonely Planet Offices
Australia Locked Bag 1, Footscray, Victoria 3011
USA 150 Linden St, Oakland CA 94607
UK 2nd Floor, 186 City Rd, London EC1V 2NT

Cover illustration
by Patrick Marris

ISBN 978 1 74059 645 9

acknowledgments

about the authors

Tilahun Kebede was inspired to write an Amharic phrasebook after working as a guide/translator for travellers to Ethiopia. He's now based in Sydney where he balances a career in finance and freelance translating. Catherine Snow is an Australian researcher/writer who has spent some of her finest moments in Ethiopia and East Africa. Daniel Aberra provided the Sustainable Travel section.

from the authors

Thanks to Ethiopian diaspora everywhere for keeping community life and the internet alive with Ethiopian music and culture. Special thanks to Tilahun's parents, Roman for medical expertise and Kebede for general assistance. Thanks to Kefyalew Mekonnen for insightful advice, and other friends, colleagues and family who gave support and assistance.

from the publisher

Publishing Manager Jim Jenkin was a blur through the smoke from the starting pistol's retort – the Amharic marathon had begun. He ran with ease through the opening stages to set his team up for a pain-free race. Commissioning Editors Karina Coates and Karin Vidstrup Monk ensured that every foot landed in the right place. Ben Handicott kept hurting his, but set the pace and edited out the pain. Adrienne Costanzo weeded out the weaklings with her proofer's eye. Sophie Putman showed late dictatorial form, so launching the weary competitors towards the end. Patrick Marris found it such a breeze, he had time to stop and draw the pretty pictures. He then helped fellow designers Yukiyoshi Kamimura and Belinda Campbell (in a swan-song performance) get it all on to the printed page. The final touches were applied by assisting editors Branislava Vladisavljevic and Laura Crawford, managing editor Annelies Mertens and layout designer David Kemp. Natasha Velleley and Wayne Murphy created the map. Project Managers Fabrice Rocher and Rachel Williams kept the team neat and tidy throughout, while cheering it past the wall and over the finish line with encouraging cries of əg·zer yi·ma·rəh, just before lighting up.

make the most of this phrasebook ...

Anyone can speak another language! It's all about confidence. Don't worry if you can't remember your school language lessons or if you've never learnt a language before. Even if you learn the very basics (on the inside covers of this book), your travel experience will be the better for it. You have nothing to lose and everything to gain when the locals hear you making an effort.

finding things in this book

For easy navigation, this book is in sections. The Pronunciation and Grammar chapters are the ones you'll thumb through time and again. The Getting Around and Accommodation chapters cover basic travel situations like catching transport and finding a bed. The Meeting People and Interests chapters give you conversational phrases and the ability to express opinions – so you can get to know people. Food has a section all of its own: gourmets and vegetarians are covered and local dishes feature. The Health and Emergencies chapters equip you with health and police phrases, just in case. The Sustainable Travel section, finally, completes this book. Use the comprehensive Index to find everything easily. Otherwise, check the traveller's Dictionary for the word you need.

being understood

Throughout this book you'll see coloured phrases on each page. They're phonetic guides to help you pronounce the language. Start with them to get a feel for how the language sounds. The Pronunciation chapter will explain more, but you can be confident that if you read the coloured phrase, you'll be understood.

communication tips

Body language, ways of doing things, sense of humour – all have a role to play in every culture. The boxes included throughout this phrasebook give you useful cultural and linguistic information that will help you communicate with the locals and enrich your travel experience.

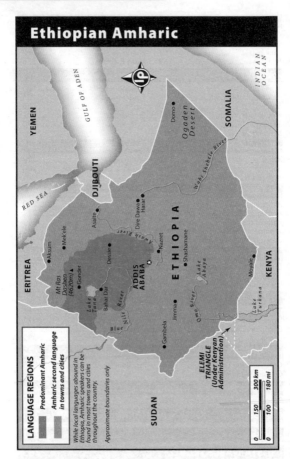

Ethiopian Amharic

LANGUAGE REGIONS

Predominant Amharic

Amharic second language in towns and cities

While local languages abound in Ethiopia, Amharic speakers can be found in most towns and cities throughout the country.

Approximate boundaries only

YEMEN

GULF OF ADEN

INDIAN OCEAN

SOMALIA

Domo

Ogaden Desert

Wabi Shebele River

DJIBOUTI

RED SEA

Asaïta

Dire Dawa

Harar

ERITREA

Aksum

Mek'ele

Awash River

Nazret

ETHIOPIA

Mt Ras Dashen (4620m)▲

Gonder

Dessie

ADDIS ABABA

Shashamane

Lake Abaya

Bahar Dar

Lake Tana

Blue Nile River

Jimma

Omo River

Lake Turkana

Moyale

KENYA

Gambela

SUDAN

ELEMI TRIANGLE (Under Kenyan Administration)

0   150   300 km
0   100   180 mi

INTRODUCTION

Amharic is indigenous to Ethiopia and is the most widely used and understood language in the country. Just a few basic phrases will guide you through stunning landscapes to mystical churches, ancient sites and the bustling backstreets of Ethiopian towns. Here, bold Ethiopic script adorns shop fronts, murals and drink bottles, stamping everything with a distinct regional flavour.

Amharic is the official language of the media and government, and widely used in cross-cultural communications. It's the mother tongue of the Amhara people, who originate from the central and north-western highlands. There are over 80 other indigenous languages spoken in Ethiopia, including Tigrinya, Oromo and Gurage. English is also spoken, but mainly by educated urban people.

Like Arabic, Hebrew and Assyrian, Amharic is a Semitic language, belonging to the Afro-Asiatic family. There are three main subgroups of this family in Ethiopia: the Ethiopic subgroup, including Amharic and Tigrinya; the Cushitic subgroup, including Somali and Oromo languages; and Omotic, including the Wolayitta language. In Ethiopia's south-west, you'll also come across Nilo-Saharan languages, including Nuer and Mursi dialects. For many Ethiopians, Amharic remains a second language; learning a few words in local languages will be a boon to your travels.

Historical Origins

Ethiopia's rich and ancient culture is reflected in the history of its languages. Around the first millennium BC, the people of northern Ethiopia and present-day Eritrea began to establish solid contacts with the people of south-west Arabia, just over the Red Sea. New languages began to emerge from this interaction, including Ge'ez.

Ge'ez is the current liturgical language of the Ethiopian Orthodox Church – used in church chants, and sacred manuscripts even to this day. The current Ethiopic alphabet, used to write Amharic and Tigrinya, is adapted from Ge'ez.

INTRODUCTION

Ge'ez began as the language of the Aksum Empire that dominated northern Ethiopia from the 1st to the 6th centuries AD. As the empire went into decline, the power base shifted to the Amhara region. From the 10th to the 12th centuries, the use of Amharic became more widespread.

Over following centuries, ruling regimes tended to be Amhara-led. This, combined with the region's mountainous terrain and geographic isolation, ensured the spread and development of the language continued. Apart from the Italian occupation from 1936 to 1941, Ethiopia escaped long periods of European colonial domination. Extensive bodies of Amharic literature and sophisticated grammar and vocabulary were able to evolve unhindered. Although the written language was initially the domain of the church and the elite, modernisation in the 19th and 20th centuries encouraged its use among Ethiopians from all backgrounds. The last decade has seen a greater emphasis on regional languages for literacy, learning and the bureaucracy, so more people in Oromo regions are using Oromo, more people in Tigre are using Tigrinya, and so on.

As a visitor to the country, you'll invite both hospitality and curiosity. By speaking Amharic and throwing in some local words and phrases, your finest moments will be encounters with local people – the chat with a farmer after he ushers you into his hut to escape the rain, the jokes with kids at streetside markets, and the camaraderie with local bus passengers as you travel across the country.

ABBREVIATIONS USED IN THIS BOOK

adj	adjective	n	noun
f	feminine	pl	plural
inf	informal	pol	polite
lit	literal translation	sg	singular
m	masculine	v	verb

Tune into the sounds of Ethiopia's streets for tips on pronunciation: a mini-bus worker trilling his r as he calls the destination, a·rat ki·lo!; a vendor clicking her ķ's as she advertises her spicy snacks, ķo·lo, ķo·lo!; a man waving down a friend from a street-side café, weun·dəm!, 'Hey brother!'. Though some Amharic sounds have no English equivalents, with a bit of practice, you'll be told you're gob·beuz, 'brilliant', by native Amharic speakers.

VOWEL SOUNDS

Listen for eu and ə, the most common Amharic vowels. They can sound quite similar to non-native speakers, but they are different. Be on the 'look out' and you'll soon discover the subtleties for yourself.

a	as the 'a' in 'father'
ai	as the 'ai' in aisle
ay	similar to the 'ay' in 'day'
e	as the 'e' in 'bed'
eu	as the 'e' in 'her' (without the 'r' sound); similar to the 'eu' in the French *neuf*
ə	as the 'e' in 'garden'
i	as the 'i' in 'bit'
o	similar to the 'o' in 'hot'
ow	similar to the 'ow' in 'cow'
ō	as the 'o' in 'both'
u	as the 'u' in 'flute'

CONSONANT SOUNDS

The following consonants are used throughout the book and pronounced pretty much as you'd expect in English:

b , d , f , m , n , v , w

The consonants below are pronounced as specified:

ch	as the 'ch' in 'chew'
g	as the 'g' in 'get'
h	as the 'h' in 'horse'
k	as the 'k' in 'kin'
j	as the 'j' in 'jaw'
l	as the 'l' in 'light'
ny	similar to 'ny' in 'canyon' (never as the 'ny' in 'pony')
p	as the 'p' in 'pot'
r	trilled, like the Spanish 'r'
s	as the 's' in 'plus'
sh	as the 'sh' in 'ship'
t	as the 't' in 'time', but the tongue touches the teeth
y	as the 'y' in 'yes'
z	as the 'z' in 'zoo'
zh	as the 's' in 'pleasure'

PRONUNCIATION

DOUBLE TALK

Double consonants indicate a longer, clearer sound than a single consonant – however don't divide them completely, as they're not two separate sounds.

Double consonant:	al·leu	'there is'
Single consonant:	a·leu	'he said'

Glottalic Consonants

Glottalic consonant sounds are made by tightening and releasing the glottis (the space between the vocal chords) when pronouncing a consonant, and may require some practice.

They're similar to the vocal movements made in 'uh-oh' or the cockney 'tt' in 'butter'. Try the following with basic vowels (eg, ḳa, ḳeu, ḳi, ḳo, ḳu, etc) before rolling them into words like ṭeuj, 'honey wine', ḳeuz·ḳaz·za, 'cold', and ṣeu·hai, 'sun'. Pronouncing these sounds as if the under-dot wasn't there is often OK, but beware of exceptions. For example, 'he hit' is meut·ta, while 'he came' is meuṭ·ṭa.

ch   like an emphasised 'tch' in 'witch'
ḳ   like an emphasised 'ck' in 'yuck'
p   a short, popping 'p', as the first 'p' in 'pop'
ṣ   a hissing 's' sound like an emphasised 's' in 'its'
ṭ   a spitting 't' sound like an emphasised 't' in 'hot'
'   as the 'tt' in the cockney 'butter'

PRONUNCIATION

STRESS

In general, stress falls equally on each syllable in Amharic. Pace things slowly and evenly to start with – for example, bun·na meug·zat ə·feul·lə·gal·lō, 'I want to buy coffee'. You'll loosen up as you develop a feel for the rhythms used.

INTONATION

In Amharic, a rising tone at the end of a sentence signifies a question – and there is no re-ordering of words as there often is in English sentences. For example, the English 'Is he going?' would simply be yi·he·dal? (lit: he is going?). 'Does it work?' in Amharic is simply yi·seu·ral? (lit: it works?).

PRONUNCIATION

TRANSLITERATION

There's not always a clear relationship between the spelling of Amharic script and its pronunciation. The spelling of words transliterated into Roman script in this book has therefore been modified to enable you to pronounce words more easily and accurately. Be aware that there is a range of transliteration schemes used in Amharic language courses, dictionaries and software – always look at the transliteration/pronunciation guides to avoid confusion.

SCRIPT

As well as helping you to read public signs and notices, the Amharic alphabet will help you to communicate – if you have trouble pronouncing a phrase, just point to the script!

Alphabet – *Fidel*

The unique Ethiopic alphabet (commonly referred to as a syllabary) was adapted from Ge'ez and is used to write Amharic and several other regional languages, including Tigrinya and Tigre. Oromo is now mainly written in roman script.

In a syllabary, characters usually represent consonant-vowel clusters. The Amharic version (known as fi·deul) consists of 33 basic characters. Each character combines with an additional stroke or symbol to produce one of seven possible consonant-vowel combinations or single vowels. As with roman script, the characters run from left to right across the page.

Note that some sounds have more than one character – this reflects historical changes to the writing system and, like English spelling, Amharic spelling is not always regular.

AMHARIC SYLLABARY

	eu	u	i	a	e	ə	o
h	ሀ	ሁ	ሂ	ሃ	ሄ	ህ	ሆ
l	ለ	ሉ	ሊ	ላ	ሌ	ል	ሎ
h	ሐ	ሑ	ሒ	ሓ	ሔ	ሕ	ሖ
m	መ	ሙ	ሚ	ማ	ሜ	ም	ሞ
s	ሠ	ሡ	ሢ	ሣ	ሤ	ሥ	ሦ
r	ረ	ሩ	ሪ	ራ	ሬ	ር	ሮ
s	ሰ	ሱ	ሲ	ሳ	ሴ	ስ	ሶ
sh	ሸ	ሹ	ሺ	ሻ	ሼ	ሽ	ሾ
k	ቀ	ቁ	ቂ	ቃ	ቄ	ቅ	ቆ
b	በ	ቡ	ቢ	ባ	ቤ	ብ	ቦ
t	ተ	ቱ	ቲ	ታ	ቴ	ት	ቶ
ch	ቸ	ቹ	ቺ	ቻ	ቼ	ች	ቾ
h	ኀ	ኁ	ኂ	ኃ	ኄ	ኅ	ኆ
n	ነ	ኑ	ኒ	ና	ኔ	ን	ኖ
ny	ኘ	ኙ	ኚ	ኛ	ኜ	ኝ	ኞ
vowel	አ	ኡ	ኢ	ኣ	ኤ	እ	ኦ
k	ከ	ኩ	ኪ	ካ	ኬ	ክ	ኮ
h	ኸ	ኹ	ኺ	ኻ	ኼ	ኽ	ኾ
w	ወ	ዉ	ዊ	ዋ	ዌ	ው	ዎ
vowel	ዐ	ዑ	ዒ	ዓ	ዔ	ዕ	ዖ
z	ዘ	ዙ	ዚ	ዛ	ዜ	ዝ	ዞ
zh	ዠ	ዡ	ዢ	ዣ	ዤ	ዥ	ዦ
y	የ	ዩ	ዪ	ያ	ዬ	ይ	ዮ
d	ደ	ዱ	ዲ	ዳ	ዴ	ድ	ዶ
j	ጀ	ጁ	ጂ	ጃ	ጄ	ጅ	ጆ
g	ገ	ጉ	ጊ	ጋ	ጌ	ግ	ጎ
t	ጠ	ጡ	ጢ	ጣ	ጤ	ጥ	ጦ
ch	ጨ	ጩ	ጪ	ጫ	ጬ	ጭ	ጮ
p	ጰ	ጱ	ጲ	ጳ	ጴ	ጵ	ጶ
s	ጸ	ጹ	ጺ	ጻ	ጼ	ጽ	ጾ
s	ፀ	ፁ	ፂ	ፃ	ፄ	ፅ	ፆ
f	ፈ	ፉ	ፊ	ፋ	ፌ	ፍ	ፎ
p	ፐ	ፑ	ፒ	ፓ	ፔ	ፕ	ፖ

PRONUNCIATION

LOST IN THE TRANSLATION

Colonial powers were shameless in their efforts to conquer Ethiopia, even resorting to a tactic of mistranslating state documents.

In 1889, Ethiopia's Emperor Menelik II signed the Treaty of Wechale with the Italian government. The treaty allowed for an Italian protectorate to be established over Ethiopia. At least, that's what the Italian version said – the Amharic version mentioned no such thing! Menelik only discovered the deception when Britain and Germany refused invitations to his coronation on the grounds that he was meant to communicate with them 'via the Italian government'. Menelik stopped the Italian expansion into the country by famously defeating them at the Battle of Adwa (northern Ethiopia) in 1896.

A few points on grammar will help you construct your own basic sentences in Amharic. Before you dive in, it's wise to take heed of an old Amharic saying: ƙeus beu ƙeus ən·ƙu·lal beug·ru yi·he·dal, 'Slowly, slowly an egg learns to walk'. Take things bit by bit and, slowly but surely, it'll start to come together.

Note that the system used to represent Amharic in this chapter differs to that described in the Pronunciation chapter and used in the rest of the book. This is to help illustrate the grammatical structure of words and phrases.

SENTENCE STRUCTURE

The word order of Amharic sentences is generally subject-object-verb:

Lydia wants coffee.	lidiya bunna təfeulləgalleuch
	(lit: Lydia coffee she-wants)
David bought a shirt.	david sheumiz geuzza
	(lit: David shirt he-bought)

However, the subject and object is often built into the verb:

They bought it.	geuzzut
	(lit: they-bought-it)

DON'T GET IN AF-FIX

One Amharic word often carries the same meaning as two or three English words, for example, abbate (lit: father-my) or yihedal (lit: he-is-going).

This is because Amharic uses many affixes (letters attached to words) instead of separate words to indicate things like tense, subject, object and gender. These include suffixes (letters attached to the end of words) and prefixes (letters attached to the beginning of words). Recognising the sound and meaning of these affixes will benefit you in your efforts to learn Amharic.

ARTICLES

The indefinite articles 'a' and 'an' aren't used in Amharic:

> I want a taxi.   taksi əfeulləgallō
> (lit: taxi I-want)

The definite article 'the' is used in Amharic.

When nouns are the subject of a sentence, the definite article appears as a suffix attached to the end of the noun, as follows:

- When nouns are the subject of a verb ('what' or 'who' is performing the action) you generally use -u after a consonant or -w after a vowel:

  > The bus is going.   owtobəs-u yihedal
  > (lit: bus-the it-is-going)

  Note that when the definite article -w follows a vowel, it often changes the sound of that vowel. Following an 'a', for example, the sound will be ow, as in 'cow'. In contrast, after an 'o', the sound is ō as in 'toe'.

- If the subject is female, small, or the object of affection, use -wa, -itu or -itwa:

  > The child sings.   ləj-itwa təzeufeunalleuch
  > (lit: girl-the she-sings)

- When sō, 'man', or set, 'woman', is the subject of a sentence, use the following endings:

  > sō-yō   (lit: man-the)
  > setə-yowa (lit: woman-the)

Nouns that are the object of a sentence (what or whom the verb is referring to, or acting on) also take the definite article. Add -n to the appropriate subject suffixes for the definite article listed above:

> I see the bus.   owtobəs-u-n aiyō
> (lit: bus-the I-see)
> Call the man.   sō-yō-n ţəra (m)
> (lit: man-the you-call)

NOUNS
Plurals

There's no need to mark a noun plural in Amharic if the number is clear from the context. Take, for example, the phrase bəzu kʼərchat (lit: many basket) – bəzu implies more than one, so the notion of 'plural' is clear. Or if you point to a bunch of flowers, and say, kʼonjo abeuba (lit: beautiful flower), it's obvious you mean the whole bunch.

If the quantity is not obvious from the context, nouns are made plural by attaching the suffix -och to words ending in a consonant or -woch to words ending in a vowel:

I want to see a lion.   anbeussa mayeut əfeulləgallō
                           (lit: lion to-see I-want)
I want to see lions.   anbeussa-woch mayeut əfeulləgallō
                           (lit: lion-s to-see I-want)

The plural suffix comes before the definite article suffix (in this example, the object definite article, -un):

Look at the lions.   anbeussa-woch-un teumeulkeut (m)
                           (lit: lion-s-the you-look-at)

YOU TALKIN' TO ME?

You'll notice the use of (m), 'masculine', and (f), 'feminine', after a number of the phrases throughout this book. These refer to the gender of the person you're speaking to, not your own gender. So, if you're speaking to a woman, use the (f) form, whether you're a man or a woman.

You'll also see (pol), 'polite', and (pl), 'plural' – if you're speaking to elders or authority figures, use the (pol) form, and if you're speaking to a group of people, use the (pl) form.

ADJECTIVES

Adjectives generally precede the noun:

I want a cheap umbrella.   rəkash janṭəlla əfeulləgallō
                           (lit: cheap umbrella I-want)

Attach definite articles to the adjective, not the noun:

The big bus is going.   təlləḳ-u owtobəs yihedal
                        (lit: big-the bus it's-going)
Look at the small bird.   tənnish-wan weuf teumeulkeut
                          (lit: small-the bird look-at)

Adjectives often change form if the noun is plural:

təlləḳ meukina   (lit: big car)
tələlləḳ meukinawoch (lit: big cars)

Using the singular form of an adjective with a plural noun will
still get the message across though.

Forming Adjectives

Some adjectives are formed by attaching the prefix yeu (meaning
'of' or 'pertaining to') to the noun:

cultural performance   yeu bahəl cheuwata
                       (lit: of culture performance)

yeu- is also often used to indicate possession (see page 24).

Descriptive Verbs

Often the subject and descriptive word is itself a verb in Amharic,
for example:

I'm hot.   mokeuny
           (lit: hot-I'm)
I'm cold.   beureudeuny
            (lit: cold-I'm)

Comparatives

There are a number of ways to form comparatives in Amharic.
One way is to place keu, 'from', between the subjects:

He's taller than me.   əssu keu əne reujim nō
                        (lit: he from I tall he-is)

You can do the same thing using descriptive verbs instead of adjectives. A few descriptive verbs even have comparative meanings:

Trousers are better   suri keu ķeumiss yishalal
    than a dress.   (lit: trousers from dress it's-better)

Sometimes the words for 'more', yiləķ or yibeulṭ, are used
between the items being compared, for emphasis:

Wine's better than beer.   keu bira yiləķ wain ṭəru nō
                           (lit: from beer more wine good it-is)

Superlatives

There are no specific superlative adjectives in Amharic. However,
you can form something close to a superlative by using beuṭam,
'very', before the adjective and attaching the definite article (-u or
-wa) to the adjective:

the cheapest hotel   beuṭam rəkash-u hotel
                        (lit: very cheap-the hotel)
the nearest monastery   beuṭam ķərb-wa deubər
                        (lit: very near-the monastery)

GRAMMAR

ADVERBS

Adverbs generally come before the verb in Amharic. It's not necessary to make them agree in number, gender, etc:

Please go slowly.	əbakəh ḵeuss beul(m)
	(lit: please slow you-be)
Please come quickly.	əbakəsh tolo nay(f)
	(lit: please quick you-come)

The prefix beu- is sometimes attached to abstract nouns to form adverbs:

He drives fast.	beu-fətneut yineudal
	(lit: by-speed he-drives)

PRONOUNS
Personal Pronouns

Amharic subject pronouns in the 2nd and 3rd person singular, 'you' and 'he/she/it', have a polite form, a masculine form and a feminine form. Use the polite form when addressing people older than you or people in positions of authority. The feminine form is also used for people or things that are small or the object of affection (the diminutive form).

You'll find that subject and object pronouns are often omitted in Amharic sentences, as they're built onto the verb stem (see Verbs, page 24).

Personal Pronouns			
I/me	əne	she/it	əsswa, ərswa
you	anteu/anchi (m/f)	you (pl)	ənnanteu
	ərswo/əsswo (pl/pol)	we	ənya
he/it	əssu, ərsu	they	ənneussu

GRAMMAR

Possessive Pronouns

Possessive pronouns are indicated by attaching a suffix to the noun.
They can also be formed with the use of yeu.

	nouns ending in consonants	noun ending in vowels
my	-e	-ye
your (m)	-əh	-h
your (f)	-əsh	-sh
your (pol)	-wo	-wo
his/its	-u	-w
her/its	-wa	-wa
your (pl)	-achu	-chu
our	-achən	-chən
their	-achō	-chō

my bag	shanṭa-ye
	(lit: bag-my)
your name	səm-əh (m)
	səm-əsh (f)
	(lit: name-your)
our dinner	ərat-achən
	(lit: dinner-our)

GRAMMAR

If the noun is the object of a sentence, attach the definite article
-n after the possessive pronoun:

Give me my ticket.	tiket-e-n səṭeuny (m)
	(lit: ticket-my-the you-give-me)

POSSESSION

The prefix yeu is commonly used to indicate that something belongs to or pertains to something else:

the man's hat	yeu sōyō ķob
	(lit: of man-the hat)

Similarly, yeu is rolled into pronouns to form possessive pronouns:

It's your towel.	yanchi foṭa nō (f)
	(yeu + anchi = yanchi)
	(lit: of-you towel it-is)
She's my friend.	yeune gwadeunya nat
	(yeu + əne = yeune)
	(lit: of-me friend she-is)

VERBS

Verbs in Amharic change form to agree in tense, number and gender with the subjects and objects they refer to. This is achieved by attaching suffixes and prefixes to the verb stem. The meu- or ma- form is generally the infinitive. Some examples of verb stems you can use are:

hed	from	meuhed (to go)
geuz	from	meugzat (to buy)
beul	from	meublat (to eat)

These verb stems act as a kind of bare branch onto which leaves (affixes) are added to make the word whole. This will become clearer as you read through the examples below.

Present & Future

In Amharic, the present and future tenses are not distinguished by changes to the verb – exactly the same words (the same stems and affixes) are used for both:

I	ə...allō	she/it	tə...alleuch
you	tə...alleuh (m)	he/she/it	yi...allu (pol)
	tə...alleush (f)	we	ən...alleun
you	yi...allu (pol)	you (pl)	tə...allachu
he/it	yi...al	they	yi...allu

Take, for example, the verb stem hed from meuhed, 'to go':

She goes/is going/will go.	tə-hed-alleuch
They go/are going/will go.	yi-hed-allu
You go/are going/will go.	tə-hej-alleush (f)

Note that spelling is often adjusted with 2nd person feminine.

As a rule, the above forms used alone indicate present tense – the future tense is usually indicated by context or time words:

She'll go tomorrow.   neugeu tə-hed-alleuch
(lit: tomorrow she-goes)

Simple Past

For simple past tense (actions that have already been completed), add the following suffixes to the verb stem. Note that suffixes can vary depending on the type of infinitive verb.

I	...ow/ku
you	...h/kh (m)
you	...sh/sh (f)
you	...u (pol)
he/it	...a/eu
she/it	...ch/euch
you (pl)	...chu/achu
we	...n/ən
they	...u

For example:

She went.	hed-euch
We drank.	teuṭa-n
I arrived.	deurreus-ku

Continuous

To form a continuous past tense, attach the prefix əyeu- to the simple past tense, outlined above, and then add neubbeur, 'was'.

She was going.   əyeu-hedeuch neubbeur

For present continuous tense, use nō, 'is', instead of neubbeur.

Objects in Verbs

Amharic verbs often contain objects as well as subjects. This is done by attaching special object pronoun affixes, such as -aw- or -euw-, 'him/it' or -at-, 'her/it':

he'll bring	yameuṭal
He'll bring it.	yameuṭawal
I want	əfeulləgallō
I want it.	əfeulləgeuwallō
Let's ask.	ənṭeuyik̠
Let's ask her.	ənṭeuyik̠at

Negatives

There isn't a word for 'no' in Amharic. Instead, affixes are attached to verbs to form negative verbs. The most common are:

yeulleum	'there isn't/it's not there'
aideulleum	'it's not/it isn't'

Others include:

alfeulləgəm	(lit: I don't want)
alchəlləm	(lit: I can't)
yeuleunem	(lit: we don't have)

GRAMMAR

To make present/future tense verbs negative, you generally attach the following suffixes and prefixes to the verb stem. Suffixes may alter their vowel sounds depending on which verb stem is used:

I	al...m (əm)
you	at...m (əm)/at...m (im) (m/f)
you	ai...um (pol)
he/it	ai...m (əm)
she/it	at...m (əm)
you (pl)	at...um
we	an...m (əm)
they	ai...um

You can't.	atchəlləm
We don't like ...	... anweuddəm
They're not going.	aihedum

Note that in contrast to English, the answer to a negative question in Amharic is, in part, a positive response:

You're not eating?	atbeuyim? (f)
Yes, I'm not eating.	ow, albeulam

TO HAVE

The verb of existence – 'there exists', alleu, and 'there doesn't exist', yeulleum – is sometimes used on its own in place of 'have' and 'don't have', particularly when asking if something is available.

Do you have a candle?	shama alleu?
	(lit: candle there-exists)

In other situations, use the following words as you would in English:

I have	alleuny
you have	alleuh/alleush (m/f)
you have	allot (pol)
he/it has	allō
she/it has	allat
you (pl) have	allachu
we have	alleun
they have	allachō

GRAMMAR

TO BE

Note that in Amharic, the verb of existence – 'there exists' (alleu) and 'there doesn't exist' (yeulleum) – is often used where in English, the verb 'to be' would be used:

I am	neuny
you are	neuh/neush (m/f)
you are	not (pol)
he/it is	nō
she/it is	neuch
you (pl) are	nachu
we are	neun
they are	nachō
I'm a tourist.	gobəny neuny
	(lit: tourist I-am)
You're kind.	deugg neuh (m)
	(lit: kind you-are)

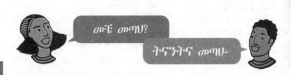

ESSENTIAL VERBS

Remember that verbs change their form according to tense, subject and gender. You can try extracting verb stems derived from the infinitives below and using them with the affixes outlined in Present & Future tense, page 24. There may be some adjustments you need to make to the verb stem (eg, eu may be needed for consonants without a vowel between them) – the following table is intended as a general guide only.

GRAMMAR

Essential Verbs

to arrive	meudreus
it arrived	deurswal
to ask	meuţeuyeuķ
ask him	ţeuyəkō
to buy	meugzat
I bought	geuzow
to come	meumţat
we came	meuţan
to do	madreug
she's doing	tadeurgalleuch
to drink	meuţeuţat
they're drinking	yiţeutallu
to give	meusţeut
give me	səţeuny
to go	meuhed
it isn't going	anhedəm
to know	maweuķ
I don't know	alawəkəm
to learn	meumar
he's learning	yimaral
to like	meuwdeud
do you like?	yiweudallu? (pol)
to live (somewhere)	meunor
you live ...	... tənoralleuh (m)
to love	mafķeur
he loves her	yafeukratal
to make	meusrat
you (pl) are making	təseurallachu
to meet	meugeunanyeut
let's meet	ənəgeunany
to pay	meukfeul
he paid	keufəlwal
to read	manbeub
you read (past)	anəbeushal (f)
to return	meumeulleus
she'll return	təmeulleusalleuch

Essential Verbs (cont)	
to stay	meukoyeut
I'm staying	əkoyallō
to see	mayeut
you see	aiyeuh (m)
to speak	meunageur
I speak	teunageurku
to write	meuşaf
you write	yişafu (pol)

MODALS

To indicate 'must', 'can' or 'want' in Amharic, use the Amharic equivalent of an infinitive – eg, meuhed, 'to go', mayeut, 'to see' – then add the modal ('must', 'can' or 'want'). The modal must agree with the subject in number and gender:

I want to go.   meuhed əfeulləgallō
                       (lit: to-go I-want)

Must

I must	alleubəny
you must	alleubəh/alleubəsh (m/f)
you must	alleubəwot (pol)
he/it must	alleubeut
she/it must	alleubat
you (pl) must	alleubachu
we must	alleubən
they must	alleubachō

We must go today.   zare meuhed alleubən
                       (lit: today to-go we-must)

Can

I can	əchəlallō
you can	təchəlalleuh/təchəyalleush (m/f)
you can	yichəlallu(pol)
he/it can	yichəlal
she/it can	təchəlalleuch
you (pl) can	təchəlallachu
we can	ənchəlalleun
they can	yichəlallu

We can go.	meuhed ənchəlalleun
	(lit: to-go we-can)

Want

I want	əfeullǝgallō
you want	təfeullǝgalleuh/
	təfeullǝgiyalleush (m/f)
you want	yifeullǝgallu (pol)
he/it wants	yifeullǝgal
she/it wants	təfeullǝgalleuch
you (pl) want	təfeullǝgallachu
we want	ənfeullǝgalleun
they want	yifeullǝgallu

We want to go by bus.	beu owtobəs meuhed
	ənfeullǝgalleun
	(lit: by bus to-go we-want)

QUESTIONS

In Amharic, a raised tone at the end of a sentence signifies a question
and there's no reordering of words as there often is in English (see
Intonation, page 13).

Amharic question words include:

What?	mən/məndən?
When?	meuche?
Who?	man?
Where?	yeut?
Why?	leumən/leuməndən?
How much/many?	sənt?

You'll most often see these with ... nō?, '... is it?', eg, sənt nō?,
'how much is it?', məndən nō?, 'what is it?' – but they can be
used in many different contexts:

What are you doing?	mən tareugalleuh? (m) (lit: what you're-doing)
When does it leave?	meuche yineusal? (lit: when it-leaves)
Who is it?	man nō? (lit: who it-is?)
Where can I find a coffee pot?	jeubeuna yeut yigeunyal? (lit: coffee-pot where it's-found)
Why didn't you come?	leumən almeutashəm? (lit: why you-didn't- come?)
How much time will it take?	sənt gize yiweusdal? (lit: how-much time it-takes)

GRAMMAR

CONJUNCTIONS

The conjunctions əna, 'and', and waym, 'or', appear between the two words they connect, as in English (note that if əna follows a word ending in a vowel, it becomes the suffix -na):

I see a donkey and a horse.   ahəya-na feureus aiyō
(lit: donkey-and horse I-see)

Some conjunctions like gən/neugeur gən, 'but', are used to join clauses (much as they are in English):

It's good but it's very   təru nō gən beuṭam wədd nō
expensive.   (lit: good it-is but very
    expensive it-is)

COW IN THE SKY

You'll find an Amharic saying to suit any situation – here are a few:

I have a cow in the sky and   lam a·leuny beu seu·mai
I haven't seen the milk.   weu·teut·wa·nəm a·lai
    (Nothing has come of it.)

A person who has too much   yeu·deu·low muk
will start chewing porridge.   yan·yə·ḳal
    *(A person who has too
    much will do useless
    things.)*

Spider webs joined   dər bi·ya·bər
together can catch a lion.   an·beus·sa yas·sər
    *(Much can be
    accomplished by
    joining together.)*

GRAMMAR

PREPOSITIONS & POSTPOSITIONS

Prepositions (like 'in', 'at', 'on' or 'before') are attached to nouns
as prefixes. In this book they appear separated from the noun to
make them easier to read:

of	yeu
at/from	ə, keu
in/at/by	beu
for/to	leu
to	weudeu

Some common Amharic postpositions (those that go after the
noun) include lai, 'up/on/over', wəch, 'out', and wəsṭ, 'in'. They're
often used in conjunction with prepositions like keu and beu:

It's outside the car.	keu meukinow wəch nō
	(lit: from car-the out it-is)

But this is not always necessary:

It's in the bus.	owtobəs wəsṭ nō
	(lit: bus-the in it-is)

ሰዎችን መተዋወቅ

MEETING PEOPLE

One of the first things you'll notice when meeting people in Ethiopia is the əj meun·sat (bow or head nod) used in greetings, goodbyes, acknowledgment or thanks.

YOU SHOULD KNOW   ማወቅ ያለብዎት

Many Amharic words and phrases, including greetings, change form, depending on whether a male (m), female (f), elder person/ authority figure (pol) or group (pl) is being addressed. In most cases, only (m) and (f) have been provided here, except in some of the most common phrases where you'll also see (pl) or (pol) forms used.

Yes.	ow	አዎ
OK/Yes.	ə·shi	እሺ
There is.	al·leu	አለ
There isn't.	yeul·leum	የለም
Excuse me.	yi·kạr·ta	ይቅርታ
Please.	ə·ba·kạh (m)	እባክህ
	ə·ba·kạsh (f)	እባክሽ
	ə·ba·kon (pol)	እባክዎን
	ə·ba·ka·chu (pl)	እባካችሁ
Thank you.	a·meu·seu·gạ·nal·lō	አመሰግናለሁ
Sorry.	az·nal·lō	አዝናለሁ

ሰላም ደህና ነህ?

ደህና ነኝ

Amharic uses negative verb forms in place of 'no'. The main forms are: yeul·leum, 'there isn't', it's not there/available' and ai·deul·leum, 'it isn't'. See Grammar, page 26, for more details.

GREETINGS & GOODBYES ሰላምታ መስዋወጥ

Ethiopian greetings range from a passing bow or 'hello', to several minutes of polite inquiries about how you and your family or loved ones are. When you meet, bow and offer your right hand – or wrist if you can't offer your hand – for a handshake. Once you know someone, you're likely to shake hands, embrace lightly and touch cheeks – right, left, then right again. The following greetings can be used any time of the day:

Hello./Greetings./Goodbye.
    ţe·na yis·ţəl·ləny   ጤና ይስጥልኝ
                                (lit: may health be given
                                   to you)

Hello.
    seu·lam   ሰላም
How are you?
    deu·na neuh? (m)   ደህና ነህ?
    deu·na neush? (f)   ደህና ነሽ?
    deu·na not? (pl)   ደህና ነዉት?

You'll also hear ən·deu·mən, a polite way of asking 'how', instead of deu·na 'fine':

How are you?
    ən·deu·mən neuh? (m)   እንደምን ነህ?
    ən·deu·mən neush? (f)   እንደምን ነሽ?
I'm fine,
    deu·na neuny   ደህና ነኝ

On a more informal level, you might hear:

Hello/Hi.
    ta·di·yass   ታዲያስ
How are things?
    ən·det nō?   እንዴት ነው-?
So, what's new?
    mən ad·dis neu·geur al·leu? ምን አዲስ ነገር አለ?

There are also different greetings for different times of the day:

How is your morning?

deu·na ad·deurk? (m)	ደህና አደርክ?
deu·na ad·deursh? (f)	ደህና አደርሽ?
deu·na ad·deu·ru? (pol)	ደህና አደሩ?

How's your day going?

deu·na walk? (m)	ደህና ዋልክ?
deu·na walsh? (f)	ደህና ዋልሽ?
deu·na wa·lu? (pol)	ደህና ዋሉ?

How are you this evening?

deu·na a·meu·sheuh? (m)	ደህና አመሸህ?
deu·na a·meu·sheush? (f)	ደህና አመሸሽ?
deu·na a·meu·shu? (pol)	ደህና አመሹ?

Good night.

deu·na deur (m)	ደህና ደር
deu·na deu·ri (f)	ደህና ደሪ
deu·na yi·deu·ru (pol)	ደህና ይደሩ

Goodbyes   መሰያየት

A useful lead-up to goodbye is ə·shi meu·he·de nō, 'OK, I'm about to go'. Bow or shake hands as you say goodbye.

Bye/See you!

chow!	ቻው!

Have a nice day.

deu·na wal (m)	ደህና ዋል
deu·na wai (f)	ደህና ዋይ

Goodbye.

deu·na hun (m)	ደህና ሁን
deu·na hu·nyi (f)	ደህና ሁኚ
deu·na hu·nu (pl)	ደህና ሁኑ

Goodbye. (when leaving for some time)

deu·na seun·bət (m)	ደህና ሰንብት
deu·na seun·bəch (f)	ደህና ሰንብች
deu·na seun·bə·tu (pl)	ደህና ሰንብቱ

Come back safely!

   beu·cheur yi·meul·lə·səh! (m)　　በፍር ይመልስህ!

   beu·cheur yi·meul·lə·səsh! (f)　　በፍር ይመልስሽ!

People may say teu·cha·weut geu·na nō (m), 'Keep us company, it's still early'. If you need to go, some polite responses are:

Sorry, I have to go now.

   yi·kər·ta a·hun meu·hed　　ይቅርታ አሁን መሄድ

   al·leu·bəny　　አለብኝ

Sorry, I have an appointment.

   yi·kər·ta keu·teu·ro al·leu·bəny　　ይቅርታ ቀጠሮ አለብኝ

We'll meet again.

   le·la gi·ze ə·nə·geu·na·nyal·leun　　ሌላ ጊዜ እንገናኛለን

CIVILITIES　　ሰዎችን ማስተናገድ

Hospitality is a major part of Ethiopian social life, and you'll often be invited for a coffee, drink or meal. If you're invited to someone's house, leave your shoes at the entrance if your host does the same. Bow as you receive tea, coffee and snacks, or say əg·zer yis·təl·ləny (lit: may God give to you).

Welcome.

   ən·kwan deu·na meu·tah (m)　　እንኳን ደህና መጣህ

   ən·kwan deu·na meu·tash (f)　　እንኳን ደህና መጣሽ

   ən·kwan deu·na meu·tu (pol)　　እንኳን ደህና መጡ

Come in.

   gə·ba/gə·bi/yig·bu (m/f/pol)　　ግባ/ግቢ/ይግቡ

Please sit down.

   ə·ba·kəh kuch beul (m)　　እባክህ ቀጮ በል

   ə·ba·kəsh kuch bay (f)　　እባክሽ ቀጮ በይ

Thank you for your hospitality.

   sə·leu meus·teun·gə·dō　　ስለ መስተንግዶው

   a·meu·seu·gə·nal·lō　　አመሰግናለሁ

You're very kind.

   beu·tam deugg not　　በጣም ደግ ነዎት

Don't mention it.

   mə·nəm ai·deul·leum　　ምንም አይደለም

MEETING PEOPLE

FORMS OF ADDRESS   ስም

When addressing someone in Ethiopia, always use their first name. In more formal situations, use the first name preceded by a title. For example, Dawit Sissay is a·to da·wit, 'Mr Dawit'. Ethiopians often use their father's first name where Westerners use surnames. After marriage, women retain their maiden names, and only change their title.

Ethiopians also use friendly terms to address people: weun·dəm, 'brother', for a man around your own age; ə·hət, 'sister', for a woman around your own age; ab·bab·ba, 'papa', for old men; ə·maṁ·ma, 'mama', for old women; and ga·she, 'my shield', for a man slightly older than you. There are also yeu·kə·ṣəl səm, 'nicknames'.

Mr	a·to	አቶ
Mrs	way·zeu·ro	ወይዘሮ
Miss	way·zeu·rit	ወይዘሪት

Asking Names   ስም መለዋወጥ

Asking names is a friendly ice-breaker in Ethiopia. Sometimes people will explain the meaning of their name in English. For example, ṭə·la·hun (Tilahun) means 'be my shade', ṣeu·hai (Sehay) means 'sun' and a·beub·ba (Abeba) means 'flower'.

What's your name?
sə·məh man nō? (m)	ስምህ ማነው?
sə·məsh man nō? (f)	ስምሽ ማነው?
sə·mə·wot man nō? (pol)	ስምዎት ማነው?

My name's ...
| sə·me ... nō | ስሜ ... ነው |

This is ...
| yi·he ... nō (m) | ይህ ... ነው |
| yi·chi ... nat (f) | ይቺ ... ናት |

FIRST ENCOUNTERS   ለመጀመሪያ ጊዜ መገናኘት

A simple smile, nod or yi·k̠ər·ta, 'excuse me', followed by a greeting is a common way to initiate conversation.

Do you like ...?	... tə·weud·dal·leuh? (m)	... ትወዳለህ?
	... tə·weu·jal·leush? (f)	... ትወጃለሽ?
our country	a·geu·ra·chən	አገራችን
this place	yi·hen bo·ta	ይህን ቦታ

I like it (a lot).
(beu·t̠am) ə·weud·dal·lō   (በጣም) እወዳለሁ·

When did you arrive?
meu·che meu·t̠ah? (m)   መቼ መጣህ?
meu·che meu·t̠ash? (f)   መቼ መጣሽ?

I arrived (yesterday/last week).
(tə·nan·t̠ə·na; ya·leu·fō   (ትናንትና/ያለፈው·
sam·mənt) meu·t̠ow   ሳምንት) መጣሁ·

Why did you come here?
leu·mən meu·t̠ah? (m)   ለምን መጣህ?
leu·mən meu·t̠ash? (f)   ለምን መጣሽ?

For tourism/a holiday.
leu gub·bə·nyit; leu ə·reuft   ለጉብኝት/ለእረፍት

For work/study.
leu sə·ra; leu təm·hərt   ለስራ/ለትምህርት

Which places have you been to?
mən mən bo·ta·wo·chən   ምን ምን ቦታዎችን
a·yeuh/a·yeush? (m/f)   አየህ/አየሽ?

I've been to (Lalibela) and (Harar).
(la·li·beu·lan) ə·na (ha·ra·rən) (ላሊበላን) እና (ሃረርን)
ai·chal·lō   አይቻለሁ·

Did you like (Gonder)?
(gon·deur) teus·ma·mah/   (ጎንደር) ተስማማህ/
teus·ma·mash? (m/f)   ተስማማሽ?

MEETING PEOPLE

Where are you staying?
  yeut nō ya·reuf·kō? (m)   የት ነው- ያረፍከው-?
  yeut nō ya·reuf·shyu? (f)   የት ነው- ያረፍሽው-?
Where are you going?
  yeut tə·he·dal·leuh? (m)   የት ትሄዳለህ?
  yeut tə·he·jal·leush? (f)   የት ትሄጃለሽ?
  yeut yi·he·dal·lu? (pol)   የት ይሄዳሉ?
I'm/We're going to ...
  weu·deu ... ə·he·dal·lō/   ወደ ... እሄዳለሁ-/
  ən·he·dal·leun   እንሄዳለን
Who are you with?
  keu man gar neuh? (m)   ከማን ጋር ነህ?
  keu man gar neush? (f)   ከማን ጋር ነሽ?

I'm with ...	keu ... gar neuny	ከ ... ጋር ነኝ
a tour group	go·bə·nyi·woch	ጉብኝዎች
my friend/ friends	gwa·deu·nya·ye/ gwa·deu·nyo·che	ጓደኛዬ/ ጓደኞቼ
my wife/ husband	ba·leu·be·te	ባለቤቴ

BEAUTIFUL!

One of the great Ethiopian phrases is ḳon·jo nō, 'It's beautiful', which can be used to describe anything, from a delicious meal to a panoramic view of the Simien Mountains.

It's beautiful!
  ḳon·jo nō!   ቆንጆ ነው-!
This place is beautiful!
  yi·he bo·ta ḳon·jo nō!   ይህ ቦታ ቆንጆ ነው-!
Isn't it beautiful?
  ḳon·jo nō ai·deul·leum?   ቆንጆ ነው- አይደለም?
What a beautiful baby/child!
  ḳon·jo ləj!   ቆንጆ ልጅ!

Is there a problem?	chig·gər al·leu?	ችግር አለ?
No problem.	chig·gər yeul·leum	ችግር የለም
Just a minute.	and gi·ze	አንድ ጊዜ
It's possible.	yi·cha·lal	ይቻላል
It's not possible.	ai·chal·ləm	አይቻልም
Good luck!	meul·kam ə·dəl!	መልካም እድል!
I'm joking.	ķeul·den nō	ቀልዴን ነው·
That's amusing!	ya·sə·ķal!	ያስቃል!

KEEP TALKING

Ethiopians love chatting and there are lots of friendly interjections in Amharic conversation. One you may hear sounds like a small gasp or hiccup. This means 'Please continue/I'm listening'. The word teu·çha·weut!/teu·çha·weu·chi!/teu·çha·weu·tu! (m/f/pl) means 'Play!' and is a friendly way of saying, 'Let's have a chat!' or 'Keep chatting!'. The word ən·teu·wa·weuķ, 'Let's get to know each other', is an offer of friendship.

How was it?	ən·det neub·beur?	እንዴት ነበር?
OK./Yes./Go on.	ə·shi	እሺ
Really?	əw·neut?	እው·ነት?
Maybe.	mə·nal·bat	ምናልባት
That's surprising!	yi·geur·mal!	ይገርማል!
It's true!	əw·neut nō!	እው·ነት ነው·!
It's a lie!	wu·sheut nō!	ውሸት ነው·!
Brilliant!	gob·beuz!	ጎበዝ!
Oh!	a·ra!	እራ!

Be strong/Chin up!		
ai·zoh/ai·zosh! (m/f)		አይዞህ/አይዞሽ!
What did you say?		
mən alk/alsh? (m/f)		ምን አልክ/አልሽ?

It's important.
as·feul·la·gi nō አስፈላጊ ነው።

It's not important.
as·feul·la·gi ai·deul·leum አስፈላጊ አይደለም

What's this/that?
yi·he/ya mən·dən nō? ይሄ/ያ ምንድን ነው?

Look!
teu·meul·keut! (m) ተመልከት!
teu·meul·keuch! (f) ተመልከች!
teu·meul·keu·tu! (pl) ተመልከቱ!

Listen!
sə·ma!/sə·mi!/sə·mu! (m/f/pl) ስማ!/ስሚ!/ስሙ!

Can you please help me?
ə·ba·kəh ər·dany? (m) እባክህ እርዳኝ?
ə·ba·kəsh ər·jiny? (f) እባክሽ እርጂኝ?

What are you doing?
mən ta·reu·gal·leuh? (m) ምን ታረጋለህ?
mən ta·reu·gi·yal·leush? (f) ምን ታረጊየለሽ?
mən ta·reu·gal·la·chu? (pl) ምን ታረጋላችሁ?

NATIONALITIES   ዜግነት

Ethiopians will be keen to hear which country you're from.
The following question can also be used to ask which region
Ethiopian people come from.

Where are you from?
    keu yeut a·geur neuh? (m)   ከየት አገር ነህ?
    keu yeut a·geur neush? (f)   ከየት አገር ነሽ?

I'm from ...	keu ... neuny	ከ ... ነኝ
(South) Africa	(deu·bub) af·ri·ka	(ደቡብ) አፍሪካ
Asia	əs·ya	እስያ
Australia	ow·stra·li·ya	አውስትራሊያ
Canada	ka·na·da	ካናዳ
Egypt	gəbs	ግብጽ
England	ən·gliz	እንግሊዝ
Ethiopia	i·tə·yo·pi·ya	ኢትዮጵያ
Europe	i·rop	አሮፕ
France	feu·reun·sai	ፈረንሳይ
Germany	jeur·meun	ጀርመን
Greece	grik	ግሪክ
India	hənd	ሕንድ
Ireland	aiyr·land	አየርላንድ
Israel	əs·ra·el	እስራኤል
Italy	ţal·yan	ጣሊያን
Japan	ja·pan	ጃፓን
the USA	a·me·ri·ka	አሜሪካ

I live in the ...	... ə·no·ral·lō	... እኖራለሁ
city	keu·teu·ma wəsţ	ከተማ ውስጥ
countryside	geu·ţeur	ገጠር

Which region/city are you from?
    keu yeu·tə·nyow kəl·ləl/   ከየትኛው ክልል/
    keu·teu·ma neuh? (m)   ከተማ ነህ?
    keu yeu·tə·nyow kəl·ləl/   ከየትኛው ክልል/
    keu·teu·ma neush? (f)   ከተማ ነሽ?

STAYING IN TOUCH   መጠያየቅ

People won't be shy about asking if you can meet again or exchange addresses. When someone hasn't seen you for a while, they'll probably say ṭeu·fah!/ṭeu·fash! (m/f), 'You've been lost!'.

Can we meet again?
  ən·deu·geu·na   እንደገና እንገናኘለን?
  ə·nə·geu·na·nyal·leun?
When/Where will we meet?
  meu·che/yeut   መቼ/የት
  ə·nə·geu·na·nyal·leun?   እንገናኘለን?
Let's meet at Piazza at (six o'clock).
  (sə·dəst seu'at) lai pi·yas·sa   (ስድስት ሰዓት) ላይ
  ə·nə·geu·nany   ፒያሳ እንገናኝ
We'll meet tomorrow/tonight.
  (neu·geu; za·re ma·ta)   (ነገ/ዛሬ ማታ)
  ə·nə·geu·na·nyal·leun   እንገናኛለን
I'll visit you (on my way back).
  (sə·meul·leuss) ə·meu·ṭal·lō   (ስመለስ) እመጣለሁ
I'll be back in (two weeks).
  beu (hu·leutt sam·mənt)   በ (ሁለት ሳምንት)
  wəsṭ ə·meul·leu·sal·lō   ውስጥ እመለሳለሁ
I'll send you a letter.
  deub·dab·be ə·lə·kal·lō   ደብዳቤ እልካለሁ
I'll call you.
  səlk ə·deu·wə·lal·lō   ስልክ እደወላለሁ
Please give me your address/
phone number.
  ə·ba·kəh (ad·ra·sha·hən;   እባክህ (አድራሻህን/
  yeu səlk kuṭ·rə·hən) sə·ṭuny (m)   የስልክ ቁጥርህን) ስጠኝ
  ə·ba·keush (ad·ra·sha·shən;   እባክሽ (አድራሻሽን/
  yeu səlk kuṭ·rə·shən) sə·chiny (f) የስልክ ቁጥርሽን) ስጭኝ

BODY LANGUAGE & ETIQUETTE   ሥነ ምግባር

Ethiopia tolerates a range of different customs and beliefs. The general rule of thumb is to observe what the locals do. For tips on eating, see page 144, and for religion, see page 191. In general, social etiquette carries enormous weight in Ethiopia. The idea of yə·luny·ta, concern about the opinions of others, is common, as is the phrase neu·wər nō!, 'It's impolite!'.

Displays of affection between men and women are unacceptable in public, but moderate displays of affection between members of the same sex is fine.

Dress fairly conservatively. Women should avoid wearing shorts, miniskirts or crop tops, particularly in rural and Muslim areas. Men should always wear a shirt and avoid torn clothing and short shorts.

If you're staying with a family or at the receiving end of hospitality, fruit or raw coffee beans are appropriate gifts.

It's usual to give informal guides or porters 'tea money' to thank them for their services, but use discretion. Some people will be offended by an offer of money, so instead you might like to invite them for coffee or a meal.

Respect for authority figures and older people is highly valued.

Be discreet about smoking and drinking in public, particularly in rural and Muslim areas. Women should be especially discreet.

Belching and breaking wind are considered totally unacceptable. Say yi·kər·ta!, 'Excuse me!', if you slip up.

Most Ethiopian body language, like nodding, shaking the head, and waving goodbye, carries the same meaning as it does in English. You'll notice Ethiopians use very expressive hand gestures in day-to-day conversation – a great benefit to non-Amharic speakers!

CULTURAL DIFFERENCES   የባህል ልዩነት

Is this a local custom?

    yi·he yeu a·ka·ba·bi·yu   ይህ የ አካባቢው

    ba·həl nō?   ባህል ነው?

I don't want to offend you.

    las·ķeu·yə·məh al·feul·lə·gəm (m)   ላስቀይምህ አልፈልግም

    las·ķeu·yə·məsh al·feul·lə·gəm (f)   ላስቀይምሽ አልፈልግም

I'm sorry, it's not the custom
in my country.

    yi·ķər·ta ya·geu·re   ይቅርታ ያገሬ

    ba·həl ai·deul·leum   ባህል አይደለም

Thank you, but I'd rather just watch.

    a·meu·seu·gə·nal·lō ma·yeut   አመሰግናለሁ ማየት

    bə·cha ə·feul·lə·gal·lō   ብቻ እፈልጋለሁ

I'll give it a go!

    ə·mo·kə·reu·wal·lō!   እሞክረዋለሁ!

I'm sorry, it's	yi·ķər·ta yeu·ne ...	ይቅርታ የኔ ...
against my ...	ai·feuķ·deu·wəm	አይፈቅደውም
beliefs	əm·neut	እምነት
culture	ba·həl	ባህል
religion	hai·ma·not	ሃይማኖት

AGE   ዕድሜ

It's impolite for men to ask women their age, but fine for a woman
to inquire about another woman's age. See Numbers & Amounts,
page 223, for your age.

How old are you?

    əd·meh sənt nō? (m)   ዕድሜህ ስንት ነው?

    əd·mesh sənt nō? (f)   ዕድሜሽ ስንት ነው?

I'm (20) years old.

    (ha·ya) a·meu·te nō   (ሃያ) አመቴ ነው

MEETING PEOPLE

OCCUPATIONS   ሥራ

What's your job?

sə·rah mən·dən nō? (m)		ሥራህ ምንድን ነው?
sə·rash mən·dən nō? (f)		ሥራሽ ምንድን ነው?

I'm (a/an) ...	... neuny	... ኘኝ
accountant	yeu hi·sab seu·ra·teu·nya	የሂሳብ ሠራተኛ
artist	seu'al·li	ሰዓሊ
businessperson	neug·ga·de	ነጋዴ
cook	mə·gəb seu·ri	ምግብ ሰሪ
doctor	ha·kim	ሐኪም
engineer	meu·han·dis	መሃንዲስ
farmer	geu·beu·re	ገበሬ
homemaker	yeu bet ə·meu·bet	የቤት እመቤት
journalist	ga·ze·teu·nya	ጋዜጠኛ
lawyer	ṭeu·beu·ḳa	ጠበቃ
nurse	neurs	ነርስ
office worker	yeu bi·ro seu·ra·teu·nya	የቢሮ ሠራተኛ
scientist	teu·meu·ra·ma·ri	ተመራማሪ
student	teu·ma·ri	ተማሪ
teacher	as·teu·ma·ri	አስተማሪ
tour guide	as·gob·nyi	አስጎብኚ
tradesperson	yeu əj ba·leu·mu·ya	የእጅ ባለሙያ
unemployed	sə·ra feut	ሥራ ፈት

I'm retired.

ṭu·reu·ta weu·ṭə·chal·lō	ጡረታ ወጥቻለሁ

What are you studying?

mən tə·ma·ral·leuh? (m)	ምን ትማራለህ?
mən tə·ma·ri·yal·leush? (f)	ምን ትማሪያለሽ?

I'm studying ...	... ə·ma·ral·lō	... እማራለሁ
business	nəgd	ንግድ
computer science	kom·pyu·teur	ኮምፒዉተር
engineering	in·jə·neu·riny	ኢንጂነሪንግ
fine arts	ki·neu țə·beub	ኪነ ጥበብ
languages	kwan·kwa	ቋንቋ
law	həg	ሕግ
medicine	hə·kə·mə·na	ሕክምና
science	sai·yəns	ሳይንስ
social studies	həb·reu təm·hərt	ሕብረ ትምህርት

FEELINGS   ስሜቶች

In Amharic, feelings are often expressed as verbs with the subject attached, so you only need to use one word.

I'm ...

angry	teu·na·də·jal·lō	ተናድጃለሁ
cold	beu·reu·deuny	በረደኝ
depressed	deu·bro·nyal	ደብሮኛል
happy	deus blo·nyal	ደስ ብሎኛል
hot	mo·keuny	ሞቀኝ
hungry	ra·beuny	ራበኝ
sad	a·zə·nyal·lō	አዝኛለሁ
thirsty	wu·ha țeu·many	ውሃ ጠማኝ
tired	deu·keu·meuny	ደከመኝ

BREAKING THE   የቋንቋ አለመግባባትን
LANGUAGE BARRIER   ማስወገድ

To form a language name in Amharic, add the suffix -ə·nya to the language or region. Local languages include o·ro·mə·nya (Oromo) and ti·grə·nya (Tigrinya) while common foreign languages include feu·reun·sai·ə·nya (French) and a·ra·bə·nya (Arabic).

Do you speak (English/Amharic)?

ən·gli·zə·nya/a·ma·rə·nya	እንግሊዝኛ/አማርኛ
tə·chə·lal·leuh? (m)	ትችላለህ?
tə·chi·yal·leush? (f)	ትችያለሽ?

Does anyone here speak (English)?
  (ən·gli·zə·nya) yeu·mi·chəl al·leu?   (እንግሊዝኛ) የሚችል አለ?

Yes, I speak (a little).
  ow (tən·nish tən·nish)   አዎ (ትንሽ ትንሽ)
  ə·cha·lal·lō   እችላለሁ

I don't speak (Amharic).
  (a·ma·rə·nya) al·chəl·ləm   (አማርኛ) አልቸልልም

Do you understand?
  geub·bah? (m)   ገባህ?
  geub·bash? (f)   ገባሽ?

I understand/don't understand.
  geub·to·nyal/al·geu·ba·nyəm   ገብቶኛል/አልገባኝም

Please speak slowly.
  ə·ba·kəh ḳeuss bə·leuh   እባክህ ቀስ ብለህ
  teu·na·geur (m)   ተናገር
  ə·ba·kəsh ḳeuss bə·leush   እባክሽ ቀስ ብለሽ
  teu·na·geu·ri (f)   ተናገሪ

What does it mean in
Amharic/English?
  beu a·ma·rə·nya/   በ አማርኛ/እንግሊዝኛ
  ən·gli·zə·nya mən ma·leut nō?   ምን ማለት ነው-?

Please write it down in
roman/Amharic script.
  ə·ba·kon beu (ən·gli·zə·nya/   እባክዎን በ (እንግሊዝኛ/
  a·ma·rə·nya) yi·ṣa·fu·liny   አማርኛ) ይፃፉልኝ

Is there a translator?
  as·teur·gwa·mi al·leu?   አስተርጓሚ አለ?

I want someone who speaks
(Oromo) and (English).
  (o·ro·mə·nya) na (ən·gli·zə·nya)   (ኦሮምኛ) ና (እንግሊዝኛ)
  yeu·mi·chəl sō ə·feul·lə·gal·lō   የሚችል ሰው- እፈልጋለሁ

Whether making friends on the bus, enjoying breathtaking views from the comfort of a plane, or rolling along in a horse and cart, half the fun is in the gu·zo, 'journey'. However you travel, meul·kam gu·zo!, 'Enjoy your trip!'.

FINDING YOUR WAY   የሚሄዱበትን ማወቅ

Start with a greeting or yi·ḵər·ta, 'Excuse me'. An optional extra is meun·geud ṭeuf·to·bə·nyal, 'I've lost my way'.

Where's the	(yeu·mi·ḵeur·bō)	(የሚቀርበው)
(nearest) ...?	... yeut nō?	... የት ነው·?
airport	ai·ro·plan	አይሮፕላን
	ma·reu·fi·ya	ማረፊያ
bus stop	ow·to·bəs	አው·ቶብስ
	ma·ḵo·mi·ya	ማቆሚያ
(city) bus station	(yeu keu·teu·ma)	(የ ከተማ
	ow·to·bəs	አው·ቶብስ)
	ṭa·bi·ya	ጣቢያ
city centre	meu·hal keu·teu·ma	መሃል ከተማ
highway	ow·ra go·da·na	አው·ራ ጎዳና
intercity bus	yeu kəf·leu ha·geur	የ ክፍለ ሃገር
station	ow·to·bəs ṭa·bi·ya	አው·ቶብስ
		ጣቢያ
main road	wan·na meun·geud	ዋና መንገድ
road to (Goba)	weu·deu (go·ba)	ወደ (ጎባ)
	yeu·mi·weus·dō	የሚወስደው·
	meun·geud	መንገድ
... street/road	... meun·geud	... መንገድ
taxi stand	tak·si ma·ḵo·mi·ya	ታክሲ· ማቆሚያ
ticket office	ti·ket meu·sheu·cha	ትኬት
		መሸጫ
train station	ba·bur ṭa·bi·ya	ባቡ·ር ጣቢያ

GETTING AROUND

Is this the way to (Entoto)?
(ən·to·ṭo) beuz·zi beu·kul nō?   (እንጦጦ) በዚህ በኩል ነው-?

Is it (very) near/far?
(beu·tam) ḳərb/ruḳ nō?   (በጣም) ቅርብ/ሩቅ ነው-?

Can I walk there?
beu·gər yas·ke·dal?   በግር ያስኬዳል?

Please show me the way.
ə·ba·kəh meun·geud
a·sa·yeuny (m)   እባክህ መንገድ አሳየኝ
ə·ba·kəsh meun·geud
a·sa·yiny (f)   እባክሽ መንገድ አሳይኝ

Can you show me on the map?
kar·tow lai
ta·sa·yeu·nyal·leuh? (m)   ካርታው ላይ ታሳየኛለህ?
kar·tow lai
ta·sa·yi·nyal·leush? (f)   ካርታው ላይ ታሳይኛለሽ?

What town/road is this?
yi·he keu·teu·ma/meun·geud
mən yi·ba·lal?   ይህ ከተማ/መንገድ
ምን ይባላል?

Can I pass this way?
beuz·zi beu·kul ma·leuf yi·cha·lal?   በዚህ በኩል ማለፍ ይቻላል?

Is there another way?
le·la meun·geud al·leu?   ሌላ መንገድ አለ?

NO, I HAVEN'T FORGOTTEN THIS ...

If you want to answer 'no' to a question, remember to use the appropriate negative verb form:

There isn't./It's not there.	yeul·leum
It's not.	ai·deul·leum
I can't.	al·chəl·ləm
I don't want.	al·feul·lə·gəm
I don't have.	yeu·leu·nyəm
OK! I haven't forgotten!	ə·shi! a·reu·sa·hum!

DIRECTIONS   አቅጣጫ

When describing locations, Ethiopians often use nearby landmarks
such as hotels instead of street addresses. See The Sights, page 83,
for additional words.

Go (straight ahead).
  (beu·ḳeu·ṭa·ta) hid/hij (m/f)   (በቀጥታ) ሂድ/ሂጅ
When you reach (the kiosk),
turn to the left/right.
  (ki·yosk) sə·tə·deurs weu·deu   (ኪዮስክ) ስትደርስ
  gra/ḳeuny ta·teuf (m)   ወደ ግራ/ቀኝ ታጠፍ
  (ki·yosk) sə·tə·deursh weu·deu   (ኪዮስክ) ስትደርሽ
  gra/ḳeuny ta·teu·fi (f)   ወደ ግራ/ቀኝ ታጠፊ

It's ...	... nō	... ነው·
at the next	yeu·mi·ḳeu·ṭəl·lō	የሚቀጥለው·
(corner)	(meu·ta·ṭeu·fi·ya)	(መታጠፊያ)
here/there	əz·zi/əz·zi·ya	እዚህ/እዚያ
in front/behind	fit leu fit/	ፊት ለፊት/
	beus·teu·jeur·ba	በስተጀርባ
in this area	əz·zi a·ka·ba·bi	እዚህ አካባቢ
inside/outside	wəsṭ/wəch	ውስጥ/ውጭ
near to ...	... a·ka·ba·bi	... አካባቢ
next to ...	... a·ṭeu·geub	... አጠገብ
on the left/right	beu gra/ḳeuny	በ ግራ/ቀኝ
	beu·kul	በኩል
to the north	weu·deu seu·men	ወደ ሰሜን
to the south	weu·deu deu·bub	ወደ ደቡብ
to the east	weu·deu məs·raḳ	ወደ ምስራቅ
to the west	weu·deu mə'ə·rab	ወደ ምዕራብ

GETTING AROUND

GETTING THERE

የሚፈልጉበት ቦታ መድረስ

Is there a/an ...	weu·deu (jim·ma)	ወደ (ጅማ)
to (Jimma)?	... al·leu?	... አለ?
aeroplane	ai·ro·plan	አይሮፕላን
boat	jeul·ba	ጀልባ
bus	ow·to·bəs	አው·ቶ·ብስ
car	meu·ki·na	መኪና
minibus	wə·yə·yat/mi·ni·bas	ው·ይይት/ ሚኒባስ
pick-up vehicle	pik·ap	ፒክ አፕ
train	ba·bur	ባቡር
truck	yeu chə·neut meu·ki·na	የጭነት መኪና

| Let's go! | ən·hid! | እንሂድ! |
| Wait! | ḳoy/ḳo·yi!(m/f) | ቆይ/ቆዪ! |

What time does the (next) ...
leave/arrive?

(yeu·mi·ḳeu·ṭəl·lō) ... beu sənt	(የሚቀጥለው·) ... በስንት
seu'at yi·neu·sal/yi·deur·sal?	ሰዓት ይነሳል/ይደርሳል?

Does it go to (Aksum)?

weu·deu (ak·sum) yi·he·dal?	ወደ (አክሱም) ይሄዳል?

How do I get to (Harar)?

weu·deu (ha·rar) beu·mən	ወደ (ሐረር)
ə·he·dal·lō?	በምን እሄዳለሁ-?

How much to ...?

weu·deu ... sənt nō?	ወደ ... ስንት ነው-?

How long does it take?

sənt gi·ze yi·weus·dal?	ስንት ጊዜ ይወስዳል?

I'll return.

ə·meul·leu·sal·lō	እመለሳለሁ-

I'm in a hurry.

cheu·ku·yal·lō	ቸኩ·ያለሁ-

Are you ready?

teu·zeu·gaj·teu·hal?(m)	ተዘጋጅተሃል?
teu·zeu·gaj·teu·shal?(f)	ተዘጋጅተሻል?

TAXIS & GARIS   ታክሲ ና ጋሪ

In many towns, you can choose between a ga·ri (horse and cart)
or tak·si. Taxis often take up to five passengers. If the taxi isn't
going to your destination, the driver will tell you ai·he·dəm , 'I'm
not going there'. If you want a cab to yourself, ask for it 'on
contract'. Negotiate a price before leaving.

To ... please.
  ə·ba·kəh/ə·ba·kəsh   እባክህ/እባክሽ ወደ ...
  weu·deu ... (m/f)
I want it on contract.
  kon·trat meu·yaz ə·feul·lə·gal·lō ኮንትራት መያዝ እፈልጋለሁ
How much to ...?
  weu·deu ... sənt nō?   ወደ ... ስንት ነው-?
I'll pay (two) birr.
  (hu·leutt) bərr ə·keuf·lal·lō   (ሁለት) ብር እከፍላለሁ
This is my stop. *(for shared taxi)*
  wo·raj al·leu   ወራጅ አለ
Please stop here.
  əz·zi a·kum   እዚህ አቁም

Special Instructions   ልዩ መመሪያዎች

Please wait for me.
  ə·ba·kəh teu·bə·keuny (m)   እባክህ ጠብቀኝ
This is not (Hawi) hotel.
  yi·he (ha·wi) ho·tel   ይህ (ሃዊ) ሆቴል
  ai·deul·leum   አይደለም
(Please) Slow down.
  (ə·ba·kəh) keuss bə·leuh   (እባክህ)
  nə·da (m)   ቀስ ብለህ ንዳ
(Please) Hurry.
  (ə·ba·kəh) to·lo beul (m)   (እባክህ) ቶሎ በል
Please don't hit the horse so much.
  ə·ba·kəh feu·reu·sun bə·zu   እባክህ ፈረሱን ብዙ
  a·təm·tow (m)   አትምታው

GETTING AROUND

BUYING TICKETS   ትኬት መግዛት

Student discounts aren't normally given to foreigners, but children's tickets are available.

Where can I get tickets to ...?
    weu·deu ... ti·ket yeut   ወደ ... ትኬት የት ይገኛል?
    yi·geu·nyal?

You buy it on the bus.
    ow·to·bəs wəst yig·zu   አውቶብስ ውስጥ ይግዙ

There are no seats left.
    ti·ket al·ḵwal   ትኬት አልቋል

For (tomorrow morning).
    leu (neu·geu ṭeu·wat)   ለ (ነገ ጠዋት)

How much is a ticket to ...?
    weu·deu ... ti·ket sənt nō?   ወደ ... ትኬት ስንት ነው?

(Three) tickets to ...
    weu·deu ... (sost) ti·ket   ወደ ... (ሶስት) ትኬት

I want to reserve a ticket to ...
    weu·deu ... ti·ket beu·ḵəd·mi·ya   ወደ ... ትኬት በቅድሚያ
    meug·zat ə·feul·lə·gal·lō   መግዛት እፈልጋለሁ

I'd like to return my ticket.
    ti·ke·ten meu·meu·leus   ትኬቴን መመለስ
    ə·feul·lə·gal·lō   እፈልጋለሁ

IT'S A SEARCH!

It could happen on buses, trains, or as you enter buildings ... it's a fə·teu·sha, 'search'. Officials go through luggage to check for dangerous or contraband goods. If you're worried about having your dirty socks exposed to the world, rest assured the searches are usually short, painless and routine.

Please open your bag.
    ə·ba·kon shan·ṭa·won   እባክዎን ሻንጣዎን
    yik·feu·tu·liny   ይክፈቱልኝ

---

one-way ticket	meu·he·ja bə·cha ti·ket	መሄጃ ብቻ ትኬት
return ticket	deur·so meuls ti·ket	ደርሶ መልስ ትኬት
child's ticket	leu lə·joch ti·ket	ለልጆች ትኬት

AIR
የአየር መንገድ

It's a domestic/international flight.
    yeu (a·geur wəst; wəch)
    beu·reu·ra nō
የ (አገር ውስጥ/
ውጭ) በረራ ነው።

My luggage hasn't arrived.
    shan·ta·ye al·deu·reu·seum
ሻንጣዬ አልደረሰም

bag/luggage	shan·ta/gwaz	ሻንጣ/ጓዝ
pass/permit	yeu yi·leuf feu·kad	የይለፍ ፈቃድ
luggage weight	yeu shan·ta kəb·deut	የሻንጣ ክብደት

Customs & Immigration
ግምሩክ ና ኢምግሬሽን

Customs and immigration staff generally speak English, and words like pas·port and vi·za are similar to English. More words and phrases can be found in Paperwork, page 88, and Specific Needs, page 213.

I have something/nothing to declare.
    yeu·mas·meu·zeu·gə·bō ə·ka
    al·leu/yeul·leum
የማስመዘግበው ዕቃ
አለ/የለም

Do I have to declare this?
    yi·hen mas·meuz·geub
    al·leu·bəny?
ይሄን ማስመዝገብ
አለብኝ?

This is all my luggage.
    shan·ta·ye yi·he hul·lu nō
ሻንጣዬ ይሄ ሁሉ ነው።

That's not mine.
    ya yeu·ne ai·deul·leum
ያ የኔ አይደለም

I didn't know I had to declare it.
    mas·meuz·geub ən·da·leu·bəny
    a·la·weu·kum
ማስመዝገብ እንዳለብኝ
አላወኩም

GETTING AROUND

border	dən·beur	ድንበር
customs	gəm·ruk	ግምሩክ
customs form	yeu gəm·ruk ḵəṣ	የግምሩክ ቅፅ
export permit	wəch meu·la·ki·ya	ወጭ መላኪያ
	feu·ḵad	ፈቃድ
immigration office	i·mi·gre·shən bi·ro	ኢሚግሬሽን ቢሮ
receipt	deu·reu·seuny	ደረሰኝ

BUS, MINIVAN & PICK-UP TRUCK

አውቶብስ፡ ወይይት ና ፒክአፕ

Often packed with an interesting array of chickens, pots and household goods, Ethiopian inter-town buses are cheap, quite comfortable and a great way to meet people.

The word wə·yə·yət, 'conversation', is another name for mini-buses or pick-up vehicles that service urban and inter-town routes. Listen for the destination to be called, eg, *'Merkato, Merkato, Merkatooo!'*. The phrase and sō! means 'Only room for one more'. See Car, page 61, for hiring and Hitchhiking, page 65, for other pick-up truck terms.

Which (bus) goes to ...?
yeu·tə·nyow (ow·to·bəs) weu·deu ... yi·hed·al? — የትኛው (አውቶብስ) ወደ ... ይሄዳል?
Does it stop overnight?
ma·ta yi·ḵo·mal? — ማታ ይቆማል?
Where does it stop?
yeut yi·ḵo·mal? — የት ይቆማል?
Can you please tell me when we get to ...?
ə·ba·ḵəh ... sə·nə·deurs nə·geu·reuny? (m) — እባክህ ... ስንደርስ ንገረኝ?
ə·ba·ḵəsh ... sə·nə·deurs nə·geu·riny? (f) — እባክሽ ... ስንደርስ ንገሪኝ?

Do I have to catch another (minibus)?
   le·la (mi·ni·bas) meu·yaz
   al·leu·bəny?

Where should I get off?
   yeut lu·reud?

This is my stop!
   wo·raj al·leu!

ሌላ (ሚኒባስ)
መያዝ አለብኝ?

የት ልውረድ?

ወራጅ አለ!

GETTING AROUND

Is someone sitting here?
 sō al·leu?   ሰው አለ?
(Please) Put my luggage on top
 of the bus.
 (ə·ba·kəh) shan·ṭa·yen   (እባክህ) ሻንጣዬን
 sə·ḳeul·ləl·ləny (m)   ስቀልልኝ
(Please) Get my luggage down.
 (ə·ba·kəh) shan·ṭa·yen   (እባክህ) ሻንጣዬን
 owr·dəl·ləny (m)   አው-ርድልኝ

TRAIN   ባቡር

Where's my seat?
 bo·ta·ye yeut nō?   በታዬ የት ነው?
Excuse me, this is my seat.
 yi·ḳər·ta bo·ta·ye nō   ይቅርታ በታዬ ነው-
What station is this?
 yi·he ba·bur ṭa·bi·ya mən   ይህ ባቡር ጣቢያ ምን
 yi·ba·lal?   ይባላል?

TRAVEL HITCHES

The bus is leaving now!
 ow·to·bə·su teu·neus·twal!   አው-ቶብሱ ተነስቷል!
(My friend) isn't back!
 (gwa·deu·nya·ye) al·geu·bam/   (ጓደኛዬ) አልገባም!/
 al·geu·ba·chəm! (m/f)   አልገባችም!
(The train) is delayed.
 (ba·bu·ru) zeu·gi·twal   (ባቡ-ሩ) ዘግይቷል
I feel sick.
 a·meu·meuny   አመመኝ
Please open the window.
 meus·ko·tun   መስኮቱን ይክፈቱልኝ
 yi·kə·feu·tu·liny

BOAT & CANOE

ጀልባ ና ታንኳ

Can you take me to ...?

weu·deu ...
tə·weus·deu·nyal·leuh? (m)

ወደ ... ትወስደኛለህ?

Which (monasteries) do you go to?

weu·deu yeu·tə·nyow (deu·bər)
tə·he·dal·leuh? (m)

ወደ የትኛው· (ደብር)
ትሄዳለህ?

What time does it return?

beu sənt seu'at yi·meul·leu·sal?

በስንት ሰዓት ይመለሳል?

| boat | jeul·ba | ጀልባ |
| canoe | tan·kwa | ታንኳ |

See also Outdoor Sports on page 184.

CAR

መኪና

Research your route before leaving. Road and safety conditions vary, as does the availability of mechanical assistance, petrol and spare parts.

Where can
I rent a ...?

... yeut meu·keu·ra·yeut
ə·cha·lal·lō?

... የት መከራየት
እችላለሁ?

4WD	for·wil draiv	ፎር ዊል ድራይቭ
car	meu·ki·na	መኪና
minivan	mi·ni·van	ሚኒቫን

I'd like a translator/driver.

as·teur·gwa·mi/shu·fer
ə·feul·lə·gal·lō

አስተርጓሚ/
ሹፌር እፈልጋለሁ·

How much is it for (a day/a week)?

leu (and keun/sam·mənt)
sənt nō?

ለ አንድ (ቀን/ሳምንት)
ስንት ነው?

Does that include insurance?

in·shu·rans·nəm
yi·cheu·mə·ral?

ኢንሹራንስንም
ይጨምራል?

How far is	yeu·mi·keu·ṭəl·lō	የሚቀጥለው…
the next ...?	... mən ya·həl yi·rə·kal?	ምን ያህል ይርቃል?
petrol station	neu·daj ma·deu·ya	ነዳጅ ማደያ
police station	po·lis ṭa·bi·ya	ፖሊስ ጣቢያ
town	keu·teu·ma	ከተማ

Can I park here?
    əz·zi ma·kom yi·cha·lal?   እዚህ ማቆም ይቻላል?

Please fill it up.
    ə·ba·kəh ben·zin mul·la·liny   እባክህ ቤንዚን ሙላልኝ

(Six) litres of petrol please.
    ə·ba·kəh (sə·dəst)   እባክህ (ስድስት)
    li·tər ben·zin   ሊትር ቤንዚን

Is it a dirt/asphalt road?
    meun·geu·du dən·ga·yam·ma/   መንገዱ ድንጋያማ/
    as·falt nō?   አስፋልት ነው?

TRAFFIC SIGNS

መንገድ ልቀቅ	GIVE WAY
መግባት ክልክል ነው·	NO ENTRY
ማቆም ክልክል ነው·	NO PARKING
ዝግታ	SLOW
ቁም	STOP

Road Safety   የመንገድ ላይ ጥንቃቄ

It's a good idea to ask local authorities about safety conditions
before setting out.

Are there problems on the road?
    meun·geud lai chig·gər al·leu?   መንገድ ላይ ችግር አለ?

No problem. It's safe.
    chig·gər yeul·leum. seu·lam nō   ችግር የለም፤ ሰላም ነው·

There are problems. It's not safe.
    chig·gər al·leu. seu·lam yeul·leum   ችግር አለ፤ ሰላም የለም

You can't pass this way.
beuz·zi beu·kul ma·leuf
kəl·kəl nō

በዚህ በኩል ማለፍ
ክልክል ነው።

Is there another way?
le·la meun·geud al·leu?

ሌላ መንገድ አለ?

Which road is better?
yeu·tə·nyow meun·geud
yi·sha·lal?

የትኛው መንገድ ይሻላል?

Do we need police protection?
yeu po·lis ər·da·ta
yas·feul·lə·geu·nal?

የፖሊስ እርዳታ
ያስፈልገናል?

Are there likely to be bandits?
shəf·ta yi·no·ral?

ሽፍታ ይኖራል?

Car Problems

የመኪና ችግሮች

Where can I find a mechanic?
meu·ka·nik yeut yi·geu·nyal?

መካኒክ የት ይገኛል?

There's something wrong with
this car.
meu·ki·now teu·beu·lash·twal

መኪናው ተበላሽቷል

The battery's flat.
bat·ryu al·kwal

ባትሪው አልቋል

The radiator's leaking.
ra·di·ya·teu·ru ya·feu·sal

ራዲያተሩ ያፈሳል

I have a flat tyre.
gom·ma·ye teun·fəss·wal

ጎማዬ ተንፍሷል

It's overheating.
mo·teu·ru mo·kwal

ሞተሩ ሞቋል

I've lost my car keys.
yeu·meu·ki·na·ye kulf
ţeuf·to·bə·nyal

የመኪናዬ ቁልፍ
ጠፍቶብኛል

I've run out of petrol.
ben·zin al·ko·bə·nyal

ቤንዚን አልቆብኛል

Please check the ...
... ə·ba·kəh ə·yō (m)

... እባክህ እየው-

GETTING AROUND

accelerator	ben·zin meus·cha	ቤንዚን መስጫ
battery	ba·tri	ባትሪ
brakes	fren	ፍሬን
clutch	fri·si·yon	ፍሪስዮን
drivers licence	meun·ja feu·kad	መንጃ ፈቃድ
engine	mo·teur	ሞተር
fan belt	chən·ge	ችንጄ
indicator	fre·cha	ፍሬቻ
lights	meu·brat	መብራት
number plate	tar·ga	ታርጋ
oil	yeu meu·ki·na zayt	የመኪና ዘይት
puncture (tyre)	yeu·teu·neu·feu·seu gom·ma	የተነፈሰ ጎማ
radiator	ra·di·ya·teur	ራዲያተር
tyres	gom·ma	ጎማ
water	wu·ha	ውሃ
windscreen	yeu fit meus·ta·weut	የፊት መስታወት

BICYCLE   ብስክሌት

Where can I hire a bicycle?
bəs·klet yeut meu·keu·ra·yeut ə·chə·lal·lō?   ብስክሌት የት መከራየት እችላለሁ?

Is it within cycling distance?
beu bəs·klet kərb nō?   በብስክሌት ቅርብ ነው?

I have a flat tyre.
gom·ma·ye teun·feuss·wal   ጎማዬ ተንፍሷል

bike	bəs·klet	ብስክሌት
helmet	hel·met	ሄልሜት
inner tube	keu·leu·meu·da·ri·ya	ከለመዳሪያ
lights	meub·rat	መብራት
padlock	yeu kulf gan	የቁልፍ ጋን
pump	yeu gom·ma meun·fi·ya	የጎማ መንፊያ
puncture	keu·da·da/ yeu·teu·neu·feu·seu	ቀዳዳ/ የተነፈሰ
tyre repairer	go·mis·ta	ጎሚስታ

HITCHHIKING   *መኪና እየጠበቁ በነፃ መጓዝ*

While hitchhiking is risky, it's sometimes the only way to reach places off the beaten track. Always hitch in pairs. For a lift, wave your hand or hold it out in a thumbs-up gesture. Don't forget pick-ups often function as buses or taxis, so you may have to pay for the ride.

Are you going to ...?
weu·deu ... tə·he·dal·leuh? (m)   ወደ ... ትሄዳለህ?

Can I get a lift with you please?
ə·ba·kəh a·sa·freuny? (m)   እባክህ አሳፍረኝ?

Please stop here.
ə·ba·kəh əz·zi a·kum (m)   እባክህ እዚህ አቁም

TALKING ABOUT TRAVELLING   *ስለ ጉዞዎ ማውራት*

Your fellow passengers will love hearing about where you're going and where you've been. See First Encounters, page 40, for basics.

I'm a tourist.
tu·rist/go·beu·nyi neuny   ቱሪስት/ጎብኚ ነኝ

Where are you heading?
weu·det nō?   ወዴት ነው?

I'm returning to ... (tomorrow).
(neu·geu) weu·deu ...   (ነገ) ወደ ...
ə·meul·leu·sal·lō   እመለሳለሁ

(Today) I arrived from ...
(za·re) keu ... geu·bow   (ዛሬ) ከ ... ገባሁ

I'll stay around here.
əz·zi ə·seu·neu·bə·tal·lō   እዚህ እሰነብታለሁ

How long have you been travelling?
gu·zo keu·jeu·meurk   ጉዞ ከጀመርክ
sənt gi·ze ho·neuh? (m)   ስንት ጊዜ ሆነህ?
gu·zo keu·jeu·meursh   ጉዞ ከጀመርሽ
sənt gi·ze ho·neush? (f)   ስንት ጊዜ ሆነሽ?

GETTING AROUND

I've been travelling for (two) months.
gu·zo keu·jeu·meur·ku
(hu·leutt) weur ho·neuny

ጉዞ ከጀመርኩ
(ሁለት) ወር ሆኖኛል

Where have you been?
yeut a·geur neub·beurk/
neub·beursh? (m/f)

የት አገር ነበርክ/
ነበርሽ?

I've been to (Egypt).
(gəbş) neub·beur·ku

(ግብጽ) ነበርኩ

How was it?
ən·det neub·beur?

እንዴት ነበር?

It was ...	... neub·beur	... ነበር
amazing	as·deu·na·ķi	አስደናቂ
beautiful	ķon·jo	ቆንጆ
boring	deu·ba·ri	ደባሪ
expensive	wədd	ውድ
historical	ta·ri·ka·wi	ታሪካዊ
interesting	yeu·mi·yas·deu·sət	የሚያስደስት
unique	lə·yu	ልዩ
very crowded	sō beu·ţam	ሰው በጣም
	yeu·beu·za·beut	የበዛበት

They're good people.
ţa·ru sō·woch na·chō

ጥሩ ሰዎች ናቸው

What's there to see in ...?
... mən yeu·mi·tai neu·geur al·leu?

... ምን የሚታይ ነገር አለ?

When's the best time to go there?
weu·deu·zi·ya leu meu·hed
ţa·ru gi·ze meu·che nō?

ወደዚያ ለመሄድ ጥሩ
ጊዜ መቼ ነው?

Is it difficult for women travelling on
their own?
leu set tu·ris·toch
as·cheu·ga·ri nō?

ለሴት ቱሪስቶች
አስቸጋሪ ነው?

ማረፊያ ቤት ACCOMMODATION

Ask for an extra tə·rass, 'pillow', and sink back into the al·ga, 'bed' – hotels are great places for practising your Amharic.

FINDING ACCOMMODATION   ማረፊያ ቤት መፈለግ

See In the Country, page 161, for words and phrases on camping.

Where can I find a ...?	... yeut yi·geu·nyal?	... የት ይኘ&ל?
hotel	ho·tel	ሆቴል
good hotel	tə·ru ho·tel	ጥሩ ሆቴል
cheap hotel	rə·kash ho·tel	ርካሽ ሆቴል
hotel nearby	kərb ho·tel	ቅርብ ሆቴል
luxury hotel	təl·lək ho·tel	ትልቅ ሆቴል
place to sleep	ma·reu·fi·ya bo·ta	ማረፊያ ቤት

Is it near the city centre/
bus station?
  leu (meu·hal keu·teu·ma;
  ow·to·bəs ṭa·bi·ya) yi·keur·bal?   ለ (መሃል ከተማ/
  አውቶቡስ ጣቢያ) ይቀርባል?

BOOKING AHEAD   በቅድሚያ ቤት መያዝ

A 'single' often means a room with a double bed, and a 'double' a room with two beds. The Amharic word for bed, al·ga, is often used in place of kə·fəl, 'room'.

I'd like to book a room (please).
  (ə·ba·kon) al·ga
  meu·yaz ə·feul·lə·gal·lō   (እባክዎን) አልጋ
                             መያዝ እፈልጋለሁ

| double | hu·leutt | ሁለት |
| single | and | አንድ |

ACCOMMODATION

How much is it per (night/week)?
leu and (ma·ta/sam·mənt)
sənt nō?

ለ (አንድ ማታ/ሳምንት)
ስንት ነው?

Does the price include (breakfast)?
(ḳur·sə·nəm) yi·cheu·mə·ral?

(ቁርስንም) ይጨምራል?

I'll/We'll be arriving at ... o'clock.
beu ... seu'at ə·deur·sal·lō/
ən·deur·sal·leun

በ ... ሰዓት እደርሳለሁ/
እንደርሳለን

My name's ...
sə·me ... nō

ስሜ ... ነው

CHECKING IN
See Paperwork, page 89, for assistance with forms.

አልጋ መያዝ

Are there any rooms available?
al·ga al·leu?

አልጋ አለ?

We're full.
al·ga yeul·leu·nəm

አልጋ የለንም

I want to see the room.
kəf·lun ma·yeut ə·feul·lə·gal·lō

ክፍሉን ማየት እፈልጋለሁ

Can I see a different room?
le·la kə·fəl ma·yeut ə·cha·lal·lō?

ሌላ ክፍል ማየት እችላለሁ?

I/We want a   ... yal·lō kə·fəl
room with a ...   ə·feul·lə·gal·lō/
                    ən·feul·lə·gal·leun

... ያለው ክፍል
እፈልጋለሁ/
እንፈልጋለን

  bathroom   meu·ta·ṭeu·bi·ya bet
  TV   ti·vi

መታጠቢያ ቤት
ቲቪ

How long will you be staying?
sənt gi·ze tə·ḳo·yal·leuh? (m)
sənt gi·ze tə·ḳo·yal·leush? (f)

ስንት ጊዜ ትቆያለህ?
ስንት ጊዜ ትቆያለሽ?

I'm staying for ...   ... ə·ḳo·yal·lō

... እቆያለሁ

  (one) night   (and) ma·ta
  (two) weeks   (hu·leutt) sam·mənt
  (three) days   (sost) ḳeun

(አንድ) ማታ
(ሁለት) ሳምንት
(ሶስት) ቀን

I leave (tomorrow morning).

(neu·geu ṭeu·wat) ə·he·dal·lō   (ነገ ጠዋት) እሄዳለሁ

I don't know yet.

geu·na a·la·weu·kum   ገና አላወኩም

BATHROOM BASICS

Showers in cheaper hotels could be either bal·di, 'bucket', or yeu bwam·bwa wu·ha, 'running water'. You can buy soft, 'toilet paper', from local kiosks. There's often a waste basket beside toilets, as putting paper down the drain can block plumbing.

Do you have hot water (all day)?

muḳ wu·ha   ሙቅ ውሃ

(ḳeu·nun mu·lu) al·leu?   (ቀኑን ሙሉ) አለ?

The plumbing is blocked.

tu·bō teu·deuf·nwal   ቱቦው ተደፍኗል

Where's the ...?	... yeut nō?	... የት ነው?
toilet	shənt bet	ሽንት ቤት
bathroom	meu·ta·ṭeu·bi·ya bet	መታጠቢያ ቤት
shower	sha·weur	ሻወር
wash basin	yeu fit	የፊት
	meu·ta·ṭeu·bi·ya	መታጠቢያ
soap	sa·mu·na	ሳሙና
towel	fo·ṭa	ፎጣ
water for bathing	meu·ta·ṭeu·bi·ya wu·ha	መታጠቢያ ውሃ
water for laundry	yeu·ləbs ma·ṭeu·bi·ya wu·ha	የልብስ ማጠቢያ ውሃ
water for toilet	leu shənt bet wu·ha	ለሽንት ቤት ውሃ

REQUESTS & QUERIES   ጥያቄዎች

Please clean my room.
ə·ba·kəh kəf·len aṣ·da·ləny (m)   እባክህ ክፍሌን አጽዳልኝ
ə·ba·kəsh kəf·len aṣ·ja·ləny (f)   እባክሽ ክፍሌን አጽጂልኝ
Please change the bed sheets.
an·so·la ḳeu·yə·rə·ləny (m)   አንሶላ ቀይርልኝ
an·so·la ḳeu·yə·ri·ləny (f)   አንሶላ ቀይሪልኝ
Where's the dining room?
mə·gəb be·tu yeut nö?   ምግብ ቤቱ የት ነው?
Is there somewhere to wash clothes?
ləbs ma·ṭeu·bi·ya bo·ta al·leu?   ልብስ ማጠቢያ ቦታ አለ?
Is there a laundry service?
yeu·lown·deu·ri a·geul·glot al·leu?   የላውንደሪ አገልግሎት አለ?
Can I use the telephone?
səlk meu·ṭeu·ḳeum ə·chə·lal·lö?   ስልክ መጠቀም እችላለሁ?
I've locked myself out of my room.
ḳul·fen kəf·lu wəşt reu·sow   ቁልፈን ክፍሉ ውስጥ እረሳሁ
Please wake me up at (one o'clock).
ə·ba·kəh (and seu'at)   እባክህ (አንድ ሰዓት)
lai ḳeuss·kəs·seuny (m)   ላይ ቀስቀሰኝ
ə·ba·kəsh (and seu'at)   እባክሽ (አንድ ሰዓት)
lai ḳeuss·kə·shiny (f)   ላይ ቀስቅሺኚ
Do you arrange tours to ...?
weu·deu ... gub·bə·nyit   ወደ ... ጉብኝት
ta·zeu·ga·jal·la·chu?   ታዘጋጃላችሁ?
Can you recommend a guide/
translator?
yeu·mə·tow·ḳut as·gob·nyi/   የምታወቁት አስጎብኚ/
as·teur·gwa·mi al·leu?   አስተርጓሚ አለ?
Is there a message for me?
leu·ne meu·lə·kət al·leu?   ለኔ መልእክት አለ?
Could I have a receipt please?
ə·ba·kon deu·reu·seuny?   እባክዎን ደረሰኝ?

I want another ...   le·la ... ə·feul·lə·gal·lö   ሌላ ... እፈል.ጋለሁ
blanket   bərd ləbs   ብርድ ልብስ
pillow   tə·rass   ትራስ

COMPLAINTS

ቅሬታ

I can't open/	... meuk·feut/	... መክፈት/
close the ...	meuz·gat al·chəl·ləm	መዝጋት አልቻልም
door	beu·run	በሩን
window	meus·ko·tun	መስኮቱን

The ... doesn't work.	... ai·seu·ram	... አይሰራም
electricity	e·le·tri·ku	ኤሌትሪኩ
light	meub·ra·tu	መብራቱ
tap	bwan·bwow	ቧንቧው

This room's (very) ...	kəf·lu (beu·ṭam) ...	ክፍሉ (በጣም) ...
cold	yi·beur·dal	ይበርዳል
hot	yi·mo·kal	ይሞቃል
noisy	a·ka·ba·bi	አካባቢ
	cha·cha·ta al·leu	ጫጫታ አለ
smelly	wəsṭ meuṭ·fo	ውስጥ መጥፎ
	shə·ta al·leu	ሽታ አለ

This room's not clean.
kəf·lu nə·ṣuh ai·deul·leum ክፍሉ ንፁህ አይደለም

I want another room.
le·la kə·fəl ə·feul·lə·gal·lō ሌላ ክፍል እፈልጋለሁ

OUT IN THE COLD

Some hotels lock the grounds before midnight. If you're planning a big night out drinking a·reu·ḳi (a local liquor) with friends, it's worth checking with reception and the zeu·beu·nya, 'security guard', before you go out.

What time do you lock the grounds?
beu sənt seu'at beur በስንት ሰዓት በር
tə·zeu·gal·la·chu? ትዘጋላችሁ?

Can I get back in after (midnight)?
keu (ə·ku·leu le·lit) bo·hal·la ከ (እኩለ ሌሊት) በኋላ
meum·meu·leus ə·cha·lal·lō? መመለስ እችላለሁ?

I'm a hotel guest.
əz·zi ho·tel nō ya·reuf·kut እዚህ ሆቴል ነው ያረፍኩት

ACCOMMODATION

ACCOMMODATION

CHECKING OUT

ከሆቴል መውጣት

I'd like to check out today/tomorrow.
kəf·lun za·re/neu·geu ə·leu·ḳal·lō

ክፍሉን ዛሬ/ነገ እሊቃለሁ

I want to pay the bill (now).
(a·hun) meuk·feul
ə·feul·lə·gal·lō

(አሁን) መክፈል
እፈልጋለሁ

I have already paid.
keu·fə·yal·lō

ከፍያለሁ

There's a mistake in the bill.
deu·reu·seu·nye lai
sə·hə·teut al·leu

ደረሰኜ ላይ ስህተት አለ

I'm returning in (one) week.
keu (and) sam·mənt bo·hal·la
ə·meul·leu·sal·lō

ከ (አንድ) ሳምንት በኋላ
እመለሳለሁ

Can I leave my luggage here?
shan·ṭa·yen əz·zi
mas·keu·meuṭ ə·chə·lal·lō?

ሻንጣዬን እዚህ
ማስቀመጥ እችላለሁ?

How much per day?
beu ḳeun sənt nō?

በቀን ስንት ነው?

Please call me a taxi.
ə·ba·kəh tak·si ṭə·ral·ləny (m)
ə·ba·kəsh tak·si ṭə·ril·ləny (f)

እባክህ ታክሲ ጥራልኝ
እባክሽ ታክሲ ጥሪልኝ

SNOOZE TIME

I'm tired.
deu·kə·mo·nyal

ደክሞኛል

I'm/We're going to sleep now.
lə·teu·nya/lən·teu·nya nō

ልተኛ/ልንተኛ ነው

I want to rest.
ma·reuf ə·feul·lə·gal·lō

ማረፍ እፈልጋለሁ

I dreamt a lot.
bə·zu həlm ai·yō

ብዙ ሕልም አየሁ

LONG-TERM ACCOMMODATION

የረጅም ጊዜ መኖሪያ

I'd like to rent a room near (the university).

(yu·ni·veur·si·ti) a·teu·geub and kə·fəl meu·keu·ra·yeut ə·feul·lə·gal·lō

(ዩኒቨርስቲ) አጠገብ አንድ ክፍል መከራየት እፈልጋለሁ

Do you have a special rate for (one month)?

leu (and weur) kə·nash al·la·chu?

ለ (አንድ ወር) ቅናሽ አላችሁ?

I want to rent a house.

bet meu·keu·ra·yeut ə·feul·lə·gal·lō

ቤት መከራየት እፈልጋለሁ

How much per (month)?

leu (weur) sənt nō?

ለ (ወር) ስንት ነው?

Useful Words

ጠቃሚ ቃሎች

candle	sha·ma	ሻማ
chair	weun·beur	ወንበር
cupboard	ķum sa·ţən	ቁም ሳጥን
curtains	meu·ga·reu·ja	መጋረጃ
iron	kow·ya	ካውያ
key	ķulf	ቁልፍ
light	meub·rat	መብራት
matches	kəb·rit	ክብሪት
mattress	fə·rash	ፍራሽ
mosquito net	yeu bim·bi meu·reub	የቢምቢ መረብ
padlock	meu·ķo·leu·fi·ya gan	መቆለፊያ ጋን
porter	teu·sheu·ka·mi	ተሸካሚ
power socket	so·ket	ሶኬት
safe	ya·deu·ra ə·ķa	ያደራ ዕቃ
	mas·ķeu·meu·cha sa·ţən	ማስቀመጫ ሳጥን
security guard	zeu·beu·nya	ዘበኛ
sheet	an·so·la	አንሶላ
worker	seu·ra·teu·nya	ሰራተኛ

ACCOMMODATION

STAYING WITH A FAMILY ከቤተሰብ ጋር መሰንበት

Staying with a family is a great way to experience local life. Ethiopian households have a regular stream of visitors, including go·reu·bet, 'neighbours', teu·keu·rai, 'lodgers', zeu·meud, 'relatives', giggling yeu seu·feur lə·joch, 'local children' and yeu bet seu·ra·teu·nya, 'domestic helpers'.

Please come and stay with us.
ə·nya ga ə·reuf (m)	እኛ ጋ እረፍ
ə·nya ga ə·reu·fi (f)	እኛ ጋ እረፊ
ə·nya ga yi·reu·fu (pol)	እኛ ጋ ይረፉ

Where do you live?
yeut tə·no·ral·leuh? (m)	የት ትኖራለህ?
yeut tə·no·ri·yal·leush? (f)	የት ትኖሪያለሽ?

I'm leaving today/tomorrow.
za·re/neu·geu ə·he·dal·lō	ዛሬ/ነገ እሄዳለሁ

I'll visit you on my way back.
sə·meul·leuss ə·meu·ṭal·lō	ስመለስ እመጣለሁ

Thank you for your hospitality.
a·meu·seu·gə·nal·lō sə·leu	አመሰግናለሁ ስለ
meus·teun·gə·dō	መስተንግዱው

ACCOMMODATION

Whether you're searching for a səlk, 'phone', or in dire need of a şim·meu·la·cheut, 'shave', you'll be a·ra·da, 'street wise', with some Amharic.

LOOKING FOR ...   ... መፈለግ

Is there a	əz·zi a·ka·ba·bi	እዚህ አካባቢ
... nearby?	... al·leu?	... አለ?
bank	bank	ባንክ
hotel	ho·tel	ሆቴል
market	geu·bi·ya	ገቢያ
restaurant	mə·gəb bet	ምግብ ቤት
post office	pos·ta bet	ፖስታ ቤት
toilet	shənt bet	ሽንት ቤት
travel agency	yeu gu·zo weu·kil	የጉዞ ወኪል
Where is it?	yeut nō	የት ነው?

Where's the ...?	... yeut nō?	... የት ነው?
city centre	meu·hal keu·teu·ma	መሃል ከተማ
... embassy	yeu ... em·bas·si	የ ... ኤምባሲ
tourist office	yeu tu·rist bi·ro	የቱሪስት ቢሮ
university	yu·ni·veurs·ti	ዩኒቨርስቲ

What time does it open/close?
    beu sənt seu'at yi·keu·feu·tal/   በስንት ሰዓት ይከፈታል/
    yiz·zeu·gal?   ይዘጋል?

AT THE BANK   ባንክ

You'll find banks and international exchange facilities in major
town centres, but credit card services are more limited. Don't
forget to hold on to currency declaration/exchange forms and
receipts in case you need to show them on departure.

Where can I change money?
  geun·zeub meu·keu·yeu·ri·yow   ገንዘብ መቀየሪያው
  yeut nō?   የት ነው-?
I want to change money/
travellers cheques
  geun·zeub/trav·leur chek   ገንዘብ/ትራ·ቭለር
  meu·keu·yeur ə·feul·lə·gal·lō   ቸክ መቀየር እፈልጋለሁ-
What's the rate?
  beu sənt wa·ga?   በስንት ዋጋ?
Can I use my credit card to
withdraw money?
  geun·zeub beu kre·dit kard   ገንዘብ በክሬዲት ካርድ
  mow·tat ə·chə·lal·lō?   ማውጣት እችላለሁ-?
I'd like to get some money
transferred to me from ...
  geun·zeub keu ...   ገንዘብ ከ ...
  ən·diz·za·weur·liny ə·feul·lə·gal·lō እንዲዛወርልኝ እፈልጋለሁ-
How long will it take?
  sənt gi·ze yi·weus·dal?   ስንት ጊዜ ይወስዳል?
I'm expecting a money
transfer from ...
  geun·zeub keu ... ə·ţeu·bə·kal·lō   ገንዘብ ከ ... እጠብቃለሁ-
Has my money transfer
from ... arrived?
  geun·zeub keu ... meu·to·lə·nyal?   ገንዘብ ከ ... መቶልኛል?

coins	san·tim	ሳንቲም
currency	yeu geun·zeub ai·neut	የገንዘብ ዓይነት
exchange bureau	yeu geun·zeub	የገንዘብ
	meu·keu·yeu·ri·ya bi·ro	መቀየሪያ ቢሮ

AT THE POST OFFICE

ፖስታ ቤት

Postal staff read and write English. Words such as 'postcard', 'telegram' and 'telex' retain their English names. See Stationery & Publications, page 133, for other useful words.

Where can I post this?
yeut las·geu·bow?   የት ላስገባው?

I'd like to   ... meu·lak   ... መላክ
send a ...   ə·feul·lə·gal·lō   እፈልጋለሁ
   gift   sə·ṭo·ta   ስጦታ
   letter   deub·dab·be   ደብዳቤ
   package   ṭə·ḳəl   ጥቅል

How much is it to ...?
weu·deu ... sənt nō?   ወደ ... ስንት ነው?

(Three) stamps please.
ə·ba·kon (sost) tem·bər   እባክዎን (ሶስት) ቴምብር

A (three)-birr stamp.
ba·leu (sost) bərr tem·bər   ባለ (ሶስት) ብር ቴምብር

Am I allowed to send (this)?
(yi·hen) meu·lak ə·chə·lal·lō?   (ይህን) መላክ እችላለሁ?

Could I borrow a pen please?
əs·krip·to an·de lə·was?   እስክሪፕቶ አንዴ ልዋስ?

Where's the (poste restante) section?
(post res·tant) al·leu?   (ፖስት ሬስታንቴ) አለ?

Do you have mail for me?
My name's ...
leu·ne deub·dab·be al·leu?   ለኔ ደብዳቤ አለ?
sə·me ... nō   ስሜ ... ነው

airmail	ya·yeur meul'əkt	የአየር መልእክት
box	sa·ṭən	ሳጥን
envelope	pos·ta	ፖስታ
express post/EMS	as·cheu·kwai/i·em·es	አስቸኳይ/ኢኤምኤስ
mailbox	yeu pos·ta sa·ṭən	የፖስታ ሳጥን
registered post	ya·deu·ra deub·dab·be	ያደራ ደብዳቤ
stamp	tem·bər	ቴምብር
surface mail	yeu·yeubs meul'əkt	የየብስ መልእክት

ADDRESSES   አድራሻ

What's the address?

ad·ra·show yeut nō?   አድራሻው የት ነው?

Is that the postal/residential
address?

yeu (pos·ta; meu·no·ri·ya bet)   የ (ፖስታ/መኖሪያ ቤት)
ad·ra·sha nō?   አድራሻ ነው?

Use roman script for writing postal addresses. Many Ethiopian
postal addresses are PO boxes, but you'll sometimes see words
like *woreda* (wo·reu·da, 'region'), *kebele* (ķeu·beu·le, 'local
administration') and a suburb name.

> Lakiya Tasew
> PO Box: 6122
> Woreda 17, Kebele 25, Gerj
> Addis Ababa, Ethiopia

TELECOMMUNICATIONS   ስልክ ቤት

You can make long-distance/international calls and send/receive
faxes from a *səlk bet*, where telecommunications staff generally
speak English. You can also use public phones and local shops for
local/national calls.

Is there a	əz·zi a·ka·ba·bi	እዚህ አካባቢ
... nearby?	... al·leu?	... አለ?
fax service	yeu faks	የፋክስ
	a·geul·glot	አገልግሎት
public telephone	yeu həzb səlk	የሕዝብ ስልክ
shop with	səlk yal·lō suk	ስልክ ያለው ሱቅ
a telephone		
telecommunications	səlk bet	ስልክ ቤት
building		

I want to make a local/international call.

(a·geur wəsṭ; wəçh a·geur) səlk   (አገር ውስጥ/ውጭ አገር)
meu·deu·weul ə·feul·lə·gal·lō   ስልክ መደወል

I want to send/receive a fax.
faks meu·lak/meu·ķeu·beul
ə·feul·lə·gal·lō

ፋክስ መላክ/መቀበል
እፈልጋለሁ

I want to call ...
weu·deu ... meu·deu·weul
ə·feul·lə·gal·lō

ወደ ... መደወል
እፈልጋለሁ

The number is ...
ķu·ţru ... nō

ቁጥሩ ... ነው

I want to reverse the charges/
make a collect call.
teu·zeu·wa·wa·ri ə·feul·lə·gal·lō

ተዘዋዋሪ እፈልጋለሁ

How much does it cost
for ... minute(s)?
leu ... deu·ķi·ķa sənt nō?

ለ ... ደቂቃ ስንት ነው?

How much is it for ... page(s)?
leu ... geuş sənt nō?

ለ ... ገጽ ስንት ነው?

I want to speak to the operator.
o·pə·re·teur ə·feul·lə·gal·lō

ኦፐራተር እፈልጋለሁ

The number for ... (please).
(ə·ba·kon) yeu ... ķu·ţər

(እባክዎን) የ ... ቁጥር

I'd like to speak to ...
... ma·neu·ga·geur
ə·feul·lə·gal·lō

... ማነጋገር እፈልጋለሁ

The number is ...
ķu·ţru ... nō

ቁጥሩ ... ነው

It's engaged.
tay·zwal

ተይዟል

Nobody answered.
ma·nəm a·ya·neu·sa·wəm

ማንም አያነሳውም

I've been cut off.
meus·meur teu·ķwar·ţwal

መስመር ተቋርጧል

deposit	meu·ya·zha	መያዣ
mobile phone	mo·bail fon	ሞባይል ፎን
phone book	yeu səlk mow·cha	የስልክ ማውጫ
urgent	as·cheu·kwai	አስቸኳይ

Making a Call
ስልክ መደወል

When using the polite form, use a·to, 'Mr', or way·zeu·ro, 'Mrs', before a person's first name.

Hello, is ... there?
al·lo ... a·leu/
al·leuch/al·lu? (m/f/pol)
አሎ ... አለ/አለች/አሉ-?

Who's calling?
man lə·beul?
ማን ልበል?

It's ... speaking.
... ə·ba·lal·lō
... እባላለሁ-

One moment (please).
and gi·ze (ə·ba·kon)
አንድ ጊዜ (እባክዎን)

He's/She's gone out.
weu·ṭa bə·leu·wal
ወጣ ብለዋል

ሰላም ደህና ነህ?

ደህና ነኝ

He's/She's not here.
yeul·leum/yeul·leu·chəm
የለም/የለችም

Can I leave a message?
meul'əkt meu·tō ə·cha·lal·lō?
መልእክት መተው- እችላለሁ-?

Please tell him/her ... called.
... deu·wəl·lo neub·beur
yi·beu·lu·ləny
... ደውሎ ነበር ይበሉልኝ

My number is ...
səlk ḳu·ṭre ... nō
ስልክ ቁጥሬ ... ነው-

I'll call back later.
bo·hal·la ə·deu·wə·lal·lō
በኋላ እደውላለሁ-

What time should I call?
beu sənt seu'at lə·deu·wəl?
በስንት ሰዓት ልደውል?

COMPUTING SERVICES

የኮምፒውተር
አገልግሎት

Terms like kom·pyu·teur and mo·deum are easy to recognise, being so similar to English. There are few Internet services outside Addis. See Stationery & Publications, page 133, and Business, page 215, for document services.

Is there an internet café?
   yeu in·teur·net a·geul·glot
   al·leu?

የኢንተርኔት
አገልግሎት አለ?

Is there a place to send email?
   i·mel meu·la·ki·ya bo·ta al·leu?

ኢ.ሜል መላኪያ ቦታ አለ?

I'd like to receive/send email.
   i·mel meu·keu·beul/meu·lak
   ə·feul·lə·gal·lō

ኢ.ሜል መቀበል/
መላክ እፈልጋለሁ

How much for (10 minutes)?
   leu (a·sər deu·ki·ka) sənt nō?

ለ (አስር ደቂቃ) ስንት ነው?

SIGHTSEEING

አገር ማየት

Castles, historical ruins and island monasteries are amongst Ethiopia's key attractions. Ethiopians are happy to share their unique heritage with others, but ask people before taking their photograph or before wandering into areas that may be off limits. There are restrictions on photographing certain sights.

Where's the tourist office?
   yeu tu·rist bi·rō yeut nō?

የቱሪስት ቢሮው የት ነው?

Do you have a map?
   kar·ta al·leuh/al·leush? (m/f)

ካርታ አለህ/አለሽ?

What are the main attractions?
   meu·ta·yet ya·leu·ba·chō
   bo·ta·woch yeu·tə·nyo·chu
   na·chō?

መታየት ያለባቸው
ቦታዎች የትኞቹ ናቸው?

How much is the entry fee?
   meug·bi·ya sənt nō?

መግቢያ ስንት ነው?

Is there a discount for (children)?

leu (lə·joch) kə·nash al·leu?   ለ (ልጆች) ቅናሽ አለ?

Am I allowed to take
photographs here?

əz·zi fo·to man·sat yi·cha·lal?   እዚህ ፎቶ ማንሳት ይቻላል?

How much is it to take
a video/picture?

vi·di·yo/fo·to leu man·sat   ቪ·ዲዮ/ፎቶ ለማንሳት
sənt nō?   ስንት ነው?

Can I take your photograph?

fo·to lan·sah? (m)   ፎቶ ላንሳህ?
fo·to lan·sash? (f)   ፎቶ ላንሳሽ?
fo·to lan·sa·chu? (pl)   ፎቶ ላንሳችሁ?

Can you please take my
photograph?

ə·ba·kəh fo·to an·sany? (m)   እባክህ ፎቶ አንሳኝ
ə·ba·kəsh fo·to an·shiny? (f)   እባክሽ ፎቶ አንሺኚ

I'll send you the photo.

fo·to·wən ə·lə·kal·lō   ፎቶውን አልካለሁ

The Sights   የሚነበቤ ቦታዎች

Can you show me ...?

... li·ya·sa·yuny yi·chi·lal·lu?   ... ሊያሳዩኝ ይችላሉ?

Can I have a look at ...?

... ma·yeut yi·cha·lal?   ... ማየት ይቻላል?

Can I touch/hold it?

meun·kat/meu·yaz yi·cha·lal?   መንካት/መያዝ ይቻላል?

Can I see inside?

wəst ma·yeut yi·cha·lal?   ውስጥ ማየት ይቻላል?

Excuse me, what's this/that?

yi·kər·ta, yi·he/ya   ይቅርታ ይህ/ያ
mən·dən nō?   ምንድን ነው?

What's this/that called?

yeuz·zi/yeuz·za sǝm   የዚህ/የዛ
mən·dən nō?   ስም ምንድን ነው?

building	hən·ṣa/foḳ	ሕንፃ/ፎቅ
church	be·teu krəs·ti·yan	ቤተ ክርስቲያን
court (of law)	fərd bet	ፍርድ ቤት
hall	a·da·rash	አዳራሽ
hot spring baths	fəl wu·ha	ፍል ውሃ
library	be·teu meu·ṣə·haf	ቤተ መጻሐፍ
market area	meur·ka·to/a·ra·da	መርካቶ/አራዳ
monastery	deu·bər	ደብር
museum	be·teu meu·zeu·kər	ቤተ መዘክር
national (theatre)	bə·he·ra·wi (ti·ya·tər)	ብሔራዊ (ትያትር)
parliament	par·la·ma; mə·kər bet	ፓርላማ/ምክር ቤት
park/gardens	meu·na·feu·sha	መናፈሻ
swimming pool	meu·wa·nya bo·ta	መዋኛ ቦታ
sports	sport	ስፖርት
square	ad·deu·ba·bai	አደባባይ
stadium	sta·di·yeum	ስታዲየም
statue/monument	ha·wəlt	ሐውልት
tourist office	yeu tu·rist bi·ro	የቱሪስት ቢሮ
university	yu·ni·veurs·ti	ዩኒቨርስቲ
wall	gəd·gəd·da	ግድግዳ
zoo	zu	ዙ

AROUND TOWN

NAME DROPPING

Emperor Menelik	a·ṣe mi·ni·lik	አጼ ሚኒሊክ
Lion of Judah	yeu yi·hu·da	የይሁዳ
	an·beus·sa	አንበሳ
Lucy	dənḳ·neush	ድንቅነሽ
(the hominoid)		
Mohammed	grany	ግራኝ መ ሃመድ
the Left-Handed	meu·ham·meud	
Prince Taferi	ras teu·feu·ri	ራስ ተፈሪ
Queen of Sheba	nə·gəst sa·ba	ንግስት ሳባ

TALKING HISTORY

How old is it?
    əd·ma·yō sənt nō?   እድሜዉ· ስንት· ነዉ?
What period is it from?
    keu·yeu·te·nyow
    kə·fə·leu zeu·meun nō?   ከየትኛዉ· ክፍለ
                                                ዘመን ነዉ?

the Stone Age	yeu dən·gai zeu·meun	የድንጋይ ዘመን
civilization	sə·lə·ṭa·ne	ስልጣኔ
(Aksum)	yeu (ak·sum)	የ(አክሱም)
(Zagwe)	(za·gō) zeu·meu·neu	(ዛጔ·)
dynasty	meun·gəst	ዘመነ መንግስት
(20th) century	ha·ya·nyow kəf·leu	ሃያኛዉ·
	zeu·meun	ክፍለ ዘመን
time of Italian	beu ṭal·yan	በጣልያን
occupation	weu·reu·ra gi·ze	ወረራ ጊዜ
ancestor	kəd·meu a·yat	ቅድመ አያት
ancient buildings	ṭən·ta·wi gəmb	ጥንታዊ ግምብ
antique	ṭən·ta·wi	ጥንታዊ
Aksum monoliths	yeu ak·sum ha·wəl·toch	የአክሱም ሐውልቶች
castle	gəmb	ግምብ
emperor	nə·gu·seu neu·geust	ንጉሰ ነገስት
excavation	ḵu·feu·ra	ቁፈራ
feudalism	ba·la·ba·ta·wi a·geu·zaz	በላባታዊ አገዛዝ
fortress	təl·ləḵ mə·shəg	ትልቅ ምሽግ
fossil/remains	a·ṣəm/ḵə·rit	አፅም/ቅሪት
fragments	sə·bər·ba·ri	ስብርባሪ
grave/tomb	meu·ḵa·bər	መቃብር
history	ta·rik	ታሪክ
monarchy	nə·gu·sa·wi a·geu·zaz	ንጉሣዊ አገዛዝ
palace	be·teu meun·gəst	ቤተ መንግስት
patriot	ar·beu·nya	አርበኛ
revolution	a·bə·yot	አብዮት
rock hewn	keu a·leut yeu·teu·seu·ru	ከአለት የተሰሩ
churches	be·teu krəs·ti·ya·noch	ቤተ ክርስቲያኖች
ruins	fə·rash	ፍራሽ
stele	ha·wəlt	ሐውልት
tools	meu·sa·ri·ya·woch	መሣሪያዎች

AROUND TOWN

TOURS, GUIDES & TRANSLATORS

ጉብኝቶች፣ አስጎብኚዎችና
አስተርጓሚዎች

Are there regular tours to ...?

weu·deu ... ḳwa·mi yeu·ho·nu
gu·bə·nyi·toch al·lu?

ወደ ... ቋሚ የሆኑ
ጉብኝቶች አሉ?

Is there a guide/translator available?

as·gob·nyi/as·teur·gwa·mi
al·leu?

አስጎብኚ /አስተርጓሚ
አለ?

How much for (one hour/
two hours)?

leu (and seu'at/hu·leutt seu'at)
sənt nō?

ለ (አንድ ሰዓት/
ሁለት ሰዓት) ስንት ነው-?

How long is the tour?

gu·bə·nyi·tu sənt gi·ze
yi·weus·dal?

ጉብኝቱ ስንት
ጊዜ ይወስዳል?

Does the tour go to ...?

gu·bə·nyi·tu weu·deu ...
yi·hed·al?

ጉብኝቱ ወደ ...
ይሄዳል?

I've lost my group.

a·breu·wəny yeu·meu·ṭut
sō·woch ṭeu·fu·bəny

አብረው-ኝ የመጡ-ት
ሰዎች ጠፉ-ብኝ

ON THE STREET

መንገድ ላይ

Ethiopian streets attract a fascinating crowd of street vendors,
beggars, shoe cleaners and roaming orators. Many have migrated
from country areas in search of work or more stability. Never refuse
a beggar – simply say əg·zər yis·ṭəh/yis·ṭəsh/yis·ṭə·ləny (m/f/pol),
'May God give you', if you don't want to give money.

I want it.

ə·feul·lə·gal·lō

እፈልጋለሁ-

I don't want it.

al·feul·lə·gəm

አልፈልግም

Sorry, I don't have any change.

az·nal·lō zər·zər yeul·leu·nyəm

አዝናለሁ- ዝርዝር የለኝም

AROUND TOWN

beggar	məs·kin	ምስኪን
city dweller	keu·teu·me	ከተሜ
footpath	yeu·gər meun·geud	የግር መንገድ
hawkers	suk̟ beu·deu·reu·te	ሱቅ በደረቴ
newspaper seller	ga·ze·t̟a shach̟	ጋዜጣ ሻጭ
shoe shiner	lis·tro	ሊስትሮ
snack seller	k̟o·lo shach̟	ቆሎ ሻጭ
street	meun·geud	መንገድ
street children	yeu go·da·na teu·da·da·ri	የጎዳና ተዳዳሪ
	hə·s̟a·nat	ሕፃናት
street lamp	yeu meun·geud meub·rat	የመንገድ መብራት
street stall	gul·lət	ጉልት
traffic lights	yeu tra·fik meub·rat	የትራፊክ መብራት

AROUND TOWN

UNWANTED ATTENTION   ሰውን ማስቸገር

Often the most difficult part of travelling in Ethiopia is dealing with unwanted attention, ranging from an occasional 'You! You! You!' to a steady crescendo of feu·reunj! feu·reunj!, 'Foreigner!/ White person!', from groups of giggling children. Try to remember that no malice is intended – it's usually a sign of curiosity or excitement. Saying hid! (m) or hij! (f), 'Go away!', or zəm·beul!, 'Shut up!', often only makes things worse. The best approach is to either ignore it, or to use some friendly Amharic phrases like sə·ma·chu man nō?, 'What are your names?'. See also Talking with Children, page 105.

PAPERWORK   የሚሞሉ ፎርሞች

While officials generally speak English, and official forms show English translations, the following may be useful:

I'd like ...	... ə·feul·lə·gal·lō	... እፈልጋለሁ
to extend	vi·za·yen	ቪዛዬን ማሳደስ
my visa	ma·sa·deuss	
to visit the	(bə·he·ra·wi park)	(ብሔራዊ ፓርክ)
(National Park)	meu·go·bə·nyeut	መጎብኘት
Is a/an ... required?	... yas·feul·lə·gal?	... ያስፈልጋል?
I have a/an ...	... al·leuny	... አለኝ
entry permit	meug·bi·ya feu·kad	መግቢያ ፈቃድ
form	kəş (form)	ቅፅ (ፎርም)
letter of	yeu feu·kad	የፈቃድ ደብዳቤ
permission	deub·dab·be	
pass/permit	yeu yi·leuf feu·kad	የይለፍ ፈቃድ
police report	yeu po·lis ri·port	የፖሊስ ሪፖርት
proof of	yeu meu·ta·weu·ki·ya	የመታወቂያ
identity	weu·reu·keut	ወረቀት
receipt	deur·reu·seuny	ደረሰኝ

AROUND TOWN

Forms

ፎርሞች

name	sət	ሰም
address	a·dra·sha	አድራሻ
age	əd·me	እድሜ
sex	ṣo·ta	ፆታ
nationality	ze·gə·neut	ዜግነት
religion	hai·ma·not	ሃይማኖት
occupation	sə·ra	ስራ
date of arrival	yeu geu·bu·beut ķeun	የገቡበት ቀን
date of birth	yeu tu·ləd ķeun	የተውልድ ቀን
date of departure	yeu weu·țu·beut ķeun	የወጡበት ቀን
country of birth	yeu tu·ləd a·geur	የትውልድ አገር
domicile	meu·no·ri·ya	መኖሪያ
duration of stay	yeu mi·ķo·yu·beut gi·zay	የሚቆዩበት ጊዜ
passport number	yeu pas·port ku·țar	የፓስፖርት ቁጥር
valid until	yeu·mi·şeu·na·beut gi·zay	የሚፀናበት ጊዜ
purpose of stay	yeu mi·ķo·yu·beut mək·ni·yat	የሚቆዩበት ምክኒያት

SIGNS

ማስታወቂያ	INFORMATION
እንግዳ መቀበያ	RECEPTION
ክፍት ነው	OPEN
ተዘግቷል	CLOSED
መግቢያ	ENTRANCE
መውጫ	EXIT
መግባት ክልክል ነው	ENTRY PROHIBITED
ዝግ ነው	NO ENTRY
ማቆም ክልክል ነው	NO PARKING
ፎቶ ማንሳት ክልክል ነው	NO PHOTOGRAPHS
ማጨስ ክልክል ነው	NO SMOKING
ሽንት ቤት	TOILETS
የወንዶች	MALE
የሴቶች	FEMALE
አደገኛ	DANGER
ተጠንቀቅ	CAUTION

HAIR STYLES

Elaborate ornaments and manicuring objects often support traditional hair designs. In some areas in the south, wooden headrests instead of pillows are used to keep clay caps, feathers or jewellery in place. Butter or fat is often used to moisturise dry hair. See also Souvenirs, page 128.

hair braids (traditional afro)	shu·ru·ba	ሹሩባ
hair braids (Tigre style, tight to head, then frizzed out)	ḳun·dal·la	ቀንዳላ
shaved head with tuft (on children)	ḳun·cho	ቀንጮ
wooden comb	mi·do	ሚዶ

AROUND TOWN

ለመዝናናት መውጣት

GOING OUT

Ethiopia enjoys a vibrant night-time bar and music scene. While az·ma·ri bet, 'music clubs', bubble with wine and song, local bun·na bet, 'coffee houses', serve up drinks, conversation and casual entertainment. In the city, you'll also find nightclubs and theatres.

WHERE TO GO

ወዴት ነው·

What's there to do in the evenings here?

məsh·at lai mən ai·neut
meuz·na·nya bo·ta al·leu?

ምሽት ላይ ምን እይነት
መዝናኛ ቦታ አለ?

I'm/We're thinking of going to ...

weu·deu ... meu·hed feul·lə·ge/
feul·lə·geun neub·beur

ወደ ... መሄድ
ፈልጌ/ፈልገን ነበር

Where can I find a good ...?	tə·ru ... yeut yi·geu·nyal?	ጥሩ ... የት ይገኛል?
bar/coffee house	bun·na bet	ቡና ቤት
cinema	si·ni·ma bet	ሲኒማ ቤት
nightclub	dans bet	ዳንስ ቤት
restaurant	mə·gəb bet	ምግብ ቤት
theatre	ti·ya·tər bet	ትያትር ቤት
traditional music venue	az·ma·ri bet	አዝማሪ ቤት

Where can I see a good film/play?

tə·ru si·ni·ma/dra·ma yeut
yi·ta·yal?

ጥሩ ሲኒማ/ድራማ የት
ይታያል?

What's showing?

mən yi·ta·yal?

ምን ይታያል?

Is it in English/Amharic?

beu ən·gli·zə·nya/
a·ma·rə·nya nō?

በ እንግሊዝኛ/
አማርኛ ነው·?

GOING OUT

91

Are there any tickets for ...?
   leu ... ti·ket al·leu?   ለ ... ትኬት አለ?
I want (three) tickets.
   (sost) ti·ket ə·feul·lə·gal·lō   (ሶስት) ትኬት እፈልጋለሁ
What's the entry fee/cover charge?
   meug·bi·ya sənt nō?   መግቢያ ስንት ነው?
How much is a (first-class ticket)?
   (an·deu·nya ma·ə·reug)   (አንደኛ ማዕረግ)
   sənt nō?   ስንት ነው?
We're sold out.
   ti·ket al·ḵwal   ትኬት አልቋል

 ሰላም ደህና ነህ? ደህና ነኝ

INVITATIONS   ግብዣ

It's common to 'shout' someone a few drinks or a meal when you invite them out. A common phrase is yeu·ne gəb·zha nō!, 'My treat!'.

Let's go for (a) ...   leu ... ən·hid   ለ ... እንሂድ
   coffee   bun·na   ቡና
   dance   dans   ዳንስ
   dinner   ə·rat   እራት
   drink (beer)   bi·ra   ቢራ

We're having a party (tonight).
   (za·re ma·ta) par·ti al·leun   (ዛሬ ማታ) ፓርቲ አለን
Please come!
   ə·ba·kəh na! (m)   እባክህ ና!
   ə·ba·kəsh nay! (f)   እባክሽ ነይ!
   ə·ba·ka·chu nu! (pl)   እባካችሁ ኑ!
We'll have a great time!
   tə·ru gi·ze ə·na·sa·lə·fal·leun!   ጥሩ ጊዜ እናሳልፋለን!

Responding to Invitations

ለግብዣ መልስ
መስጠት

Yes, OK! Where shall we go?
  ə·shi! yeut ən·hid?

እሺ! የት እንሂድ?

I'm afraid I'm busy.
  sə·ra al·leuny

ስራ አለኝ

What about (tomorrow)?
  (neu·geu) yi·meu·chə·hal/
  yi·meu·chə·shal? (m/f)

(ነገ) ይመቸሃል/
ይመቸሻል?

I'll try to make it.
  leu meum·ṭat
  ə·mo·kə·ral·lō

ለመምጣት
እሞክራለሁ

ARRANGING TO MEET

ቀጠሮ መያዝ

When/Where will we meet?
  meu·che/yeut
  ə·nə·geu·nany?

መቼ/የት እንገናኝ?

Let's meet at (eight o'clock) at ...
  beu (sə·mənt seu'at) ...
  ə·nə·geu·nany

በ (ስምንት ሰዓት) ...
እንገናኝ

Sorry I'm late.
  yi·ḳər·ta zeu·geu·yō

ይቅርታ ዘገየሁ

Never mind.
  gəd yeul·leum; mə·nəm
  ai·deul·leum

ግድ የለም/ምንም
አይደለም

TRADITIONAL DANCE & MUSIC

የአገር ባህል
ጨዋታና ሙዚቃ

You can enjoy Ethiopia's lively traditional dance and music at special restaurants, theatres and bars. Performances often include dances from the Gurage, Amhara, Oromo and Tigre regions. An appreciative audience places money on dancers' foreheads or belts as they move. If dancers try and entice you into əs·kəs·ta, a skillful shoulder dance, give it a go! Even timid efforts will be warmly received.

GOING OUT

At an az·ma·ri bet, az·ma·ri, 'minstrels', sing satirical songs or complimentary tunes for audience members. Traditional instruments include the delightful ma·sin·ko, a single-stringed violin.

Where can I see traditional
dance and music?
    yeu ba·həl cheu·wa·ta yeut   የባህል ጨዋታ የት
    yi·ta·yal?   ይታያል?
Which region is this dance from?
    yi·he dans keu·yeut nō?   ይህ ዳንስ ከየት ነው?
This singer is brilliant.
    beu·ṭam gob·beuz zeu·fany   በጣም ጎበዝ ዘፋኝ
Great performance!
    kon·jo cheu·wa·ta!   ቆንጆ ጨዋታ!
What are they singing about?
    sə·leu mən·dən nō   ስለ ምንድነው
    yeu·mi·zeuf·nut?   የሚዘፍኑት?

About ...	sə·leu ...	ስለ ...
love	fə·kər	ፍቅር
heroic deeds	jeug·nə·neut	ጀግንነት

band	yeu mu·zi·ka gwad	የሙዚቃ ጓድ
dancer	dan·seu·nya	ዳንሰኛ
drum	keu·beu·ro	ከበሮ
Ethiopian flute	wa·shint	ዋሽንት
Ethiopian harp	beug·geu·na	በገና
Ethiopian lyre	kə·rar	ክራር
Ethiopian violin	ma·sin·ko	ማሲንቆ
musician	mu·zi·keu·nya	ሙዚቀኛ
performance	cheu·wa·ta	ጨዋታ
shoulder dance	əs·kəs·ta	እስክስታ
trumpet	ṭə·rum·ba	ጥሩምባ

NIGHTCLUBS & BARS

ዳንስ ቤትና መጠጥ ቤት

What would you like?
    mən lə·ta·zeuz?

ምን ልታዘዝ?

How about a game of (billiards)?
    (bil·yard) ə·nə·cha·weut?

(ቢልያርድ) እንጫወት?

Are there any good (nightclubs)
around here?
    əz·zi a·ka·ba·bi tə·ru
    (dans bet) al·leu?

እዚህ አካባቢ ጥሩ
(ዳንስ ቤት) አለ?

What should I wear?
    mən ləl·beus?

ምን ልልበስ?

What kind of music do they have?
    mən ai·neut mu·zi·ka al·la·chō?

ምን አይነት ሙዚቃ አላቸው?

Do you want to dance?
    meu·da·neus tə·feul·lə·gal·leuh/
    tə·feul·lə·gi·yal·leush? (m/f)

መደነስ ትፈልጋለህ/
ትፈልጊያለሽ?

What type of music do you prefer?
    mən ai·neut mu·zi·ka
    tə·weud·dal·leuh/
    tə·wa·ja·leush? (m/f)

ምን አይነት ሙዚቃ
ትወዳለህ/ትወጃለሽ?

I really like (reggae).
    (re·ge) beu·tam ə·weud·dal·lō

(ሬጌ) በጣም እወዳለሁ

This place is great!
    kon·jo bet!

ቆንጆ ቤት!

The music here isn't very good.
    mu·zi·kow tə·ru ai·deu·leum

ሙዚቃው ጥሩ አይደለም

Shall we go somewhere else?
    le·la bo·ta ən·hid?

ሌላ ቦታ እንሂድ?

THEY MAY SAY ...	
ən·det nō?	How is it?
a·rif nō!	It's cool!
keul·den nō	Just joking!
yeu·ne kon·jo!	My baby!
a·bo at·deub·reun/	Don't be boring!
at·deub·rin! (m/f)	

DATING & ROMANCE   ቀጠሮ መያዝና ፍቅር

People often use the English terms for boyfriend/girlfriend.
Usually, yeu weund gwa·deu·nya (lit: boy friend) just means
a male friend, and yeu set gwa·deu·nya, a female friend.

Do you have anywhere
to go (tomorrow)?
   (neu·geu) yeu·mət·he·də·beut   (ነገ) የምትሄድበት
   bo·ta al·leu? (m)   ቦታ አለ?
   (neu·geu) yeu·mət·he·jə·beut   (ነገ) የምትሄጅበት
   bo·ta al·leu? (f)   ቦታ አለ?
Can we meet?
   meu·geu·na·nyeut ən·chə·lal·leun?   መገናኘት እንችላለን?

See also Invitations and Arranging to Meet, pages 92 and 93.

What can I get y
   mən lə·gab·zəl
   mən lə·gab·zəsh
Do you have a light?
   lai·teur al·leuh/al·le
Do you mind if I sit here
   sō al·leu?
Shall we get some fresh air?
   weu·deu wəch weu·ta ən·b
You have a beautiful smile.
   kon·jo feu·geug·ta al·leuh/
   al·leush (m/f)
Do you have a girlfriend/boyfriend?
   geurl frend al·leuh? (m)
   boy frend al·leush? (f)

              ድ አለሀ?
              ንድ አለሽ?

She's just a friend; He's just a friend.
   əs·swa gwa·deu·nya·ye nat;
   əs·su gwa·deu·nya·ye nō
Can I take you home?
   bet la·dər·səh? (m)
   bet la·dər·səsh? (f)

እሷ ጓደኛዬ ናት/
እሱ ጓደኛዬ ነው

ቤት ላድርስህ?
ቤት ላድርስሽ?

Classic Rejections   ግብዣን አለመቀበል

In Ethiopia, you may come across meug·deur·deur, the concept
of modestly declining an offer (such as a date) even though you
would like to accept. To ensure 'No thanks' is not misinterpreted
as 'OK', be polite but insistent.

No, thank you.
   aiy a·meu·seu·gə·nal·lō   አይ አመስግናለሁ
I don't drink.
   meu·ţeuţ al·ţeu·ţam   መጠጥ አልጠጣም
I don't smoke.
   a·la·cheu·səm   አላጨስም
I don't chew *chat*.
   chat al·kə·məm   ጫት አልቅምም

I'm waiting for someone.
Excuse me; I'm with al·jewu.
I have another appointment.

.....meone.   ሌላ ቀጠሮ አለኝ

..... o gar neuny   ይቅርታ ከሰው ጋር ነኝ

.....g for (my husband/wife).

  (.....eu·be·ten)   (ባለቤቴን)

  ə·yeu·ţeu·beu·ku nō   እየጠበኩ ነው.

Excuse me, I have to go now.

  yi·ḳər·ta a·hun meu·hed   ይቅርታ አሁን መሄድ

  al·leu·bəny   አለብኝ

Leave me/us alone!

  a·bo teu·weun!   አቦ ተወን!

DATE SAFE

I don't want to.

  al·feul·lə·gəm   አልፈልግም

I've had enough.

  beu·ḳany   በቃኝ

I don't feel well. *(after food or drink)*

  al·teus·ma·ma·nyəm   አልተስማማኝም

Please call me a taxi.

  ə·ba·keh tak·si ţə·ral·ləny (m)   እባክህ ታክሲ ጥራልኝ

  ə·ba·kesh tak·si ţə·ril·ləny (f)   እባክሽ ታክሲ ጥሪልኝ

Let's use a condom.

  kon·dom ə·nə·ţeu·ḳeum   ኮንዶም እንጠቀም

Love   ፍቅር

I love you.

  ə·weud·də·hal·lō (m)   እወድሃለሁ.

  ə·weud·də·shal·lō (f)   እወድሻለሁ.

Do you love me?

  tə·weud·deu·nyal·leuh? (m)   ትወደኛለሁ?

  tə·weu·jə·nyal·leush? (f)   ትወጀኛለሽ?

Do you want to be with me?
keu·ne gar meu·hon	ከኔ ጋር መሆን
tə·feul·lə·gal·leuh/	ትፈልጋለህ/
tə·feul·lə·gi·yal·leush? (m/f)	ትፈልጊየለሽ?

Let's move in together.
| ab·reun ə·nə·nur | አብረን እንኑር |

Will you marry me?
| ta·geu·ba·nyal·leuh? (m) | ታገባኛለህ? |
| ta·geu·bi·nyal·leush? (f) | ታገቢኛለሽ? |

date	keu·teu·ro	ቀጠሮ
to date	meuk·teur	መቅጠር
to go out with	ab·ro mō·tat	አብሮ መውጣት
relationship	yeu fə·ḳər gə·nu·nyə·neut	የፍቅር ግኑኝነት

LEAVING & BREAKING UP መሰናበትና መለያየት

I have to leave (tomorrow).
(neu·geu) meu·hed al·leu·bəny (ነገ) መሄድ አለብኝ

I'll miss you.
| ə·na·fə·ḳə·hal·lō (m) | እናፍቅሀለሁ- |
| ə·na·fə·ḳə·shal·lō (f) | እናፍቅሽለሁ- |

Let's write to/phone each other.
ə·nə·ṣa·ṣaf/ə·nə·deu·wa·weul እንፃፍ/እንደዋወል

I don't think it's working out.
| fə·ḳə·ra·chən yeu·mi·ḳeu·ṭəl | ፍቅራችን የሚቀጥል |
| ai·meu·səl·leu·nyəm | አይመስለኝም |

I want to stay friends.
| gwa·deuny·neu·ta·chə·nən | ጓደኝታችንን ባናቆም |
| ba·na·ḳom deus yi·leu·nyal | ደስ ይለኛል |

HOUSE OF EVERYTHING

bet, 'house', is used to refer to all sorts of places, from the divine to the everyday, including:

cinema	si·ni·ma bet
coffee house	bun·na bet
heaven	seu·mai bet
hut	go·jo bet
post office	pos·ta bet
prison	ə·sər bet
toilet	shənt bet

GOING OUT

Ethiopians love chatting about lə·joch, 'children', and zeu·meud, 'relatives'. Even if you've never met an acquaintance's family, it's courteous to ask be·teu·seub deu·na nō?, 'Is your family well?'.

QUESTIONS   ጥያቄዎች

Are you married?
| a·gəb·teu·hal? (m) | አግብተሃል? |
| a·gəb·teu·shal? (f) | አግብተሻል? |

Do you have any children?
| lə·joch al·luh? (m) | ልጆች አሉህ? |
| lə·joch al·lush? (f) | ልጆች አሉሽ? |

How many children do you have?
| sənt lə·joch al·luh/al·lush? (m/f) | ስንት ልጆች አሉህ/አሉሽ? |

How many brothers and sisters
do you have?
| sənt weun·də·moch na | ስንት ወንድሞችና እህቶች |
| ə·hə·toch al·luh/al·lush? (m/f) | አሉህ/አሉሽ? |

Do you have family photos?
| yeu be·teu·seub fo·to·graf | የቤተሰብ ፎቶግራፍ |
| al·leuh/al·leush? (m/f) | አለህ/አለሽ? |

Who's this?
| yi·he man nō? (m) | ይሄ ማነው? |
| yi·chi man neuch? (f) | ይቺ ማነች? |

Do you miss them?
| tə·na·fə·kal·leuh? (m) | ትናፍቃለህ? |
| tə·na·fə·ki·yal·leush? (f) | ትናፍቂያለሽ? |

Where do they live?
| yeut nō yeu·mi·no·rut? | የት ነው የሚኖሩት? |

101

FAMILY

REPLIES   መልሶች

I'm married.
  ag·bə·chal·lō   አግብቻለሁ

I'm engaged.
  ə·cho·nya al·leuny   እጮኛ አለኝ

I'm not married.
  a·la·geu·ba·hum   አላገባሁም

I'm divorced.
  keu ba·leu·be·te gar   ከባለቤቴ ጋር
  teu·fa·tə·chal·lō   ተፋትቻለሁ

I have one child.
  and ləj al·leuny   አንድ ልጅ አለኝ

I have (three) children.
  (sost) lə·joch al·luny   (ሶስት) ልጆች አሉኝ

I don't have any children.
  lə·joch yeul·lu·nyeum   ልጆች የሉኝም

I have a daughter/son.
  and (set ləj; weund ləj)   አንድ (ሴት ልጅ/
  al·leuny   ወንድ ልጅ) አለኝ

I have one (brother).
  and (weun·dəm) al·leuny   አንድ (ወንድም) አለኝ

I have two (sisters).
  hu·leutt (ə·hə·toch) al·luny   ሁለት (እህቶች) አሉኝ

I'm the oldest/youngest child.
  yeu meu·jeu·meu·ri·yow/   የ መጀመሪያው/
  meu·cheu·reu·show ləj neuny   መጨረሻው ልጅ ነኝ

My ... died.
  yeu·ne ... mo·teu·wal   የኔ ... ሞተዋል

My parents are divorced.
  ə·nat·na ab·ba·te teu·fa·teu·wal   እናትና አባቴ ተፋተዋል

FAMILY MEMBERS የቤተሰብ አባሎች

Family terms are used with great flexibility. For example, ə·hət, 'sister', can be used to refer to female nieces, cousins and friends.

aunt	a·kəst	አክስት
brother	weun·dəm	ወንድም
(younger) brother	(tən·nish) weun·dəm	(ትንሽ) ወንድም
child/children	ləj/lə·joch	ልጅ/ልጆች
cousin	ya·got ləj (m)	ያጎት ልጅ/
	ya·kəst ləj (f)	ያክስት ልጅ
daughter	set ləj	ሴት ልጅ
family	be·teu·seub	ቤተሰብ
father	ab·bat	አባት
fiance/e	ə·cho·nya	እጮኛ
foster child	yeu ma·deu·go ləj	የማደጎ ልጅ
friend	gwa·deu·nya	ጓደኛ
god(child)	yeu kə·rəs·tən·na (ləj)	የክርስትና (ልጅ)
grandchildren	yeu ləj lə·joch	የልጅ ልጆች
grandfather	weund a·yat	ወንድ አያት
grandmother	set a·yat	ሴት አያት
husband	bal	ባል
man/men	sō/sō·woch	ሰው/ሰዎች
mother	ə·nat	እናት
sister	ə·hət	እህት
(older) sister	(təl·lək) ə·hət	(ትልቅ) እህት
step (mother)	ən·jeu·ra (ə·nat)	እንጀራ (እናት)
uncle	a·got	አጎት
wife	mist	ሚስት
woman/women	set/se·toch	ሴት/ሴቶች

WHOSE WHOSE?

To form the possessive 'my', add e or use yeu·ne:

ab·ba·te	my father
yeu·ne ə·nat	my mother

To form a possessive like 'my friend's brother' add yeu:
yeu gwa·deu·nya·ye weun·dəm
(lit: of friend-my brother)

FAMILY

TALKING WITH PARENTS   ከወላጆች ጋር ማውራት

How old are your children?
yeu lə·jo·chu əd·me sənt nō?   የልጆቹ ዕድሜ ስንት ነው?

How many (girls/boys) are there?
sənt (se·toch/weun·doch) al·lu?   ስንት (ሴቶች/ወንዶች) አሉ?

Does he/she attend school?
təm·hərt bet jeu·mə·rwal/   ትምህርት ቤት ጀምሯል/
jeu·mə·ral·leuch?   ጀምራለች?

What's the baby's name?
yeu hə·șa·nu səm man nō?   የሕፃኑ ስም ማነው?

Is it a boy or a girl?
weund nō ways set neuch?   ወንድ ነው ወይስ ሴት ነች?

What a beautiful baby/child!
beu·țam ḳon·jo ləj!   በጣም ቆንጆ ልጅ!

Who does he/she look like?
ma·nən yi·meus·lal/   ማንን ይመስላል/
tə·meus·lal·leuch?   ትመስላለች?

He looks like you.
an·teun yi·meus·lal   አንተን ይመስላል

She looks like you.
an·chən tə·meus·lal·leuch   አንችን ትመስላለች

EMIGRATION BLUES

(My brother) lives in ...
(weun·də·me) ... yi·no·ral   (ወንድሜ) ... ይኖራል

Yes, there are many Ethiopians
in (Toronto).
ow (to·ron·to) bə·zu   አዎ (ቶሮንቶ) ብዙ
i·tə·yo·pi·ya·noch yi·no·ral·lu   ኢትዮጵያኖች ይኖራሉ

I want to go to your country.
weu·deu (an·teu/an·chi) a·geur   ወደ (አንተ/አንቺ) አገር
meu·hed ə·feul·lə·gal·lō (m/f)   መሄድ እፈልጋለሁ

TALKING WITH CHILDREN ከልጆች ጋር ማውራት

Ethiopian children are a mixed bunch – some work, some go to school and some do both! Whichever the case, most kids love sport and games, are proud of their religion and cultural heritage and have a terrific sense of humour. Chatting to them will sometimes take the heat out of 'foreigner frenzy' (see Unwanted Attention in Around Town, page 88).

FAMILY

What's your name?
   sə·məh/sə·məsh man nō? (m/f)   ስምህ/ስምሽ ማነው-?
How old are you?
   əd·meh/əd·mesh sənt nō? (m/f)   ዕድሜህ/ዕድሜሽ ስንት ነው-?
Do you have brothers and sisters?
   weun·də·mə·na ə·hət   ወንድምና እህት
   al·leuh/al·leush? (m/f)   አለህ/አለሽ?
Do you go to school?
   təm·hərt bet tə·he·dal·leuh/   ትምህርት ቤት ትሄዳለህ/
   tə·he·jal·leush? (m/f)   ትሄጃለሽ?
Do you have a good teacher?
   tə·ru as·te·ma·ri al·leuh? (m)   ጥሩ አስተማሪ አለህ?
   tə·ru as·te·ma·ri al·leush? (f)   ጥሩ አስተማሪ አለሽ?
Do you study English?
   ən·gli·zə·nya tə·ma·ral·leuh? (m)   እንግሊዝኛ ትማራለህ
   ən·gli·zə·nya tə·ma·ri·yal·leush? (f)   እንግሊዝኛ ትማሪያለሽ?
What's your favourite game?
   yeu·mət·weud·dō-/   የምትወደው-/
   yeu·meut·weu·ju cheu·wa·ta   የምትወጀው ጨዋታ
   mən·dən nō? (m/f)   ምንድን ነው-?
What will we play?
   mən ə·nə·cha·weut?   ምን እንጫወት?

I like ...   ... ə·weud·dal·lō   ... እወዳለሁ-
   football   ə·gər kwass   እግር ኳስ
   hide and seek   də·bəb·bə·kosh   ድብብቆሽ
   hopscotch   seu·nyo mak·seu·nyo   ሰኞ ማክሰኞ
   skipping   geu·meud zə·lai   ገመድ ዝላይ
   swings   zhə·wa·zhə·we   ዥዋዥዌ

FAMILY

BIRTHDAYS
ልደቶች

Birthdays are only celebrated during childhood in Ethiopia.

When's your birthday?
ለ·deu·təh/lə·deu·təsh
meu·che nō? (m/f)

ልደትህ/ልደትሽ
ሙቴ ነው?

My birthday is on (25 January).
lə·deu·te beu
(ha·ya a·məst ja·nu·wa·ri) nō

ልደቴ በ
(ሃያ አምስት ጃኑዋሪ) ነው·

Happy birthday!
meul·kam lə·deut!

መልካም ልደት!

LIFE STAGES		
baby	hə·ṣan	ሕፃን
child	ləj	ልጅ
boy	weund ləj	ወንድ ልጅ
girl	set ləj	ሴት ልጅ
youth	weu·ṭat	ወጣት
middle age	gol·ma·sa	ጎልማሳ
old man	shə·ma·gə·le	ሽማግሌ
old woman	a·ro·git	አሮጊት

ፍላጎቶች INTERESTS

Radios blaring with mu·zi·ḳa, 'music', cafés abuzz with weu·re, 'chatter', and walls adorned with sə'əl, 'art' – Ethiopians love their home-grown entertainment. Sport (see Activities, page 179) and theatre are also very popular.

COMMON INTERESTS የጋር ፍላጎቶች

What do you do in your spare time?

beu tərf gi·zeh mən		በትርፍ ጊዜህ ምን
ta·deur·gal·leuh? (m)		ታደርጋለህ?
beu tərf gi·zesh mən		በትርፍ ጊዜሽ ምን
ta·deur·gi·yal·leush? (f)		ታደርጊያለሽ?

I like/I don't like ...	... ə·weud·dal·lō/ al·weud·dəm	... እወዳለሁ/ አልወድም
cooking	mə·gəb meus·rat	ምግብ መስራት
gardening	at·kəlt	አትክልት
	meun·keu·ba·keub	መንከባከብ
listening to music/the radio	mu·zi·ḳa/ra·di·yo meus·mat	ሙዚቃ/ራድዮ መስማት
meeting friends	keu·gwa·deu nyoch gar meu·geu·na·nyeut	ከጓደኞች ጋር መፈናነት
painting	sə'əl meu·sal	ስዕል መሳል
photography	fo·to man·sat	ፎቶ ማንሳት
playing (cards)	(kar·ta) meu·cha·wot	(ካርታ) መጫወት
reading	meu·sə·haf man·beub	መጽሐፍ ማንበብ
sport	sport	ስፖርት
theatre	ti·ya·teur	ትያትር
travelling	a·geur meu·go·bə·nyeut	አገር መኖብኘት
visiting relatives	zeu·meud meu·ṭeu·yeuḳ	ዘመድ መጠየቅ
watching movies	film ma·yeut	ፊልም ማየት
watching TV	ti·vi ma·yeut	ቲቪ ማየት
writing (letters)	(deub·dab·be) meu·ṣaf	(ደብዳቤ) መፃፍ

INTERESTS

107

MUSIC & RADIO   መ-ዚ-ቃና ራ-ዲ-ዮ

Ethiopia has a thriving home-grown music industry that includes
jazz, pop and traditional tunes. Music also has an important
community function – on the farm, during special events and
in the church. Radio is the most popular form of broadcast
entertainment in Ethiopia.

Which is a good	leu ... yeu·tə·nyow	ለ ... የት·ኛው ራ·ድዮ
station for ...?	ra·di·yo ṭa·bi·ya yi·sha·lal?	ጣቢ·ያ ይሻ·ላል?
traditional	ba·həl	ባህል
music	mu·zi·ḳa	መ-ዚ·ቃ
Western	feu·reunj	ፈረንጅ
music	mu·zi·ḳa	መ-ዚ·ቃ
the news	ən·gli·zə·nya	እንግሊ·ዝኛ
in English	ze·na	ዜና

Which is the English station?
   yeu ən·gli·zə·nya ḳwan·ḳwa   የእንግሊዝኛ ቋንቋ
   ṭa·bi·ya yeu·tə·nyow nō?   ጣቢ·ያ የት·ኛው ·ነው-?
What frequency is it on?
   beu·yeu·tə·nyow mo·geud lai nō?   በየት·ኛው ሞ·ገድ ላይ ነው-?
What music do you like?
   mən ai·neut mu·zi·ḳa   ምን አይነት መ-ዚ·ቃ
   tə·weud·dal·leuh/   ት·ወዳ·ለህ/ት·ወ·ጃለሽ?
   tə·weu·jal·leush?(m/f)
Who's your favourite (singer)?
   yeu·mət·weud·dō/   የም·ት·ወደ·ው-/
   yeu·mət·weu·ju   የም·ት·ወ·ጁ
   (zeu·fany) man nō?(m/f)   (ዘፋ·ኝ) ማን ነው-?
My favourite singer is (Bob Marley).
   yeu·mə·weud·dō zeu·fany   የም·ወደ·ው- ዘፋ·ኝ
   (bob mar·li) nō   (ቦብ ማር·ሊ) ነው-
What instrument do you play?
   mən ai·neut yeu mu·zi·ḳa   ምን አይነት የመ-ዚ·ቃ
   meu·sa·ri·ya tə·cha·wo·tal·leuh/   መሳሪ·ያ ት·ጫ·ወታ·ለህ/
   tə·cha·wo·chal·leush?(m/f)   ት·ጫ·ወቻ·ለሽ?

INTERESTS

I play the ...

| ... ə·cha·weu·tal·lō | ... እጫወታለሁ |

Shall we try it together?

| ab·reun ən·mo·kər? | አብረን እንሞክር? |

Do you like ...?	... tə·weud·dal·leuh? (m)	... ትወዳለህ?
	... tə·weu·jal·leush? (f)	... ትወጃለሽ?
dancing	meu·da·neus	መደነስ
listening to music	mu·zi·ka meus·mat	ሙዚቃ መስማት
singing	meuz·feun	መዝፈን
playing music	mu·zi·ka meu·cha·wot	ሙዚቃ መጫወት

band	yeu mu·zi·ka gwad	የሙዚቃ ጓድ
guitar	gi·tar	ጊታር
musician	mu·zi·keu·nya	ሙዚቀኛ
show/concert	zə·gə·jət	ዝግጅት
singer	zeu·fany	ዘፋኝ
song	zeu·feun	ዘፈን
stage	meud·reuk	መድረክ
voice	dəmş	ድምፅ
whistling	fu·cheut	ፉጨት

INTERESTS

For traditional instruments, dancing and music venues, see page 93.

ART   ኪነ ጥበብ

Church art is Ethiopia's most famous traditional art form. See also Religion, page 191.

Where can I see some good ...?	tə·ru ... yeut ma·yeut ə·chə·lal·lō?	ጥሩ ... የት ማየት እችላለሁ?
church art	yeu be·teu krəs·ti·yan sə'ə·loch	የቤተክርስቲያን ስዕሎች
modern painting	zeu·meu·na·wi sə'ə·loch	ዘመናዊ ስዕሎች
painting by (Afwerke Tekle)	yeu (af·weurķ teuk·len) sə'ə·loch	የ (አፈወርቅ ተክሌን) ስዕሎች
traditional painting	yeu ba·həl sə'ə·loch	የባህል ስዕሎች

Who's the painter?
man nō seu·al·yu? ማን ነው· ሰዓሊዉ·?
When was it done/painted?
meu·che nō yeu·teu·seu·row/ መቼ ነው· የተሰራዉ·/
yeu·teu·sa·lō? የተሳለዉ·?

architecture	yeu hən·ṣa a·seu·rar	የሕንፃ አሰራር
art (painting)	sə'əl	ስዕል
artwork	yeu ki·neu ṭə·beub sə·ra·woch	የኪነ ጥበብ ስራዎች
artist	yeu ki·neu ṭə·beub sō	የኪነ ጥበብ ሰዉ·
calligraphy	yeu ḳum ṣeu·ha·fi	የቁም ፀሐፊ
canvas	sheu·ra	ሸራ
exhibition	eg·zi·bi·shən	ኤግዝቢሽን
paintbrush	yeu ḳeu·leum bu·rash	የቀለም ቡርሽ
paints	ḳeu·leum	ቀለም
photographer	fo·to an·shi	ፎቶ አንሺ
print	ə·təm	እትም
sculpture	ḳar·ṣa ḳarṣ	ቅርፃ ቅርፅ
style	sta·yil/zeu·de	ስታይል/ዘዴ

INTERESTS

CINEMA ሲኒማ

What's on at the cinema tonight?
za·re mən·dən nō ዛሬ ምንድነዉ·
yeu·weu·ṭow? የወጣዉ·?
What type of movie is it?
mən ai·neut film nō? ምን አይነት ፊልም ነዉ·?
Have you seen ...?
... ai·teu·hal/ai·teu·shal? (m/f) ... አይተኻል/አይተሻል?
What films do you like?
mən ai·neut film ምን አይነት ፊልም
tə·weud·dal·leuh/ ትወዳለህ/ትወጃለሽ?
tə·weu·jal·leush? (m/f)

I like/I don't	... ə·weud·dal·lō/	... እወዳለሁ/
like ...	al·weud·dəm	አልወድም
action	ak·shən film	አክሽን ፊልም
comedy	yeu·mi·ya·səḳ film	የሚያስቅ ፊልም
drama	ta·rik ya·lō film	ታሪክ
		ያለው ፊልም
films from	yeu (hənd) film	የ (ህንድ) ፊልም
(India)		

WAXING LYRICAL

Allusion and double meanings play a major role in Amharic verse and literature, which are said to have səm əna weurḳ (wax and gold). The wax is the apparent meaning, and the gold, the hidden but true meaning.

THEATRE, LITERATURE   ትያትር፣
& STORIES   ስነ ጹሑፍና ታሪኮች

Ethiopia's rich literary tradition finds expression in theatre, poetry, song and the novel. Oral narratives are also popular. You can see these at various entertainment venues. Even if you don't understand a word that's said, the colourful gestures, expressions and clever use of pauses and intonation should keep you entertained.

I want to go to the theatre.

weu·deu ti·ya·tər bet	ወደ ትያትር ቤት
meu·hed ə·feul·lə·gal·lō	መሄድ እፈልጋለሁ

I'd like to	... ma·yeut	... ማየት
see a ...	ə·feul·gal·lō	እፈልጋለሁ
comedy	yeu·mi·ya·səḳ	የሚያስት
	dra·ma	ድራማ
(historical)	(yeu ta·rik)	(የታሪክ)
drama	dra·ma	ድራማ
variety show	yeu·teu·leu·ya·yu	የተለያዩ
	tər'i·toch	ትርኢቶች

Can you recommend one?
yeu·tə·nyow yi·sha·lal
tə·la·lah/tə·ya·leush? (m/f)

የትኛው ይሻላል
ትላለህ/ትያለሽ?

Did you like it?
weu·deud·kō? (m)
weu·deud·shyu? (f)

ወደድከው?
ወደድሽው?

I really liked it!
beu·ṭam weud·də·jeu·wal·lō!

በጣም ወድጄዋለሁ!

The main actor was great!
wan·now ak·teur
as·deu·na·ḳi neub·beur!

ዋናው አክተር
አስደናቂ ነበር!

I didn't understand much.
bə·zu al·geu·ba·nyəm

ብዙ አልገባኝም

ወደድከው?

በጣም
ወድጄዋለሁ!

COLOURFUL CHARACTERS

Amharic is full of colourful words to describe people's status and characters.

big man	təl·ləḳ sō	ትልቅ ሰው
commoner	teu·ra sō	ተራ ሰው
a gossip	a·lu·bal·teu·nya	አሉባልተኛ
jealous	ḳeu·na·teu·nya	ቀናተኛ
loyal	ta·many	ታማኝ
modern person	zeu·meu·na·wi	ዘመናዊ
nice/gentle	cheu·wa	ጨዋ
poor	deu·ha	ደሃ
rich	hab·tam	ሃብታም
rude	ba·leu·ge	ባለጌ
shy	ai·neu a·far	አይነ አፋር
talkative	weu·re·nya	ወሬኛ
worldly	a·leu·ma·wi	ዓለማዊ

READING   ማንበብ

See also Stationery & Publications, page 133.

Do you like reading?
  man·beub tə·weud·dal·leuh/   ማንበብ ትወዳለህ/
  tə·weu·jal·leush? (m/f)   ትወጃለሽ?
I like/I don't like it.
  ə·weud·dal·lō/al·weud·dəm   እወዳለሁ·/አልወድም
What do you like to read?
  mən man·beub   ምን ማንበብ
  tə·weud·dal·leuh/   ትወዳለህ/
  tə·weu·jal·leush? (m/f)   ትወጃለሽ?

I like to read ...   ... man·beub   ... ማንበብ
                        ə·weud·dal·lō   እወዳለሁ·
  books   meu·sə·haf   መጽሐፍ
  comics   a·sə·kiny   አስቂኝ
                      meu·sə·haf   መጽሐፍ
  crime novels   yeu weun·jeul ləb   የወንጀል
                      weu·leud   ልብ ወለድ
  fables   teu·reut   ተረት
  fiction/novels   ləb weu·leud   ልብ ወለድ
  magazines   meu·sə·het   መጽሔት
  newspapers   ga·ze·ta   ጋዜጣ
  non-fiction   ləb weu·leud   ልብ ወለድ
                      yal·ho·neu meu·sə·haf   ያልሆነ መጽሐፍ
  poetry   gə·təm   ግጥም
  romance   yeu fə·kər   የፍቅር
                      ləb weu·leud   ልብ ወለድ
  short stories   a·cha·chər   አጫጭር
                      ta·ri·koch   ታሪኮች

Do you have any books (in English)?
  beu (ən·gli·zə·nya) yeu·teu·sa·feu   በ (እንግሊዝኛ)
  meu·sə·haf al·la·chu?   የተፃፈ መጽሐፍ አላችሁ?
Can I borrow it?
  meu·was yi·cha·lal?   መዋስ ይቻላል?

OPINIONS

አስተያየት

INTERESTS

It looks ...	... yi·meus·lal	... ይመስላል
crowded	sō yeu·beu·za·beut	ሰው የበዛበት
empty	ba·do	ባዶ
(like) a painting	sə'əl	ስዕል

It smells ...	shə·ta al·lō	... ሽታ አለው
awful	a·ṣeu·ya·fi	አጸያፊ
beautiful	ḳon·jo	ቆንጆ
like (butter)	yeu (ḳə·be)	የ (ቅቤ)
	ai·neut	አይነት

It's ...	... nō	... ነው
rough	sheu·ka·ra	ሽካራ
soft/smooth	leus·las·sa	ለስላሳ

It's noisy.
bə·zu cha·cha·ta al·leu　ብዙ ጫጫታ አለ

It's quiet.
ṣeuṭ ya·leu nō　ጸጥ ያለ ነው

Did you like it?
weu·deud·kō? (m)　ወደድከው?
weu·deud·shyu? (f)　ወደድሽው?

It was ...	... neub·beur	... ነበር
boring	deu·ba·ri	ደባሪ
entertaining	yeu·mi·yaz·na·na	የሚያዝናና
sad	yeu·mi·ya·sa·zən	የሚያሳዝን
very funny	beu·ṭam	በጣም
	yeu·mi·ya·səḳ	የሚያስቅ

| ... is better. | ... yi·sha·lal | ... ይሻላል |

ማሕበራዊ ጉዳዮች SOCIAL ISSUES

Ethiopians have a strong interest in the world around them, and may ask questions about your home country. Be discreet about discussing politics and sensitive social issues, particularly in relation to cultural practices.

EXPRESSING OPINIONS

አስተያየትን መግለጽ

What do you think of ...?
  sə·leu ... mən as·teu·ya·yeut
  al·leuh/al·leush? (m/f)

ስለ ... ምን አስተያየት
አለህ/አለሽ?

It's good/bad.
  tə·ru/meut·fo nō

ጥሩ/መጥፎ ነው

I think/believe ...
  ə·ne ən·deu·ma·sə·bō ...

እኔ እንደማስበው ...

Do you like ...?
  ... tə·weud·dal·leuh? (m)
  ... tə·weu·jal·leush? (f)

... ትወዳለህ?
... ትወጃለሽ?

I like/don't like ...
  ... ə·weud·dal·lō/al·weud·dəm

... እወዳለሁ/አልወድም

IN THE NEWS

ዜና

Did you hear today's news?
  yeu za·re ze·na seum·teu·hal/
  seum·teu·shal? (m/f)

የዛሬ ዜና ሰምተሃል/
ሰምተሻል?

There are problems in
(the Middle East).
  (meu·ha·keu·leu·nyow məs·rak)
  wəst chig·gər alleu

(መካከለኛው ምስራቅ)
ውስጥ ችግር አለ

Yes, it's a serious matter.
  ow a·sa·sa·bi gu·dai nō

አዎ አሳሳቢ ጉዳይ ነው

affair/issue	gu·dai	ጉዳይ
bomb	bomb	ቦምብ
civil war	yeurs beurs ṭor·neut	የርስ በርስ ጦርነት
civilian	seu·la·ma·wi sō	ሰላማዊ ሰው
conflict	wə·gi·ya	ውጊያ
crime	weun·jeul	ወንጀል
demonstration	seu·la·ma·wi seulf	ሰላማዊ ሰልፍ
headline	ar'əs·teu ze·na	አርእስተ ዜና
hijacking	yeu ai·ro·plan	የአይሮፕላን
	ṭeu·leu·fa	ጠለፋ
international	a·leum a·ḵeuf	አለም አቀፍ
landmine	feunj	ፈንጅ
newspaper	ga·ze·ṭa	ጋዜጣ
Organisation for	yeu af·ri·ka	የአፍሪካ
African Unity	an·də·neut də·rə·jət	አንድነት ድርጅት
peace	seu·lam	ሰላም
peace agreement	yeu seu·lam	የሰላም
	sə·mə·mə·neut	ስምምነት
radio	ra·di·yo	ራዲዮ
refugees	sə·deu·teu·nyoch	ስደተኞች
soldier	weu·ta·deur	ወታደር
terrorism	shə·bar	ሽብር
the United	yeu·teu·ba·beu·rut	የተባበሩት
Nations	meun·gə·stat	መንግስታት
	də·rə·jət	ድርጅት
war	ṭor·neut	ጦርነት

SOCIAL ISSUES

THEY MAY SAY ...

əw·neut nō	It's true.
weu·re nō	It's a rumour.
wu·sheut nō	It's a lie.
əw·neut ai·deul·leum	It's not true.

DEVELOPMENT ISSUES

የእንግት ጉዳዮች

What do people think about ...?

| sə·leu ... sō·woch mən | ስለ ... ሰዎች ምን |
| ya·sə·ba·lu? | ያስባሉ? |

(Agriculture) is important
for development.

| (gəb·rən·na) leu əd·geut | (ግብርና) ለእንድግት |
| as·feul·la·gi nō | አስፈላጊ ነው |

It's good for ...	leu ... tə·ru nō	ለ ... ጥሩ ነው
It's not good	leu ... tə·ru	ለ ... ጥሩ
for ...	ai·deul·leum	አይደለም
developed countries	ya·deu·gu a·geu·roch	ያደጉ አገሮች
developing countries	ta·da·gi a·geu·roch	ታዳጊ አገሮች
ordinary people	teu·ra sō	ተራ ሰው
rich people	hab·tam sō	ሃብታም ሰው
poor people	deu·ha sō	ደሃ ሰው

aid organisation	yeu ər·da·ta də·rə·jət	የርዳታ ድርጅት
aid worker	yeu ər·da·ta də·rə·jət seu·ra·teu·nya	የርዳታ ድርጅት ሠራተኛ
air pollution	yeu ai·yeur meu·beu·keul	የአየር መበከል
charity	beu·go ad·ra·got	በን አድራነት
colonialism	kəny a·geu·zaz	ቅኝ አገዛዝ
development	əd·geut	እንግት
foreign aid	yeu wəch ər·da·ta	የውጭ እርዳታ
foreign culture	yeu wəch ba·həl	የውጭ ባህል
foreign debt	yeu wəch ə·da	የውጭ እዳ
foreign investment	yeu wəch meu·wa·leu nə·wai	የውጭ መዋለ ንዋይ
free trade	neu·sa nəgd	ነጻ ንግድ
human rights	yeu sō·woch neu·sa·neut	የሰዎች ነፃነት

SOCIAL ISSUES

illiteracy	meu·ha·ye·me·neut	መሃይምነት
money	geun·zeub	ገንዘብ
poverty	de·he·neut	ድህነት
privatisation	keu meun·gest	ከመንግስት
	weu·deu gel na·breut	ወደ ግል
	ma·zeu·wa·weur	ንብረት ማዞወር
slums	ko·sha·sha seu·feur	ቆሻሻ ሰፈር
standard of living	yeu·nu·ro deu·reu·ja	የኑሮ ደረጃ
tourism	tu·ri·zem	ቱሪዝም
underprivileged	chig·ge·reu·nya	ችግረኛ
unemployment	se·ra a·te·neut	ስራ አጥነት
urbanisation	yeu keu·teu·moch	የከተሞች
	meus·fa·fat	መስፋፋት
World Bank	yeu a·leum bank	የአለም ባንክ

የዛሬ ዜና ሰምተሻል?

አዎ አሳሳቢ ጉዳይ ነው

TELL TAILS

Remember Amharic verbs have the subject attached in
the form of affixes. In the case of 'you', there are male,
female and polite forms. Listen for these sounds at the
beginning and end of verbs:

te...al·leuh (m)   (for addressing males)
te...al·leush (f)   (for addressing females)
yi...al·lu (pol)   (for addressing older people)

POLITICS   ፖለቲካ

You'll find that words like prez·dant, 'president', and so·sha·list, 'socialist', are almost identical to English.

Who is your country's
(prime minister)?
  ya·geu·ra·chu (ṭeuk·lai   ያገራችሁ (ጠቅላይ
  mi·nis·ter) man nō?   ሚኒስቴር) ማን ነው?
What is the main political party?
  wan·now yeu po·leu·ti·ka   ዋናው የፖለቲካ
  par·ti man nō?   ፓርቲ ማን ነው?
What are conditions for
(immigrants) like?
  yeu (sə·deu·teu·nyoch) hu·ne·ta የ (ስደተኞች)
  ən·det nō?   ሁኔታ እንዴት ነው?
(The cost of living) is/isn't high.
  (nu·ro) wədd nō;   (ኑሮ) ውድ ነው-/
  (nu·ro) wədd ai·deu·leum   (ኑሮ) ውድ አይደለም
(Education) is free/expensive/cheap.
  (təm·hərt) neu·ṣa/wədd/   (ትምህርት) ነፃ/ውድ/
  rə·kash nō   ርካሽ ነው-
Does the government provide
(social security)?
  meun·gəst yeu·mi·seu·ṭō   መንግስት የሚሰጠው-
  (də·go·ma) al·leu?   (ድጎማ) አለ?

conservative	a·ṭə·ba·ḳi	አጥባቂ
democracy	di·mok·ra·si	ዲሞክራሲ.
economy	i·ko·no·mi	ኢኮኖሚ
education	təm·hərt	ትምህርት
election	mər·cha	ምርጫ
equality	ə·ku·lə·neut	እኩልነት
free (not bound)	neu·ṣa	ነፃ
free speech	yeu meu·na·geur	የመናገር
	neu·ṣa·neut	ነፃነት
government	meun·gəst	መንግስት
health care	yeu ṭe·na a·geul·glot	የጤና አገልግሉት

SOCIAL ISSUES

homeless	yeu go·da·na teu·da·da·ri	የጎዳና ተዳዳሪ
immigration	sə·deut	ስደት
(new) jobs	(ad·dis) sə·ra·woch	(አዲስ) ስራዎች
opposition	teu·ka·wa·mi	ተቃዋሚ
parliament	mə·kər bet	ምክር ቤት
policy	a·meu·rar	አመራር
politician	po·leu·ti·keu·nya	ፖለቲከኛ
previous	yeu ƙeud·mō	የቀድሞው
government	meun·gəst	መንግስት
racism	zeu·reu·nya·neut	ዘረኝነት
tax	gə·bər	ግብር
unemployment	sə·ra meu·ta·ṭat	ስራ መታጣት

SOCIAL ISSUES

LOOKING FOR ...   ... *መፈለግ*
At the Market & Street Stalls   *ገበያና መደብሮች*

Ethiopian geu·bi·ya, 'markets', operate daily in major towns and once a week in rural areas. People from miles around congregate to buy and sell their wares and catch up on the latest news. Use Amharic to find your way through the colourful maze of clothing, baskets, spices, trinkets and livestock. Local gul·lət, 'street stalls', are great for vegetables, eggs and small household items.

When's market day?
   yeu geu·bi·ya keun meu·che nō?   የገበያ ቀን መቼ ነው?
Where's the market area?
   wan·now geu·bi·ya yeut nō?   ዋናው ገበያ የት ነው?
Where can I find ...?
   ... yeut yi·geu·nyal?   ... የት ይገኛል?
Do you have any (sandals)?
   (neu·teu·la cham·ma) al·leu?   (ነጠላ ጫማ) አለ?
I would like to buy (this/that).
   (yi·hen/yan) meug·zat   (ይሄን/ያን) መግዛት
   ə·feul·lə·gal·lō   እፈልጋለሁ

Where is the ... stall/section?	yeu ... teu·ra yeut nō?	የ ... ተራ የት ነው?
clothes	ləbs	ልብስ
fruit and vegetable	fə·ra·fə·re na at·kəlt	ፍራፍሬና አትክልት
grains	ə·həl	እህል
pottery	sheuk·la	ሽክላ
spices	kə·meu·ma kə·meum	ቅመማ ቅመም

At the Shops

ሱቆች አካባቢ

Where's the nearest ...?	keuz·zi yeu·mi·keur·bō ... yeut nō?	ከዚህ የሚቀርበው ... የት ነው?
bakery	dab·bo bet	ዳቦ ቤት
barber	şeu·gur as·teu·ka·kai	ፀጉር አስተካካይ
bookshop	meu·şə·haf bet	መጽሐፍ ቤት
butcher	sə·ga bet	ስጋ ቤት
camera shop	fo·to bet	ፎቶ ቤት
chemist	far·ma·si bet	ፋርማሲ ቤት
clothes shop	yeu ləbs suk	የልብስ ሱቅ
curio/souvenir shop	yeu ba·həl ə·ka·woch meu·deu·bər	የባህል ዕቃዎች መደብር
electronics shop	yeu e·le·trik ə·ka·woch meu·deu·bər	የኤሌትሪክ ዕቃዎች መደብር
fruit shop	fə·ra·fə·re bet	ፍራፍሬ ቤት
general store	sheu·keu·ța sheu·keuț meu·deu·bər	ሸቀጣ ሸቀጥ መደብር
grocery	gro·seu·ri	ግሮሰሪ
hairdresser	kun·jə·na sa·lon	ቀንጅና ሳሎን
jewellery shop	ge·ța geț suk	ጌጣ ጌጥ ሱቅ
laundry	lown·deu·ri	ላውንደሪ
market	geu·bi·ya	ገቢያ
music shop	mu·zi·ka bet	ሙዚቃ ቤት
service station	neu·daj ma·deu·ya	ነዳጅ ማደያ
shop	suk	ሱቅ
tailor	ləbs seuf·fi	ልብስ ሰፊ
travel agent	yeu gu·zo weu·kil	የጉዞ ወኪል

SHOPPING

SIGNS	
ክፍት ነው·	OPEN
ተዘግቷል	CLOSED

MAKING A PURCHASE

መግዛት

How much is it?
  sənt nō?
  ስንት ነው?

I'm just looking.
  ə·ya·yō nō
  እያየሁ ነው

That's all/enough.
  yi·beu·ḳal
  ይበቃል

What is it?
  mən·dən nō?
  ምንድን ነው?

I'll come back later.
  ə·meul·leu·sal·lō
  እመለሳለሁ

I want (three).
  (sost) ə·feul·lə·gal·lō
  (ሶስት) እፈልጋለሁ

Do you have (something better/any others)?
  (yeu·teu·shal·leu/le·la) al·leu?
  (የተሻለ/ሌላ) አለ?

I want a (larger/smaller) ...
  (teu·leuḳ ya·leu/an·neus ya·leu) ... ə·feul·lə·gal·lō
  (ተለቅ ያለ/አነስ ያለ) ... እፈልጋለሁ

I want one like this.
  ən·deuz·zi ai·neut ə·feul·lə·gal·lō
  እንደዚህ አይነት እፈልጋለሁ

I want it./I don't want it.
  ə·feul·lə·gal·lō/al·feul·lə·gəm
  እፈልጋለሁ/አልፈልግም

Can I pay using credit card/cheques?
  beu (kre·dit kard; chek) meuk·feul yi·cha·lal?
  በ (ክሬዲት ካርድ/ቼክ) መክፈል ይቻላል?

Could I have a receipt please?
  deu·reu·seuny ə·ba·kon?
  ደረሰኝ እባክዎን?

Keep the change.
  yan·teu/yan·chi gur·sha nō (m/f)
  ያንተ/ያንቺ ጉርሻ ነው

I want my change.
  meuls ə·feul·lə·gal·lō
  መልስ እፈልጋለሁ

Please wrap it.
  ə·ba·kon yi·ṭeuḳ·lə·lu·ləny
  እባክዎን ይጠቅልሉልኝ

SHOPPING

OK, thank you!
  ə·shi, a·meu·seu·gə·nal·lō!   እሺ አመሰግናለሁ·!

I want something like this/that.
  yeuz·zi/yeuz·za ai·neut   የዚህ/የዛ አይነት
  ə·feul·lə·gal·lō   እፈልጋለሁ

It's too short/long.
  beu·ṭam a·çhər/reu·jim nō   በጣም አጭር/ረኺም ነው·

Returning Items   እቃዎችን መመለስ

Can I return it?
  meum·meu·leus ə·chə·lal·lō?   መመለስ እችላለሁ·?

I'd like a refund.
  geun·zeu·ben meul·lə·su·liny   ገንዘቤን መልሱልኝ

It's not good quality.
  ṭə·rat yeu·leu·wəm   ጥራት የለውም

It's broken.
  teu·seub·rwal   ተሰብሯል

THEY MAY SAY ...

yeul·leum
  We don't have any available.
beu·ka?
  Is that all?
sənt tə·feul·lə·gal·leuh? (m)
sənt tə·feul·lə·gi·yal·leush? (f)
  How many/much do you want?
yeu·tə·nya·wən?
yi·he·nya·wən?
  Which one? This one?
a·ya·wa·ṭam!
  I'll lose on that!
  (said by shopkeepers when bargaining)
deun·beu·nya ən·ho·nal·leun
  We'll deal more in future.

SHOPPING

BARGAINING   መከራከር

You may need to bargain for souvenirs, clothes and similar items, though some shops have fixed prices.

How much is it?
  sənt nō?   ስንት ነው-?
That's expensive.
  wədd nō   ው-ድ ነው-
I'll pay ... birr
  ... bərr ə·keuf·lal·lō   ... ብር እከፍላለሁ-
Do you have anything cheaper?
  rə·kash al·leu?   ርካሽ አለ?
(Please) give me a discount.
  (ə·ba·kəh) wa·ga ķeu·nəs (m)   (እባክህ) ዋጋ ቀንስ
  (ə·ba·kəsh) wa·ga ķeu·nəsh (f)   (እባክሽ) ዋጋ ቀንሽ
Is that your last price?
  yeu·meu·cheu·reu·sha wa·ga nō?   የመጨረሻ ዋጋ ነው-?
(OK), I'll take it.
  (ə·shi), ə·weus·deu·wal·lō   (እሺ) እወስደዋለሁ-

ESSENTIAL GROCERIES   አስፈላጊ ሽቀጣ ሽቀጦች
Do you have ...   ... al·leu?   ... አለ?
  batteries   ba·tri dən·gai   ባትሪ ድንጋይ
  bread   dab·bo   ዳቦ
  candle(s)   sha·ma   ሻማ
  egg(s)   ən·ķu·lal   እንቁላል
  flour   du·ķet   ዱቄት
  margarine   mar·ga·rin   ማርገሪን
  matches   kəb·rit   ክብሪት
  milk   weu·teut   ወተት
  salt   chō   ጨው
  soap   sa·mu·na   ሳሙ-ና
  sugar   sə·kwar   ስኳር
  tea (leaf)   shai kə·ţeul   ሻይ ቅጠል
  toilet paper   soft; yeu shənt bet   ሶፍት/የሽንት
                       weu·reu·ķeut   ቤት ወረቀት
  washing powder   o·mo   ኦሞ

CLOTHING   ልብሶች

bra	ṭut ma·si·ya·zha	ጡት ማስያዣ
clothes	ləbs	ልብስ
dress	ḳeu·miss	ቀሚስ
jacket	ja·ket	ጃኬት
jeans	jəns	ጅንስ
jumper/sweater	shu·rab	ሹራብ
leather jacket	ḳo·da kot	ቆዳ ኮት
rain clothes	yeu zə·nab ləbs	የዝናብ ልብስ
singlet	ka·na·te·ra	ካናቴራ
shirt	sheu·miz	ሸሚዝ
shorts	ḳum·ṭa su·ri	ቁምጣ ሱሪ
socks	kal·si	ካልሲ
trousers	su·ri	ሱሪ
underpants	wəsṭ su·ri	ውስጥ ሱሪ

Do you have something in my size?
  leu·ne yeu·mi·hon al·leu?   ለኔ የሚሆን አለ?
Can I see some samples?
  na·mu·na ma·yeut yi·cha·lal?   ናሙና ማየት ይቻላል?
I want you to take my measurements.
  meul·leu·kat ə·feul·lə·gal·lō   መለካት እፈልጋለሁ
Can I try it on?
  lə·leu·kow?   ልለካው?
Is there a mirror?
  meus·ta·weut al·leu?   መስታወት አለ?
It fits well.
  lə·ke nō   ልኬ ነው
Can it be altered?
  lə·tas·teu·ka·kəl·lō   ልታስተካክለው ትችላለህ?
  tə·cha·lal·leuh? (m)
Can you mend this?
  yi·hen sə·fal·liny? (m)   ይህን ስፋልኝ
When will it be ready?
  meu·che yi·deur·sal?   መቼ ይደርሳል?
I'll come back later.
  bo·hal·la ə·meul·leu·sal·lō   በኋላ እመለሳለሁ

button	yeu ləbs ḳulf	የልብስ ቁልፍ
fabric	cheurḳ	ጨርቅ
hem	ṭeurz	ጠርዝ
needle and thread	meur·fe·na kər	መርፌና ክር
safety pin	meur·fe ḳulf	መርፌ ቁልፍ
(long) sleeves	(reu·jim) ə·jə·ge	(ረጅም) እጅጌ
zip	zip/teu·feu·tə·leuk	ዚፕ/ተፈትለክ

Traditional Dress & Body Decorations
የአገር ባሀል ልብስና የሰውነት ጌጦች

beur·nos	woollen cape	በርኖስ
bu·lə·ko	grey-white cloth used as blanket or body wrap	ቡ-ልኮ
də·rə·ya	colourful cloth (worn by Harari women)	ድርያ
ə·jeu ṭeu·bab	men's long shirt	እጅ ጠባብ
ga·bi	thick shawl normally worn over clothing	ጋቢ
ḳeu·miss	dress	ቀሚስ
ku·ta	white cotton toga, thicker than neu·ṭeu·la	ኩታ
neu·ṭeu·la	shawl worn over a ḳeu·miss	ነጠላ
shash	female head cloth	ሻሽ
sheu·ma	light white shawl worn over clothing	ሸማ
shi·riṭ	Somali and Afar wrap	ሸርጥ
ṭə·beub	traditional women's dress, normally white; also refers to embroidered borders on material	ጥበብ
ṭəlf ṭeu·la·fi	embroidery	ጥልፍ ጠላፊ
yeu ba·həl ləbs	traditional dress/ clothing	የባህል ልብስ

SOUVENIRS   የስጦታ ዕቃዎች

Ethiopian souvenirs range from authentic carvings and paintings
to items still used in Ethiopian homes. You may need a permit to
export cultural items like parchments and antiques (or even things
that look old!). See also Jewellery & Accessories, page 130.

candle-stick holder	yeu sha·ma mas·keu·meu·cha	የሻማ ማስቀመጫ
carpet	mən·taf	ምንጣፍ
carving	kər·sa kərs	ቅርጻ ቅርጽ
comb	mi·do	ሚዶ
cross	meus·keul	መስቀል
fly whisk	cha·ra	ጭራ
knife	seun·ti	ሰንጢ
painting	(yeu ba·həl)	(የባህል)
(traditional)	sə'əl	ስዕል
parchment (of animal hide)	bə·ran·na	ብራና
pottery	yeu sheuk·la ə·ka·woch	የሸክላ ዕቃዎች
rug	yeu·gər mən·taf	የገር ምንጣፍ
rug (sheepskin)	a·go·za	አጎዛ
stool (wooden)	du·ka/beur·chu·ma	ዱካ/በርጩማ
straw mat	seu·len	ሰሌን
umbrella	jan·tə·la	ጃንጥላ
vase	yeu a·beu·ba mas·keu·meu·cha	የአበባ ማስቀመጫ

WHERE'D YEU GET IT?

Each region has its own distinctive style and speciality.
Dorze is known for colourful cotton clothes, Harar for
quality basketry, Debre Birhan for carpets, Gonder for
crosses and other areas for jewellery and pottery. To
indicate the region of origin for a requested item, simply
add yeu followed by the region and item.

yeu (dor·ze) ləbs	cloth from (Dorze)
yeu (gon·deur) meus·keul	cross from (Gonder)

SHOPPING

Baskets ቅርጫቶች

Baskets in Ethiopia have different names depending on their design and purpose.

ḳər·chat/ḳər·cha·toch ቅርጫት/ቅርጫቶች
  basket/baskets
a·geul·gəl አገልግል
  leather/animal skin food storage basket (often round, decorated and tied with leather straps)
meu·sob መሶብ
  large multi-coloured basket used for keeping ən·jeu·ra, sometimes used as a traditional eating table (meu·sob weurk)
mu·dai ሙዳይ
  small, round, often coloured/decorated basket
seu·fed ሰፈድ
  flat basket used for winnowing grain
yeu ha·rar ḳər·cha·toch የሐረር ቅርጫቶች
  baskets from the Harar region
zeun·bil ዘንቢል
  basket for carrying goods (usually shopping)

Cooking & Eating Implements
የምግብ መስሪያና መመዘቢያ እቃዎች

bə·rə·le	for drinking honey wine (ṭeuj)	ብርሌ
geu·beu·te	wooden bowl	ገበቴ
geun·bo	clay pot	ገንቦ
ən·sə·ra	large clay pot/pitcher used for storing and carrying water	እንስራ
jeu·beu·na	traditional coffee pot	ጀበና
ḳəl	gourd	ቅል
sheuk·la dəst	clay saucepan/pot	ሸክላ ድስት
wan·cha	traditional cup (horn/clay)	ዋንጫ
yeu sheuk·la ə·ḳa	earthenware pot	የሸክላ ዕቃ

SHOPPING

JEWELLERY & ACCESSORIES   ጌጣ ጌጥ

anklet	al·bo	አልቦ
belt	ḳeu·beu·to	ቀበቶ
bracelet	am·bar	አምባር
cap	ko·fə·ya	ኮፍያ
earrings	gu·tə·cha	ጉ ·ት ·ቻ
engraving	ḳərṣ	ቅርፅ
handkerchief	meu·ha·reub	መሃረብ
hat	ḳob	ቆብ
jewellery	ge·ṭa geṭ	ጌጣ ጌጥ
necklace	kə·tab	ክታብ
necklet	ha·bəl	ሃብል
purse	por·sa	ፖርሳ
ring	ḳeu·leu·beut	ቀለበት
sandals	kəft cham·ma	ክፍት ጫማ
shoelaces	yeu cham·ma ma·seu·ri·ya	የጫማ ማሰሪያ
shoes	cham·ma	ጫማ
sunglasses	yeu ṣeu·hai meu·neu·ṣər	የፀሃይ መነፅር
sun hat	bar·ne·ṭa	ባርኔጣ
wallet	yeu kis por·sa	የኪስ ፖርሳ

BODY BEAUTIFUL

Unique facial and body markings are used by different groups in Ethiopia. In the north, delicate neck and facial tattoos set off traditional white clothing and elaborate hair designs. In the south-west, some groups pattern themselves with intricate scarification and body painting. Henna (hen·na) patterns are used all over Ethiopia to enhance beauty.

kul   ኩል
    eyeliner
ən·so·səl·la   አንሶስላ
    hand and foot decoration, made from plant extracts
nə·ḳə·sat   ንቅሳት
    tattoo on the forehead, neck or hands (of women), or
    used to darken the gums of the mouth

SHOPPING

MATERIALS
ጨርቃ ጨርቅና የሽክላ እቃዎች

What's it made of?
keu mən·dən nō
yeu·teu·seu·row?

ከምንድን ነው የተሰራው?

Is it pure (gold)?
nə·şuh (weurk) nō?

ንፁህ (ወርቅ) ነው?

bronze	neu·has	ነሐስ
calico	a·bu·jeu·did	አቡጄዲድ
copper	meu·dab	መዳብ
cotton	təţ	ጥጥ
(handmade)	(beu əj yeu·teu·seu·ra)	(በእጅ የተሰራ)
glass	bər·chə·ko	ብርጭቆ
gold	weurk	ወርቅ
leather	ko·da	ቆዳ
metal	bə·reut	ብረት
rubber	las·tik/gom·ma	ላስቲክ/ጎማ
silk	harr	ሐር
silver	bərr	ብር
stainless steel	yeu·mai·zəg bə·reut	የማይዝግ ብረት
synthetic	sō seu·rash	ሰው ሰራሽ
velvet	keu·fay	ከፈይ
wax	seum	ሰም
wood	ən·cheut	እንጨት
wool	suf	ሱፍ

COLOURS
ቀለሞች

black	ţə·kur	ጥቁር
blue	seu·ma·ya·wi	ሰማያዊ
brown	bun·na ai·neut	ቡና አይነት
green	a·reun·gwa·de	አረንጓዴ
orange	bər·tu·kan ai·neut	ብርቱካን አይነት
pink	roz	ሮዝ
purple	ham·ra·wi	ሐምራዊ
red	ķai	ቀይ
white	neuch	ነጭ
yellow	bi·cha	ቢጫ

SHOPPING

TOILETRIES   የመታጠቢያ ቤትና የመኳኳያ እቃዎች

If you can't find the word for something you need in this list,
try using the English for it.

brush	bu·rash	ቡርሽ
comb	ma·beu·teu·ri·ya	ማበጠሪያ
condom	kon·dom	ኮንዶም
cosmetics	meu·kwa·kwa·ya	መኳኳያ
insect repellent	yeu bim·bi	የቢምቢ
	meu·keu·la·keu·ya krem	መከላከያ ክሬም
mirror	meus·ta·weut	መስታወት
nail clippers	yeu ṭə·fər meu·ku·reu·cha	የጥፍር መቁረጫ
perfume	shə·to	ሽቶ
razor	yeu şim mə·lach	የሊ:ም ምላጭ
sanitary pads	mo·deuss	ሞደስ
shampoo	sham·po	ሻምፖ
skin oil	yeu sō·neut ḳə·bat	የሰውነት ቅባት
soap	sa·mu·na	ሳሙና
tampons	tam·pon	ታምፖን
toilet paper	soft; yeu shənt	ሶፍት/ የሽንት
	bet weu·reu·ḳeut	ቤት ወረቀት
toothbrush	yeu ṭərs bu·rash	የጥርስ ቡርሽ
traditional	yeu ṭərs	የጥርስ
wooden	meu·fa·ḳi·ya	መፋቂያ
toothbrush		
toothpaste	yeu ṭərs	የጥርስ
	sa·mu·na/kol·get	ሳሙና/ኮልጌት

FOR THE BABY   ለሕፃናት

... for babies	leu hə·şan yeu·mi·hon ...	ለሕፃን የሚሆን ...
nappy rash cream	yeu ḳo·da ḳə·bat/krem	የቆዳ ቅባት/ክሬም
powdered milk	yeu ḳor·ḳo·ro weu·teut	የርቆሮ ወተት
tinned food	yeu ḳor·ḳo·ro mə·gəb	የርቆሮ ምግብ
feeding bottle	ṭu·ṭo	ጡጦ

STATIONERY & PUBLICATIONS

የጽሑፍት ዕቃዎችና መጽሐፍት

Ethiopian newspapers in English include the *Addis Tribune*, the *Monitor* and the *Ethiopian Herald*. See Reading, page 113, for additional book-related words.

Where are newspapers sold?
ga·ze·ta yeut yi·sheu·tal?　　　ጋዜጣ የት ይሸጣል?

I want it in (English/Amharic).
beu (ən·gli·zə·nya/　　　በ (እንግሊዝኛ/አማርኛ)
a·ma·rə·nya) ə·feul·lə·gal·lō　　እፈልጋለሁ

Do you have any books by ...?
yeu ... meu·sə·haf al·la·chu?　　የ ... መጽሐፍ አላችሁ?

I want a book about Ethiopian ...	sə·leu i·tə·yo·pi·ya ... meu·sə·haf ə·feul·lə·gal·lō	ስለ ኢትዮጵያ ... መጽሐፍ እፈልጋለሁ
art	ki·neu tə·beub	ኪነ ጥበብ
cookery	mə·gəb a·seu·rar	ምግብ አሰራር
history	ta·rik	ታሪክ
wildlife	dur a·ra·wit	ዱር አራዊት
I want a/an ...	... ə·feul·lə·gal·lō	... እፈልጋለሁ
(Ethiopian/ foreign)	yeu (i·tə·yo·pi·ya/ feu·reunj) keun	የ (ኢትዮጵያ/ ፈረንጅ) ቀን
calendar	meu·ku·teu·ri·ya	መቁጠሪያ
dictionary (English to Amharic)	meuz·geu·beu ka·lat (keu ən·gli·zə·nya weu·deu a·ma·rə·nya)	መዝገበ ቃላት (ከእንግሊዝኛ ወደ አማርኛ)
book	meu·sə·haf	መጽሐፍ
box	sa·tən	ሳጥን
card	kard	ካርድ
envelope	pos·ta	ፖስታ
exercise book	deub·teur	ደብተር
fountain pen	bə'ər	ብዕር
glue	ma·ta·beu·ki·ya	ማጣበቂያ

SHOPPING

magazine	meu·şə·het	መጽሔት
... map	yeu ... kar·ta	የ ... ካርታ
city	keu·teu·ma	ከተማ
region/zone	kəl·ləl	ክልል
road	meun·geud	መንገድ
masking tape	plas·teur	ፕላስተር
newspaper	(yeu wəçh)	(የውጭ)
(foreign)	ga·ze·ţa	ጋዜጣ
pen	əs·krip·to	እስክሪፕቶ
pencil	ər·sass	እርሳስ
scissors	meu·ķeuss	መቀስ
string	si·ba·go	ሲባጎ
writing paper	meu·şa·fi·ya	መጻፊያ ወረቀት
	weu·reu·ķeut	

Do you provide	yeu ... a·geul·glot	የ... አገልግሎት
a ... service?	al·la·chu?	አሳችሁ?
Is there a	əz·zi a·ka·ba·bi	እዚህ አካባቢ የ
... service nearby?	... a·geul·glot al·leu?	... አገልግሎትአለ?
computer	kom·pyu·teur	ኮምፒውተር
photocopying	fo·to ko·pi	ፎቶ ኮፒ
translation	as·teur·gwa·mi	አስተርጓሚ
(English) typing	(ən·gli·zə·nya)	(እንግሊዝኛ)
	taip	ታይፕ

How much to print (one) page?

(and) geuş print leu mad·reug	(አንድ) ጌ ፕሪንት
sənt nō?	ለማድረግ ስንት ነው-?

MUSIC
መ-ዚ-ቃ

For music types, see page 108 in Interests. You can buy tapes and sometimes CDs at a mu·zi·ka bet.

I want to buy	... meug·zat	... መግዛት
a/an ...	ə·feul·lə·gal·lō	እፈልጋለሁ
audio cassette	ka·set	ካሴት
blank cassette	yal·teu·keu·da·beut	ያልተቀዳበት
	yeu tep ka·set	የቴፕ ካሴት
cassette by ...	yeu ... ka·set	የ ... ካሴት
CD by ...	yeu ... si·di	የ ... ሲዲ
song by ...	yeu ... zeu·feun	የ ... ዘፈን
traditional	ya·geur ba·həl	ያገር ባህል
Ethiopian music cassette	ka·set	ካሴት

What's her/his best recording?
yeus·swa/yeus·su yeu·ta·weu·ḳō
ka·set yeu·tə·nyow nō?
የሷ/የሱ የታወቀው
ካሴት የትኛው ነው?

Can I listen to this (cassette) here?
yi·hen (ka·set) meus·mat
ə·cha·lal·lō?
ይህን (ካሴት)
መስማት እችላለሁ?

PHOTOGRAPHY
ፎቶግራፍ

For photographic goods and services, ask for a fo·to bet. English is used for many photographic terms, like 'lens' and 'flash'.

How much is it for developing/
enlarging?
maṭ·ḳo·ri·ya/ma·sa·ṭeu·bi·ya
sənt nō?
ማጥቆሪያ/ማሳጠቢያ
ስንት ነው?

Can you fix my camera?
ka·me·ra·yen lət·seu·row
tə·cha·lal·leuh? (m)
ካሜራዬን ልትሰራው
ትችላለህ?

When will it be ready?
meu·che yi·deur·sal?
መቼ ይደርሳል?

I want to buy	... meug·zat	... መግዛት
a/an ...	ə·feul·lə·gal·lō	እፈልጋለሁ
battery	ba·tri dən·gai	ባትሪ ድንጋይ
camera	ka·me·ra; fo·to man·sha	ካሜራ/ፎቶ ማንሻ
film	film	ፊልም
B&W film	tə·kur na neuch film	ጥቁርና ነጭ ፊልም
colour film	keu·leur film	ከለር ፊልም
(24/36) film	ba·leu (ha·ya a·rat; seu·las·sa sə·dəst) film	ባለ (ሃያ አራት/ ሰላሳ ስድስት) ፊልም
flash	flash	ፍላሽ
videotape	vi·di·yo ka·set	ቪድዮ ካሴት

SMOKING · ሲጋራ ማጨስ

Is it OK if I smoke here?
əz·zi si·ga·ra ma·cheus
yi·cha·lal?
እዚህ ሲጋራ
ማጨስ ይቻላል?

No smoking.
ma·cheus kəl·kəl nō
ማጨስ ክልክል ነው·

Excuse me, do you have a light?
yi·kər·ta kəb·rit al·leuh/
al·leush? (m/f)
ይቅርታ ክብሪት አለህ/
አለሽ?

Please don't smoke.
ə·ba·kəh a·ta·chəs (m)
ə·ba·kəsh a·ta·chə·shi (f)
እባክህ አታጭስ
እባክሽ አታጭሺ

I'm trying to give up.
leu·ma·kom
ə·yeu·mo·keur·ku nō
ለማቆም እየሞከርኩ· ነው·

ashtray	yeu si·ga·ra meu·teur·ko·sha	የሲጋራ መተርከሻ
cigarette (packet)	(pa·ko) si·ga·ra	(ፓኮ) ሲጋራ
cigars	si·ga·ra	ሲጋራ
lighter	lai·teur	ላይተር
matches	kəb·rit	ክብሪት
pipe	pi·pa	ፒፓ
tobacco	təm·ba·ho	ትምባሆ

SIZES & COMPARISONS ልክና ማመሳሰል

another	le·la	ሌላ
big	təl·ləķ	ትልቅ
bigger	teu·leuķ ya·leu	ተለቅ ያለ
biggest	beu·tam təl·ləķ	በጣም ትልቅ
enough	beu·ķi	በቂ
few	tən·nish	ትንሽ
heavy	keu·bad	ከባድ
many/a lot	bə·zu	ብዙ
more	beu·za ya·leu	በዛ ያለ
small	tən·nish	ትንሽ
smaller (less)	an·neus ya·leu	አነስ ያለ
smallest	beu·tam tən·nish	በጣም ትንሽ
some	an·dand	አንዳንድ
too much/many	beu·tam bə·zu	በጣም ብዙ

WEIGHTS & MEASURES ሚዛንና መለኪያዎች

Ethiopia uses the metric measurement system. Amharic metric terms sound almost exactly the same as they do in English.

centimetre	sən·ti me·tər	ሴንቲ ሜትር
metre	me·tər	ሜትር
kilometre	ki·lo me·tər	ኪሎ ሜትር
gram	gram	ግራም
half a kilogram	gə·mash ki·lo	ግማሽ ኪሎ
kilogram	ki·lo gram	ኪሎ ግራም
100 kilograms	kun·tal	ኩንታል
millilitre	mil·li li·tər	ሚሊ ሊትር
half a litre	gə·mash li·tər	ግማሽ ሊትር
litre	li·tər	ሊትC

USEFUL WORDS   ጠቃሚ ቃሎች

agent (commission)	deu·lal·la	ደላላ
to bargain	meu·keu·ra·keur	መከራከር
change	meuls	መልስ
cheap	rə·kash	ርካሽ
clean	nə·ṣuh	ንጹህ
dirty	ḳo·sha·sha	ቆሻሻ
discount	ḳə·nash	ቅናሽ
expensive	wədd	ውድ
to export	weu·deu wəch meu·lak	ወደ ውጭ መላክ
fixed price	yeu teu·weu·seu·neu wa·ga	የተወሰነ ዋጋ
to import	keu·wəch mas·meu·ṭat	ከውጭ ማስመጣት
long	reu·jim	ረጅም
new	ad·dis	አዲስ
old	a·ro·ge	አሮጌ
packet	pa·ko	ፓኮ
plastic bag	keu·reu·ṭit	ከረጢት
receipt	deur·reu·seuny	ደረሰኝ
shop/kiosk	suḳ	ሱቅ
short	a·chər	አጭር
street stalls	gul·lət	ጉልት
surcharge	teu·cheum·ma·ri wa·ga	ተጨማሪ ዋጋ
trade	nəgd	ንግድ

Most Ethiopian meals consist of ən·jeu·ra, a local flat bread, topped with a spicy meat or vegetable weuṭ, 'sauce'. Wash it all down with ṭeuj, 'honey wine', and a pot of fresh bun·na, 'coffee' – meul·kam mə·gəb!, 'Enjoy your meal!'.

THROUGH THE DAY   በቀን ውስጥ

Ethiopians usually take a light breakfast and have a solid lunch and/or dinner.

breakfast	ḳurs	ቁርስ
lunch	mə·sa	ምሳ
dinner	ə·rat	እራት
snack (evening)	meuk·seus	መክሰስ

PLACES TO EAT   መመገቢያ ቦታዎች

Eating places are generally open from early morning until late in the evening, with meal times flexible.

Is there a good/cheap (restaurant)
near here?
   əz·zi a·ka·ba·bi ṭə·ru/rə·kash   እዚህ አካባቢ ጥሩ/ርካሽ
   (mə·gəb bet) al·leu?   (ምግብ ቤት) አለ?
What's the name of the restaurant?
   yeu mə·gəb be·tu səm   የምግብ ቤቱ ስም
   man nō?   ማነው?
Where's (the restaurant)?
   (mə·gəb be·tu) yeut nō?   (ምግብ ቤቱ) የት ነው?

I want to	yeu ... mə·gəb	የ ... ምግብ
eat ... food.	ə·feul·lə·gal·lō	እፈልጋለሁ
Ethiopian	i·tə·yo·pi·ya	ኢትዮጵያ
Italian	ṭal·yan	ጣሊያን
Western	feu·reunj	ፈረንጅ

FOOD

The main places for eating out are mə·gəb bet and bun·na bet, but there are plenty of other great places to eat, drink and un-wind. Most neighbourhoods have at least one of the following:

az·ma·ri bet   አዝማሪ ቤት
    traditional music and entertainment bar, serving drinks and light snacks

bun·na bet   ቡና ቤት
    'coffee house', serving coffee, tea, soft drinks, alcoholic drinks, light snacks and sometimes full meals

kek bet or pes·tri   ኬክ ቤት
    bakery or tea shop selling cakes, pastries, tea and coffee

jus bet   ጁስ ቤት
    snack bar specialising in fresh fruit juices so thick and delicious your spoon will stand up in them

mə·gəb bet   ምግብ ቤት
    restaurant or eating house (refers to any place serving full meals)

meu·sheu·ta bet   መሸታ ቤት
    similar to a bun·na bet or az·ma·ri bet, with drinks and entertainment

țeul·la bet/țeuj bet   ጠላ ቤት/ጠጅ ቤት
    traditional bars serving Ethiopian beer, spirits and wine (usually a male domain)

EATING OUT   ውጭ መብላት

Menus aren't always available, so ask the a·sa·la·fi, 'waiter', about dishes and prices. The menu decoder on page 148 will help you decipher what the dishes mean. To attract the waiter's attention, say yi·kər·ta, 'Excuse me', or hold up your hand.

Do you serve (food) here?
    (mə·gəb) al·leu?   (ምግብ) አለ?
A table for (two).
    leu (hu·leutt) sō bo·ta   ለ (ሁለት) ሰው ቦታ
Is this seat free?
    sō al·leu?   ሰው አለ?

Do you have a menu (in English)?
me·nu (beu ən·gli·zə·nya) al·leu?   ሜኑ (በእንግሊዝኛ) አለ?

What's on the menu today?
za·re mən al·la·chu?   ዛሬ ምን አላችሁ?

Do you have (vegetables)?
(at·kəlt) al·leu?   (አትክልት) አለ?

Where can I wash my hands?
əj meu·ta·ṭeu·bi·ya yeut nō?   እጅ መታጠቢያ የት ነው?

I want (another) ...
(le·la) ... ə·feul·lə·gal·lō   (ሌላ) ... እፈልጋለሁ

I'm hungry.
ra·beuny   ራበኝ

I'm thirsty.
wu·ha ṭeu·many   ውሃ ጠማኝ

I'm full/satisfied.
ṭeu·gəb·yal·lō   ጠግቤአለሁ

The bill please.
hi·sab ə·ba·kəh/ə·ba·kəsh (m/f)   ሂሳብ እባክህ/እባክሽ

FOOD

Please bring a/an ...   ə·ba·kəh ... am·ṭa (m)   እባክህ ... አምጣ
                ə·ba·kəsh ... am·chi (f)   እባክሽ ... አምጭ

ashtray	meu·teur·ko·sha	መተርኮሻ
cup	ku·ba·ya	ኩባያ
fork	shu·ka	ሹካ
glass	bər·chə·ko	ብርጭቆ
knife	bil·la·wa	ቢላዋ
plate	sa·hən	ሳህን
spoon	man·ki·ya	ማንኪያ
towel	fo·ṭa	ፎጣ

THEY MAY SAY ...

mən lə·ta·zeuz?
   What would you like?
le·la mə·gəb yəm·ṭa?
   Do you want more food?

FOOD

Describing Your Meal

ስለ ምግብዎ መናገር

This food is delicious.
ǩon·jo mə·gəb nō
ቆንጆ ምግብ ነው።

We love Ethiopian cuisine.
yeu i·tə·yo·pi·ya mə·gəb
ən·weud·dal·leun
የኢትዮጵያ ምግብ
እንወዳለን

Our compliments to the chef.
ba·leu mu·ya nō yeu seu·row
ባለሙያ ነው የሰራው።

This food is off/not good.
məg·bu teu·beu·lash·twal
ምግቡ ተበላሽቷል

This food is too spicy.
məg·bu beur·beu·re
beuz·to·beu·tal
ምግቡ በርበሬ
በዝቶበታል

I want it mild/hot.
a·lə·ça/beur·beu·re
yi·hu·nə·ləny
አልጫ/በርበሬ
ይሁንልኝ

I don't want ...
... al·feul·lə·gəm
... አልፈልግም

I want only ...
... bə·ça ə·feul·lə·gal·lō
... ብቻ እፈልጋለሁ

It's ...   ... nō   ... ነው።

bitter	meu·ra·ra	መራራ
cold	ǩeuz·ǩaz·za	ቀዝቃዛ
cooked	yeu beu·seu·leu	የበሰለ
dry	deu·reuǩ	ደረቅ
heated	moǩ ya·leu	ሞቅ ያለ
hot	muǩ	ሙቅ
salty	çhō yeu·beu·za·beut	ጨው የበዛበት
stale	yeu teu·beu·la·sheu	የተበላሸ
sweet	ṭa·faç	ጣፋጭ

VEGETARIAN & SPECIAL MEALS

አትክልትና ልዩ ምግቦች

In fasting season, vegetarian dishes are always available. Local markets are great for raw food to supplement your diet. See the menu decoder for popular vegetarian dishes.

I don't eat meat.
sə·ga al·beul·lam
ስጋ አልበሳም

Do you have fasting food (vegetarian dishes)?
yeu şom mə·gəb al·leu?
የፆም ምግብ አለ?

I don't eat (fish).
(a·sa) al·beul·lam
(ዓሳ) አልበሳም

I can't eat dairy products.
weu·teut neuk məg·bo·chən al·beul·lam
ወተት ነክ ምግቦችን አልበሳም

Do you have any vegetable dishes?
yeu at·kəlt mə·gəb al·la·chu?
የአትክልት ምግብ አሳችሁ?

Does it contain (eggs)?
(ən·ķu·lal) al·lō?
(እንቁላል) አለው?

I'm allergic to (peanuts).
(o·cho·lo·ni) ais·ma·ma·nyəm
(ኦቾሎኒ) አይስማማኝም

USEFUL WORDS

ጠቃሚ ቃሎች

bottle opener	yeu ţeur·mus meuk·feu·cha	የጠርሙስ መክፈቻ
chair	weun·beur	ወንበር
cooking oil	yeu mə·gəb zayt	የምግብ ዘይት
to eat	meub·lat	መብላት
food	mə·gəb	ምግብ
jug	ţa·sa	ጣሳ
mortar and pestle	mu·keu·cha·na zeu·neu·zeu·na	ሙቀጫና ዘበኛ
napkin	yeu aff meuţ·reu·gi·ya	የእጅ መጥረጊያ
pot	sheuk·la	ሽክላ
recipe	mə·gəb a·seu·rar zeu·de	ምግብ አሰራር ዘዴ
saucepan	yeu weuţ sa·hən	የወጥ ሳህን
table	ţeu·reu·pe·za	ጠረጴዛ
teaspoon	yeu shai man·ki·ya	የሻይ ማንኪያ
waiter	a·sa·la·fi	አሳላፊ

FOOD

FOOD

EATING WITH FRIENDS   ከጓደኞች ጋር መብላት

Ethiopians often ask friends and visitors to join them for a meal –
usually a communal experience with several people eating from the
one large plate of ən·jeu·ra. If you're not hungry, take a little food
to thank them for the invitation, or pat your stomach and say
a·meu·seu·gə·nal·lō, ṭeu·gəb·yal·lō, 'Thank you, I'm satisfied'.

While mealtimes are relaxed and friendly, there are a few points
on etiquette to note. Try to avoid using your left hand for eating
to respect cultural sensitivities. Never pick at food, lick your
fingers, or eat food from the other side of the plate. If your hosts
raise parcels of food to your mouth, a friendly gesture known as
gur·sha, accept the mouthful. People will urge you to keep eating
until you reassure them with ṭeu·gəb·yal·lō, 'I'm satisfied'.

Please join us!	ə·nə·bla!	እንብላ!
Please eat!	bə·la/bi! (m/f)	ብላ/ብይ!
Please have a drink!	ṭeu·ṭa/ṭeu·chi! (m/f)	ጠጣ/ጠጪ!
I'll pay/My treat!	yeu·ne gəb·zha nō!	የኔ ግብዣ ነው!
It was an enjoyable meal.	ḳon·jo mə·gəb neub·beur	ቆንጆ ምግብ ነው ነበር

FEAST OF FASTS

Religion has a big influence on Ethiopian eating habits.
Devoted Orthodox Christians fast around 165 to 250
days a year, including Lent in the lead-up to Easter.
During this time, they abstain from all animal products
(meat, dairy, eggs). The main Muslim fast is Ramadan,
in which followers eat nothing between sunrise and sun-
down. Both Orthodox Christians and Muslims only eat
meat slaughtered by their own kind.

fasting	ṣom	ጾም
fasting food	yeu ṣom mə·gəb	የጾም ምግብ
feast	meu·feu·seuk	መፈሰክ

BREAKFAST
ቁርስ

The most common light breakfast is dab·bo beu shai, 'bread and tea'. Most eateries also serve honey, eggs and coffee. Spicy traditional cereals are sometimes served in people's homes.

bread/bread rolls	dab·bo	ዳቦ
coffee (with sugar/ without sugar)	bun·na (beu sə·kwar; ya·leu sə·kwar)	ቡና (በስኳር/ ያለ ስኳር)
coffee (with milk/ without milk)	bun·na (beu weu·teut; ya·leu weu·teut)	ቡና (በወተት/ ያለ ወተት)
egg(s)	ən·ku·lal	እንቁላል
boiled eggs	kə·kəl ən·ku·lal	ቅቅል እንቁላል
fried eggs	ən·ku·lal ṭəbs	እንቁላል ጥብስ
scrambled eggs	ən·ku·lal fər·fər	እንቁላል ፍርፍር
honey	mar	ማር
juice	chə·ma·ki	ጭማቂ
margarine	mar·geu·rin	ማርገሪን
milk	weu·teut	ወተት
sugar	sə·kwar	ስኳር
tea (strong/weak)	(weuf·ram/keu·chən) shai	(ወፍራም/ቀጭን) ሻይ

FOOD

Traditional Breakfast Dishes
የአገር ባህል የቁርስ ምግቦች

fət·fət
ፍትፍት
chopped up ən·jeu·ra or bread mixed with chilli or butter

geun·fo
ገንፎ
barley or wheat porridge, often served with Ethiopian butter and a spicy hot sauce

ka·teu·nya/də·rəb·rə·bosh
ቃተኛ/ድርብርበሽ
ən·jeu·ra cooked in a paste of chilli and Ethiopian butter

kən·che
ቅንጨ
boiled crushed wheat porridge with traditional butter

FOOD

TYPICAL DISHES   ዋና ምግቦች

To eat Ethiopia's main dish, *injera* (ən·jeu·ra), break a corner off with the fingers and use it to wrap or scoop up the spicy meat or vegetable topping. If you like your food on the mild side, ask for a·lə·cha food. See also the menu decoder, page 148.

The most common meats are chicken, lamb and beef. Seafood, other than fish, is rare. Pork is also rare, as it is forbidden to both Christians and Muslims.

Traditional Condiments   የአገር ባህል ቅመማ ቅመም

Powdered herb and spice mixtures are added during cooking or used as a seasoning for the main meal. The combination of the spices in beur·beu·re and spiced butter is what gives sauces their distinct Ethiopian flavour.

a·frinj   አፍሪንጅ
    mixture of red pepper seeds, ginger and garlic

a·wa·ze/də·leuh   አዋዜ/ድልህ
    butter and beur·beu·re sauce; usually eaten with raw meat

beur·beu·re   በርበሬ
    crushed chilli, garlic, ginger, basil, rue seed, cloves, cinnamon, cardamom, Bishop's weed and red onion

miṭ·mi·ṭa   ሚጥሚጣ
    powdered hot small red peppers mixed with garlic, ginger and other spices (hotter than beur·beu·re)

seu·na·fəch   ሰናፍጭ
    Ethiopian mustard

chilli sauce	də·ləh/a·wa·ze	ድልህ/አዋዜ
gravy/broth	meu·reuḳ	መረቅ
salt	chō	ጨው
sugar	sə·kwar	ስኳር
tomato sauce	yeu ti·ma·tim də·ləh	የቲማቲም ድልህ

Snacks ቀላል ምግቦች

Snacks such as fresh bread or ko·lo, 'fried barley', are eaten with tea, coffee or juices, or on their own. See Staples, page 152, for a list of bread types.

bread/bread rolls	dab·bo	ዳቦ
chips	də·nəch țəbs	ድንች ጥብስ
crackers	ki·ța	ቂጣ
fried barley	ko·lo	ቆሎ
peanuts	o·cho·lo·ni	አቾሎኒ
popcorn	a·beu·ba ko·lo	አበባ ቆሎ
samosa (lentil)	sam·bo·sa	ሳምቦሳ
wheat snacks	dab·bo ko·lo	ዳቦ ቆሎ
yogurt	ər·go	እርጎ

FOOD

KEY DISHES ዋና ዋና ምግቦች

The main vegetable dishes at eateries are məs·sər weuṭ, shi·ro, at·kəlt and kək weuṭ. The main meat dishes are do·ro weuṭ, kai weuṭ, kət·fo, țəbs and zəg·ni. All come with ən·jeu·ra. For a bit of each, ask for beu·yai·neu·tu. For a vegetarian mix, ask for yeu șom beu·yai·neu·tu.

You'll notice in the menu decoder that meat and vegetable names are often attached to the following dish types.

a·lə·cha	አልጫ
not too spicy	
mən·cheut a·bəsh	ምንቸት አብሽ
minced, cooked in spices	
shor·ba	ሾርባ
soup, not usually an entree in Ethiopia	
țəbs	ጥብስ
cut into pieces and fried in spices	
tə·re	ጥሬ
raw, usually dipped in spices	
weuṭ	ወጥ
spicy stew/sauce	

FOOD

MENU DECODER

aib   አይብ
  Ethiopian cheese (similar to cottage cheese). Sometimes
  mixed with spinach/collard greens (aib beu go·meun)

a·sa   አሳ
  fish; either dried, salted or cooked in sauce

a·sa weuṭ   አሳ ወጥ
  fish cooked in spicy sauce

at·kəlt (lit: vegetables)   አትክልት
  mixture of cooked vegetables; usually spinach, carrots,
  potatoes

bam·ya a·lə·cha   ባምያ አልጫ
  okra in a spicy mild sauce

beu·yai·neu·tu   በያይነቱ
  'of each kind'; a mixture of common ən·jeu·ra toppings,
  usually do·ro weuṭ, ṭəbs, vegetables and spicy pulse
  mixtures

bid·de·na   በዴና
  bread sometimes served in east Ethiopia, similar to
  ən·jeu·ra, but sweeter and made from millet

də·nəch seu·la·ṭa/weuṭ   ድንች ሰላጣ/ድንች ወጥ
  potato salad/stew

dab·bo   ዳቦ
  bread or bread rolls with similar flavour and texture to
  Western bread

do·ro weuṭ   ዶሮ ወጥ
  a rich and spicy chicken stew, one of Ethiopia's favourite
  national dishes, often served with a whole boiled egg

du·leut   ዱለት
  minced tripe, liver and lean beef fried in onions, butter,
  chilli, cardamom and pepper

ən·jeu·ra   እንጀራ
  large, pancake-like bread made from ṭəf (Ethiopia's native grain), yeast and water. Light and spongy in texture,
  tangy in flavour, colours vary from white to dark brown,
  depending on the flour used – sometimes millet or rice
  flour is used.

FOOD

ər·go   እርጎ
yoghurt, a cooling side dish for hot, spicy meals

ən·ku·lal weuṭ   እንቁላል ወጥ
spicy egg sauce

go·meun   ጎመን
cooked spinach/collard greens

go·meun beu sə·ga   ጎመን በስጋ
collard greens and meat mixed together

ḳai weuṭ   ቀይ ወጥ
spicy beef, lamb or goat stew

ḳə·ḳəl   ቅቅል
boiled meat

ḳək weuṭ   ክክ ወጥ
spicy split-pea sauce

ḳət·fo   ክትፎ
spicy minced beef often served with aib cottage cheese
(sometimes served raw – say leub leub if you want it cooked)

ḳi·ṭa   ቂጣ
crisp chapatti-like bread, often cooked in chilli, butter and
spices

ḳo·cho   ቆጮ
Southern Ethiopian staple ḳo·cho (made from the fermented
roots of the false banana tree), often cooked in a peppery
sauce with minced meat

ḳwa·li·ma   ቋሊማ
spicy sausage, from the Harar region

ḳwan·ṭa   ቋንጣ
strips of beef (usually dried), rubbed in chilli, butter, salt
and pepper

mən·cheut a·bəsh   ምንቾት አብሽ
minced meat curry

məs·sər weuṭ   ምስር ወጥ
lentil 'curry'; lentils cooked in onions, chilli, spices

meu·reuḳ   መረቅ
soup/broth (usually spicy lamb or beef)

FOOD

nəf·ro	ንፍሮ

dry mixture of boiled chick peas, lentils and other legumes

sə·ga weuṭ	ስጋ ወጥ

spicy beef stew

seu·la·ṭa	ሰላጣ

salad (may be coleslaw or tomato and lettuce, depending on where you are)

shi·ro	ሽሮ

spiced chick pea dhal – neuch shi·ro is mild, and mə·ṭən shi·ro is hot

ṭəbs	ጥብስ

pan fried and spiced beef or lamb slices

tə·ḳəl go·meun	ጥቅል ጎመን

cooked cabbage and carrots

tə·re sə·ga	ጥሬ ስጋ

raw beef served with butter, chilli and other spices

ti·ma·tim fət·fət	ቲማቲም ፍትፍት

mildly spiced, chopped tomato dish with ən·jeu·ra

yeu a·deun·gwa·re shor·ba	የአደንጓሬ ሾርባ

bean soup

yeu do·ro ṭəbs	የዶሮ ጥብስ

fried and spiced chicken pieces

yeu dub·ba weuṭ	የዱባ ወጥ

spicy pumpkin stew

yeu ḳa·ri·ya sən·nəny	የቃሪያ ስንኝ

uncooked hot peppers stuffed with onion

yeu məs·sər shor·ba	የምስር ሾርባ

tasty lentil soup

yeu ṣom mə·gəb	የጾም ምግብ

fasting food; a range of spicy vegetable and legume dishes

zəg·ni a·lə·ᴄha	ዝግኒ አልጫ

mild meat stew (usually lamb)

COOKING METHODS

የምግብ አሰራር ዘዴ

Ethiopian meals are time consuming to prepare. The watery ən·jeu·ra dough requires three days of fermentation, and the ubiquitous spices need careful grinding and mixing. Ethiopians are usually happy to demonstrate local cooking techniques and may encourage you to give it a go, a messy but fun experience.

What are you cooking?
mən ə·yeu·seu·rah nō? (m)	ምን እየሰራህ ነው-?
mən ə·yeu·seu·rash nō? (f)	ምን እየሰራሽ ነው-?

Can I watch?
ma·yeut yi·cha·lal?	ማየት ይቻላል?

Can I help?
meur·dat ə·chəl·lal·lō?	መርዳት እችላለሁ?

It's not cooked.
al·beu·seu·leum	አልበሰለም

baked (in an oven)	yeu·teu·ga·geu·reu	የተጋገረ
boiled	kə·kəl	ቅቅል
cooked/heated	yeu beu·seu·leu	የበሰለ
fried	yeu teu·teu·beu·seu	የተጠበሰ
raw	tə·re	ጥሬ
well done	yeu beu·seu·leu	የበሰለ

SELF-CATERING

ምግብ ማዘጋጀት

You'll find a huge range of fresh fruit, vegetables, eggs, pulses and staples from markets and street stalls. There are also prepared mixtures like shi·ro – just add water and cook! Tinned and imported food is limited to grocery shops in major towns. You can buy meat from a sə·ga bet or a live chicken from the local market – though you might get attached to it on the bus ride home! See also At the Market & Street Stalls, page 121.

FOOD

Staples
ዋና ምግቦች

bread/bread rolls (plain)	dab·bo	ዳቦ
bread (from the false banana tree; a southern staple)	ko·cho	ቆጭ
bread (northern Ethiopian round bread)	am·ba·sha	አምባሻ
flour	du·ket	ዱቄት
injera	ən·jeu·ra	እንጀራ
injera (dried)	dər·kosh	ድርቆሽ
maize (corn)	beu·ko·lo	በቆሎ
pasta	pas·ta	ፓስታ
potatoes	də·nach	ድንች
rice	ruz	ሩዝ
roasted cereal drink	beu·so	በሶ
spaghetti	spa·ge·ti	ስፓጌቲ
sweet potatoes	sə·kwar də·nach	ስኳር ድንች

Dairy Produce
ወተት ነክ የምግብ ውጤቶች

butter	ka·be	ቅቤ
Ethiopian (spiced) butter	yeu teu·neu·teu·reu ka·be	የተነጠረ ቅቤ
cheese (cottage style)	aib	አይብ
cream (usually skimmed from boiled milk)	səl·ba·bot	ስልባቦት
eggs	ən·ku·lal	እንቁላል
margarine	mar·geu·rin	ማርጋሪን
milk	weu·teut	ወተት
yogurt	ər·go	እርጎ

Meat & Poultry ሥጋና ዶሮ

beef/ox meat	yeu beu·re sə·ga	የበሬ ሥጋ
broth	meu·reuk	መረቅ
chicken	do·ro	ዶሮ
dripping	cho·ma	ጮማ
fish	a·sa	አሳ
goat meat	yeu fə·yeul sə·ga	የፍየል ሥጋ
lamb	yeu beug sə·ga	የበግ ሥጋ
meat	sə·ga	ሥጋ
offal	du·leut	ዱለት
sausage	ḳwa·li·ma/so·sej	ቋሊማ/ሶሴጅ
veal	yeu ṭə·ja sə·ga	የጥጃ ሥጋ

FOOD

Vegetables አትክልቶች

beans	a·deun·gwa·re	አደንጓሬ
beetroot	ḳai sər	ቀይ ስር
cabbage	ṭə·ḳəl go·meun	ጥቅል ጎመን
capsicum	yeu feu·reunj ḳa·ri·ya	የፈረንጅ ቃሪያ
carrot	ka·rot	ካሮት
cauliflower	a·beu·ba go·meun	አበባ ጎመን
corn	beu·ḳo·lo	በቆሎ
onion	shən·kurt	ሽንኩርት
peas	a·teur	አተር
potato	də·nəch	ድንች
pumpkin/squash	dub·ba	ዱባ
salad	seu·la·ṭa	ሰላጣ
spinach	ḳos·ṭa	ቆስጣ
sweet potato	sə·kwar də·nəch	ስኳር ድንች
tomato	ti·ma·tim	ቲማቲም
vegetables	at·kəlt	አትክልት

FOOD

Legumes, Nuts & Pulses   አተር ባቄላና ለው·ዝ

barley	geubs	ጉብስ
beans	ba·ḳe·la	ባቄላ
chick peas	shən·bra dub·be	ሽንብራ ዱቤ
kidney beans	ba·ḳe·la	ባቄላ
lentils	məs·sər	ምስር
nuts	leuwz	ለው·ዝ
peanuts	o·cho·lo·ni	አቾሎኒ
split peas	kək	ክክ
sunflower seeds	yeu suff a·beu·ba fə·re	የሱ·ፍ አበባ ፍሬ

ቆንጆ ምግብ ነው·

ባለሙ·ያ ነው· የሰራ·ው·

Fruit   ፍራ·ፍሬ

apple	pom	ፖም
avocado	a·vo·ka·do	አቮካዶ
banana	muz	ሙ·ዝ
dates	teu·mər	ተምር
fruit	fə·ra·fə·re	ፍራ·ፍሬ
grapes	wain	ዋይን
guava	zay·tun	ዘይቱን
lemon	lo·mi	ሎ·ሚ
mandarin	meun·deu·rin	መንደሪን
mango	man·go	ማንጎ
melon	bə·ṭih	ብጢ
orange	bər·tu·kan	ብርቱካን
papaya	pa·pa·ya	ፓፓያ
peach	kok	ኮክ
pineapple	a·nan·nas	አናናስ
sugar cane	sheun·ko·ra	ሽንኩራ
sultanas	zeu·bib	ዘቢብ
watermelon	kər·bush	ክርቡ·ሽ

Herbs & Spices ቅመማ ቅመም

See page 146 for traditional ready-made spice mixtures.

basil	beu·so bə·la	በሶ ብላ
Bishop's weed	neuçh az·mud	ኖጭ አዝሙ-ድ
black cumin	ṭə·ḳur az·mud	ጥቁር አዝሙ-ድ
chilli	ḳa·ri·ya	ቃሪያ
cinnamon	keu·reu·fa	ቀረፋ
cloves	ḳə·rən·fud	ቅርንፉድ
coriander	dəm·bə·lal	ድምብላል
cumin	az·mud	አዝሙ-ድ
fennel	ən·sə·lal	እንስላል
fenugreek	a·bəsh	አብሽ
garlic	neuçh shən·kurt	ኖጭ ሽንኩ-ርት
ginger	zən·jə·bəl	ዝንጅብል
pepper (black)	ḳun·do beur·beu·re	ቆንዶ በርበሬ
rue	ṭe·na a·dam	ጤና አዳም
spices	ḳə·meu·ma ḳə·meum	ቅመማ ቅመም
turmeric	ərd	እርድ

Sweet Food ጣፋጭ ምግብ

Desserts (other than fruit and yogurt) are uncommon in Ethiopia, but sweet food is a treat between meals. Try cakes and biscuits at your local kek bet. Pastries like hal·wa and bak·la·va are popular in Addis. See also Snacks on page 147.

biscuit	bəs·kut	ብስኩ-ት
cake	kek	ኬክ
chewing gum	mas·ti·ka	ማስቲካ
chocolate	cheu·ko·let	ቸኮሌት
honey	mar	ማር
ice cream	ais krem	አይስ ክሬም
popcorn	a·beu·ba ḳo·lo	አበባ ቆሎ
sugar	sə·kwar	ስኳር
sugar cane	sheun·ko·ra	ሽኩ-ራ
sweets/lollies/ fudge	keu·reu·me·la	ከረሜላ

FOOD

የቡና አፈላል

yeu bun·na a·feu·lal coffee ceremony

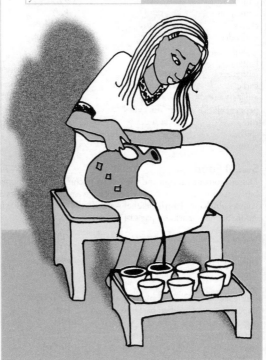

DRINKS
የሚጠጡ

Jus bet and bun·na bet (juice and coffee bars) offer cheap and delicious freshly made drinks as well as bottled drinks. Tap water should be boiled or treated before drinking.

Nonalcoholic
አልኮል ነክ ያልሆኑ

juice	cha·ma·ḳi	ጭማቂ
mixed fruit	spress	ስፕሬስ
pineapple juice	yeu a·nan·nas cha·ma·ḳi	የአናናስ ጭማቂ
without water	jus ba·cha ya·leu wu·ha	ጁስ ብቻ ያለ ውሃ
milk	weu·teut	ወተት
mineral water	am·bo wu·ha	አምቦ ውሃ
soda/soft drink	leus·las·sa	ለስላሳ
water	wu·ha	ውሃ
boiled water	yeu feu·la wu·ha	የፈላ ውሃ
sterilised water	yeu teu·ṭa·ra wu·ha	የተጣራ ውሃ
hot cereal drink	aṭ·mit/beu·so	አጥሚት/በሶ

Tea & Coffee
ሻይና ቡና

Believed to be the original home of the coffee tree, Ethiopia is a coffee lover's dream. Fresh black coffee, cappuccino and latte-style brews are served everywhere in bun·na bet.

In the traditional coffee ceremony, held frequently in people's homes, coffee is prepared, step-by-step, over a small charcoal stove. When the roasting beans are passed around for you to savour the aroma, wave the smoke towards your nose. When you're offered snacks or a si·ni (tiny cup) of coffee, nod your head in appreciation. The first round is a·bol, the second hu·leut·teu·nya and the third and most important, beu·reu·ka, which means 'blessing'. The ceremonies are a great time for conversation among friends, families and neighbours, and can last for hours.

FOOD

black coffee	ṭə·ḳur bun·na	ጥቁር ቡና
coffee ...	bun·na ...	ቡና ...
with/without sugar	beu/ya·leu sə·kwar	በ/ያለ ስኳር
with/without milk	beu/ya·leu weu·teut	በ/ያለ ወተት
with a little milk	keu tən·nish weu·teut gar	ከትንሽ ወተት ጋር
coffee beans	ṭə·re bun·na	ጥሬ ቡና
coffee ceremony	yeu bun·na a·feu·lal	የቡና አፈላል
coffee pot	yeu bun·na jeu·beu·na	የቡና ጆቤና
incense granules	ə·ṭan	ዕጣን
incense stick	neud	ነድ
coffee leaf tea (rare)	ḳu·ṭi/hoj·ja	ቄጢ/ሆጃ
black tea	ṭə·ḳur shai	ጥቁር ሻይ
tea ...	shai ...	ሻይ ...
with/without sugar	beu/ya·leu sə·kwar	በ/ያለ ስኳር
with/without milk	beu/ya·leu weu·teut	በ/ያለ ወተት
with a little milk	keu tən·nish weu·teut gar	ከትንሽ ወተት ጋር
strong/weak	weuf·ram/ḳeu·chen	ወፍራም/ቀጭን
tea with spices	ba·leu kə·meum shai	ባለ ቅመም ሻይ
tea with lemon	shai beu lo·mi	ሻይ በሎሚ
hot milk	ṭə·kus weu·teut	ትኩስ ወተት

Alcoholic   አልኮል ነክ የሆኑ መጠጦች

The most famous Ethiopian home brews are ṭeul·la and ṭeuj, available at ṭeul·la bet, ṭeuj bet and sometimes restaurants. The main drinking venue is the local bun·na bet (coffee shop/bar) which has local and imported alcoholic and nonalcoholic drinks. Most spirits retain their English or original name.

Let's drink!
ən·ṭeu·ṭa!   እንጠጣ!
Cheers!
leu·ṭe·na·chən!   ለጤናችን!

FOOD

a·reu·ki   አረቄ
warming local grain spirit; twice-filtered is da·gəm

ka·ti·ka·la   ካቲካላ
local spirit

ṭeul·la   ጠላ
refreshing mild alcoholic drink made from barley or maize

ṭeuj
wine made from honey and the local ge·sho plant, drunk out of bə·rə·le, small flasks with long, narrow necks. Variations on the main drink include deu·reuķ (dry), meu·ha·keu·leu·nya (medium sweet), leus·las·sa or bərz (wine and mild).

beer	bi·ra	ቢራ
ice	beu·reu·do	በረዶ
whiskey	wis·ki keu	ውስኪ
with (Coke)	(ko·ka ko·la) gar	ከ (ኮካ ኮላ) ጋር
wine	wain	ዋይን

IN THE BAR   ቡና ቤት ውስጥ

What'll you have?
  mən yim·ṭal·ləh? (m)   ምን ይምጣልህ?
  mən yim·ṭal·ləsh? (f)   ምን ይምጣልሽ?

I'll have ...
  ... yim·ṭa·ləny   ... ይምጣልኝ

No ice.
  beu·reu·do al·feul·lə·gəm   በረዶ አልፈልግም

Same again, please.
  yeuz·zi·hu ai·neut ə·ba·kon   የዚሁ አይነት እባክዎን

FOOD

One Too Many?

ብዙ መጠጥ?

I don't drink.
  meu·teut al·teu·tam

መጠጥ አልጠጣም

I'm tired, I'd better get home.
  deu·keu·meuny weu·deu
  bet lə·hid

ደክሞኝ ወደ ቤት
ልሂድ

I feel fantastic!
  deus blo·nyal!

ደስ ብሎኛል!

I think I've had one too many.
  bə·zu teu·tow

ብዙ ጠጣሁ

Whether hiring a beuk·lo, 'mule', or watching the ko·ko·boch, 'stars', Amharic is great for communicating with geu·beu·re, 'farmers', and a sure way to find the best scenery.

CAMPING   ድንኳን መትከል

There are few designated camp sites in Ethiopia. Always ask permission from landowners or authorities before you pitch your tent. Bury, burn or take away your rubbish.

Is there somewhere to camp nearby?
dən·kwan meut·keu·ya   ድንኳን መትከያ
bo·ta al·leu?   ቦታ አለ?

May I camp here?
əz·zi dən·kwan meut·keul   እዚህ ድንኳን መትከል
ə·chə·lal·lō?   እችላለሁ-?

Yes, you can.
ow, tə·chə·lal·leuh/   አዎ ትችላለህ/
tə·chi·yal·leush (m/f)   ትችያለሽ

No you can't.
ai·chal·ləm   አይቻልም

How much   leu (and) ...   ለ (አንድ) ...
for (one) ...   sənt nō?   ስንት ነው-?
  night   ma·ta   ማታ
  tent   dən·kwan   ድንኳን

May I light a fire here?
əz·zi ə·sat man·deud   እዚህ እሳት ማንደድ
yi·cha·lal?   ይቻላል?

IN THE COUNTRY

Where can I find ...?	... yeut yi·geu·nyal?	... የት ይገኛል?
charcoal	keu·seul	ከሰል
firewood	yeu ma·geu·do ən·cheut	የማገዶ እንጨት
kerosene	ke·ro·sin	ኬሮሲን
matches	kəb·rit	ክብሪት
water	wu·ha	ውሃ
bottle opener	yeu teur·mus meuk·feu·cha	የጠርሙስ መክፈቻ
camp site	dən·kwan	ድንኳን መትከያ
	meut·keu·ya bo·ta	ቦታ
canvas	sheu·ra	ሸራ
can opener	yeu ķor·ķo·ro meuk·feu·cha	የቆርቆሮ መክፈቻ
cooking pot	bə·reut dəst	ብረት ድስት
lamp (oil)	fa·nos	ፋኖስ
matches	kəb·rit	ክብሪት
mosquito net	yeu bim·bi meu·reub	የቢምቢ መረብ
tent	dən·kwan	ድንኳን
torch	yeuj ba·tri	የጅ ባትሪ

ON THE FARM   እርሻ

Most Ethiopians live and work in the country, their lives governed by the seasons, harvests and local religious life. While men and boys tend the animals and labour in the fields, women collect water and wood and take care of the household. Try to respect farmers' privacy, land and customs. Bow and greet people before chatting. Farmers may have a different concept of distance from you: ma·do means 'yonder'.

How has the weather been?
zeun·də·ro zə·nab / ən·det nō?   ዘንድሮ ዝናብ እንዴት ነው-?

May I pass this way?
beuz·zi beu·kul ma·leuf yi·cha·lal?   በዚህ በኩል ማለፍ ይቻላል?

May I cross your property?
beur·swo meu·ret beu·kul ma·leuf yi·cha·lal?   በርስዎ መሬት በኩል ማለፍ ይቻላል?

agriculture	gəb·rən·na	ግብርና
country person	ba·la·geur	ባላገር
crops	ə·həl	እህል
enclosure (animal)	gur·reu·no	ጉረኖ
farm	ər·sha	እርሻ
farmer	geu·beu·re	ግብሬ
fence	a·ṭər	አጥር
field/paddock	me·da	ሜዳ
granary	go·teu·ra	ጎተራ
harvest (n)	meu·hər	መኸር
hay	dər·ḳosh	ድርቆሽ
hut	go·jo bet	ጎጆ ቤት
livestock	keubt	ከብት
nomad	zeu·lan	ዘላን
planting/ sowing	meut·keul/ meuz·rat	መትከል/ መዝራት
plough	ma·reu·sha	ማረሻ
shepherd	ə·reu·nya	እረኛ
thatch/cover	kə·dan	ክዳን
village	meun·deur/seu·feur	መንደር/ሰፈር
water pump	yeu wu·ha pamp	የውሃ ፓምፕ
well	yeu wu·ha gud·gwad	የውሃ ጉድጓድ

IN THE COUNTRY

HIKING
የእግር ጉዞ

From rich green valleys and rivers to spectacular mountain ranges, Ethiopia offers great hiking opportunities. Ask authorities if you'll need a trekking permit, and check the area is safe. Walking long distances is normal for country people – the word for 'trekking' is simply yeu·gər gu·zo, 'to journey by foot'.

IN THE COUNTRY

Getting Information

መረጃ ማግኘት

Where is the local permit/
government office?
feu·kad yeu·mi·seu·ţō
meus·ri·ya bet yeut nō?

ፈቃድ የሚሰጠው መስሪያ
ቤት የት ነው?

I want to trek (in this area).
(əz·zi a·ka·ba·bi) beu·gər
meu·gwaz ə·feul·lə·gal·lō

(እዚህ አካባቢ) በግር
መንገዝ እፈልጋለሁ

Do I need a permit?
yeu yi·leuf feu·ķad
yas·feul·lə·gal?

የዶለፍ ፈቃድ
ያስፈልጋል?

Are there bandits/land mines?
shəf·ta/feunj al·leu?

ሽፍታ/ፈንጅ አለ?

I want to go from ... to ...
keu ... weu·deu ... meu·hed
ə·feul·lə·gal·lō

ከ ... ወደ ... መሄድ
እፈልጋለሁ

Are there marked trails?
yeu·gər meun·geud al·leu?

የግር ጉዞ መንገድ አለ?

Do you know this area well?
yi·hen bo·ta beu·deunb
yō·ķu·tal?

ይሄን ቦታ በደንብ
ያወቁታል?

How long will it take?
sənt gi·ze yi·weus·dal?

ስንት ጊዜ ይወስዳል?

Is there anything interesting to
see on the way?
meun·geud lai yeu·mi·tai
neu·geur al·leu?

መንገድ ላይ የሚታይ
ነገር አለ?

Is access difficult?
leu·ma·leuf as·cheu·ga·ri nō?

ለማለፍ አስቸጋሪ ነው?

How high is the climb?
weu·deu lai leu mō·ţat mən
ya·həl yi·rə·ķal?

ወደ ላይ ለመውጣት ምን
ያህል ይርቃል?

Which is the shortest route?
yeu·tə·nyow meun·geud
ya·ķwar·ţal?

የትኛው መንገድ
ያቁርጣል?

Which is the easiest route?
yeu·tə·nyow meun·geud
yi·keu·lal?

የትኛው መንገድ ይቀላል?

Where can we buy supplies?
yeu gu·zo sənk yeut
meug·zat yi·cha·lal?

የጉዞ ስንቅ የት
መግዛት ይቻላል?

Is there a (rest house) on the route?
meun·geud lai (ma·reu·fi·ya
bet) al·leu?

መንገድ ላይ
(ማረፊያ ቤት) አለ?

Guides, Porters & Hiring Animals

አስጎብኚዎች፣ ሠራተኞችና
ለኪራይ የሚሆኑ እንስሳት

We are thinking of going to ...
weu·deu ... meu·hed a·sə·beu·nal

ወደ ... መሄድ አስበናል

How many hours will we
travel per day?
beu keun leu sənt seu'at
ə·nə·gwa·zal·leun

በቀን ለስንት ሰዓት
እንጓዛለን?

Can you recommend a ...	yeu·mə·tow·kut ... al·leu?	የምታወቁት ... አለ?
guide	as·gob·nyi	አስጎብኚ
interpreter	as·teur·gwa·mi	አስተርጓሚ
porter	teu·sheu·ka·mi	ተሸካሚ
worker	seu·ra·teu·nya	ሰራተኛ

Where can I hire a ...?	... yeut meu·keu·ra·yeut ə·cha·lal·lō?	... የት መከራየት እችላለሁ?
donkey	a·hə·ya	አህያ
horse	feu·reus	ፈረስ
mule	beuk·lo	በቅሎ

How much is it for ...?	leu ... sənt nō?	ለ ... ስንት ነው?
(two) days	(hu·leutt) keun	(ሁለት) ቀን
a single journey	and gu·zo	አንድ ጉዞ

IN THE COUNTRY

I'll pay ...
    ə·keuf·lal·lō   ... እከፍላለሁ

Let's go on foot.
    beu·gər ən·hid   በግር እንሂድ

Go faster! (to mule)
    meuch!   መች!

Go faster! (to horse)
    cha!   ቻ!

On the Path   መንገድ ላይ

Local people are more likely to use terms like 'at daybreak'
(goh si·keud) and 'before sunset' (ṣeu·hai sat·geu·ba) instead
of specific times.

Let's go!
    ən·hid!   እንሂድ!

How far away is the (next town)?
    (yeu·mi·keu·ṭəl·lō keu·teu·ma)   (የሚቀጥለው ከተማ)
    mən ya·həl yi·rə·ḳal?   ምን ያህል ይርቃል?

Can I walk there?
    beu·gər yas·ke·dal?   በግር ያስኬዳል?

Would we reach it ... ?   ... ən·deur·sal·leun?   ... እንደርሳለን?
    before midday   keu ə·ku·leu   ከእኩለ
                     keun beu·fit   ቀን በፊት
    before nightfall   sai·cheu·ləm   ሳይጨልም

Is this the way to ...?
    ... beuz·zi beu·kul nō?   ... በዚህ በኩል ነው-?

Where are you going?
    yeut tə·he·dal·leuh? (m)   የት ትሄዳለህ?
    yeut tə·he·jal·leush? (f)   የት ትሄጃለሽ?

I'm going to ...
    weu·deu ... ə·he·dal·lō   ወደ ... እሄዳለሁ

What is this/that?
    yi·he/ya mən·dən nō?   ይህ/ያ ምንድ ነው-?

Look at this/that.
    yi·hen/yan teu·meul·keut (m)   ይህን/ያን ተመልከት
    yi·hen/yan teu·meul·keuch (f)   ይህን/ያን ተመልከች

What a beautiful place!
beu·țam deus yeu·mil bo·ța!
በጣም ደስ የሚል ቦታ!

What's the name of this place?
yi·he bo·ța mən yi·ba·lal?
ይህ ቦታ ምን ይባላል?

Where are we (on this map)?
(kar·tow lai)
yeut nō ya·leu·nō?
(ካርታው ላይ)
የት ነው ያለነው?

We are here (on this map).
(kar·tow lai) əz·zi lai neun
(ካርታው ላይ) እዚህ ላይ ነን

Can I pass this way?
beuz·zi beu·kul ma·leuf
yi·cha·lal?
በዚህ በኩል ማለፍ
ይቻላል?

I'd like to ...	... ə·feul·lə·gal·lō	... እፈልጋለሁ
go to the toilet	weu·deu shənt	ወደ ሽንት ቤት
	bet meu·hed	መሄድ
have a rest	ma·reuf	ማረፍ
have some tea/water	shai/wu·ha	ሻይ/ውሃ

I don't feel comfortable here.
yi·he bo·ța deus a·la·leu·nyəm
ይህ ቦታ ደስ አላለኝም

Is there another place?
le·la bo·ța yi·no·ral?
ሌላ ቦታ ይኖራል?

Is this water safe for drinking?
wu·how leu meu·țeuț yi·ho·nal?
ውሃው ለመጠጥ ይሆናል?

(Please) Slow down.
(ə·ba·kəh) ķeuss beul (m)
(እባክህ) ቀስ በል
(ə·ba·kəsh) ķeuss bay (f)
(እባክሽ) ቀስ በይ

I'm lost.
meun·geud țeuf·to·bə·nyal
መንገድ ጠፍቶብኛል

Where can we spend the night?
ma·ta yeut ə·nar·fal·leun?
ማታ የት እናርፋለን?

I'll stay overnight in ...
... ad·ral·lō
... አድራለሁ

See also Directions on page 53.

IN THE COUNTRY

altitude	keu·fə·ta	ከፍታ
Amhara duffle bag	jo·nə·ya	ጁንያ
backpack	shan·ta	ሻንጣ
bottle (skin)	ko·da	ኮዳ
binoculars	bai·no·ku·lar	ባይኖኩለር
boots	bot cham·ma	ቦት ጫማ
candle	sha·ma	ሻማ
canoe	tan·kwa	ታንኳ
canteen (traditional)	a·geul·gəl	አገልግል
to climb	mō·tat	መውጣት
compass	kom·pass	ኮምፓስ
downhill	kul·ku·leut	ቁልቁለት
drinking bottle	teur·mus	ጠርሙስ
first-aid kit	yeu meu·jeu·meu·ri·ya ər·da·ta sa·tən	የመጀመሪያ እርዳታ ሳጥን
hammer	meu·do·sha	መዶሻ
hat	bar·ne·ta	ባርኔጣ
hike	yeu·gər gu·zo	የግር ጉዞ
horse ride	feu·reus gəl·bi·ya	ፈረስ ግልቢያ
knife	seun·ti	ስንጢ
to load/harness	meu·chan	መጫን
map	kar·ta	ካርታ
mountain climbing	teu·ra·ra mō·tat	ተራራ መውጣት
pick	do·ma	ዶማ
rest house	ma·reu·fi·ya bet	ማረፊያ ቤት
rock climbing	kwa·təny mō·tat	ቋጥኝ መውጣት
rope	geu·meud	ገመድ
saddle	ko·rə·cha	ኮርቻ
steep	keut ya·leu	ቀጥ ያለ
stick	du·la	ዱላ
to unload/ unharness	ma·ra·geuf	ማራገፍ
uphill	a·keu·beut	አቀበት
waterproof clothes	yeu zə·nab ləbs	የዝናብ ልብስ
water purifier	yeu wu·ha ma·ta·ri·ya	የውሃ ማጣሪያ

SEASONS   ወቅቶች

Seasons in Ethiopia are divided into dry season and wet season.
There are also other seasonal changes referred to, particularly in
rural areas.

dry season (October to May)	beu·ga	በጋ
wet season (June to September)	kə·reumt	ክረምት
little wet season	beulg	በልግ
harvest time	yeu meu·hər weuķt	የመኸር ወቅት
spring	şeu·day	ፀደይ

WEATHER   የአየር ሁኔታ

Be prepared for some dramatic weather changes during the wet
season, and carry warm, waterproof gear with you.

What's the temperature?
ai·yeur hu·ne·ta sənt nō?   ያየር ሁኔታ ስንት ነው?

What will the weather be like
(today/tomorrow)?
yeu (za·re/neu·geu) ai·yeur   የ (ዛሬ/ነገ) ያየር ሁኔታ
hu·ne·ta mən yi·ho·nal?   ምን ይሆናል?

It'll be ...	... yi·ho·nal	... ይሆናል
Will it be ...?	... yi·ho·nal?	... ይሆናል?
cloudy	deu·meu·na·ma	ደመናማ
cold	bərd	ብርድ
fine	tə·ru	ጥሩ
hot	moķ ya·leu	ሞቅ ያለ
humid	yi·weu·bəķ	ይወብቅ
rainy	zə·na·ba·ma	ዝናባማ
stormy	neu·god·gwa·da·ma	ነጎድጓዳማ
sunny	şeu·hai·ya·ma	ፀሃያማ
windy	neu·fa·sha·ma	ነፋሻማ

IN THE COUNTRY

IN THE COUNTRY

bright	bə·ruh	ብሩህ
dark	cheul·leu·ma	ጨለማ
drought	dərk	ድርቅ
dry	deu·reuk	ደረቅ
dust	a·bwa·ra	አቧራ
flood (large)	yeu wu·ha mu·lat	የውሃ ሙላት
flood (small)	gorf	ጎርፍ
fog	gumm	ጉም
hail	beu·reu·do	በረዶ
haze	chi·gag	ጭጋግ
heat wave	ha·rur	ሃሩር
lightning	meub·reuk	መብረቅ
rain	zə·nab	ዝናብ
rainbow	keus·teu deu·meu·na	ቀስተ ደመና
shade	tə·la	ጥላ
shelter	meu·teu·leu·ya	መጠለያ
sky	seu·mai	ሰማይ
snow	beu·reu·do	በረዶ
storm (rain)	keu·bad (zə·nab)	ከባድ (ዝናብ)
sun	şeu·hai	ፀሃይ
thunder	neu·god·gwad	ነጎድጓድ
weather	ai·yeur hu·ne·ta	ያየር ሁኔታ
wind	neu·fass	ነፋስ

GEOGRAPHICAL TERMS   የጂኦግራፊ ቃሎች

bridge	dəl·dəy	ድልድይ
bush	kut·kwa·to	ቁጥቋጦ
burrow	gud·gwad	ጉድጓድ
cave	wa·sha	ዋሻ
clearing	geu·la·ta bo·ta	ግላጣ ቦታ
cliff	geu·deul	ገደል
countryside	a·geur bet	አገር ቤት
creek	jə·reut	ጅረት
dam	gəd·dəb	ግድብ
desert	beu·reu·ha	በረሃ
ditch	gud·ba	ጉድባ
dust	tə·bi·ya	ትቢያ

Earth (the)	meu·ret	መሬት
forest	cha·ka	ጫካ
gorge	geu·deul	ገደል
grass	sar	ሳር
green	a·reun·gwa·de	አረንጓዴ
highlands	keu·fə·teu·nya bo·ta	ከፍተኛ ቦታ
hill	ko·reub·ta	ኮረብታ
horizon	ad·mass	አድማስ
hot springs	fəl wu·ha	ፍል ውሃ
island	deu·set	ደሴት
lake	haik	ሐይቅ
lowlands	zə·kə·teu·nya bo·ta	ዝቅተኛ ቦታ
mountain(s)	teu·ra·ra/teu·ra·roch	ተራራ/ተራሮች
mountain peak	yeu teu·ra·ra chaff	የተራራ ጫፍ
mud	chi·ka	ጭቃ
national park	bə·he·ra·wi park	ብሔራዊ ፓርክ
pebbles	teu·teur	ጠጠር
plain	leut ya·leu meu·ret	ለጥ ያለ መሬት
plateau	am·ba	አምባ
pond	ku·re	ኩሬ
region	kəl·ləl	ክልል
river	weunz	ወንዝ
rock	kwa·təny	ቋጥኝ
sand	a·sheu·wa	አሸዋ
stone	dən·gai	ድንጋይ
swamp/marsh	reug reug	ረግ ረግ
track/footpath	yeu·gər meun·geud	የግር መንገድ
valley	sheu·leu·ko	ሸለቆ
water	wu·ha	ውሃ
waterfall	fwa·fwa·te	ፏፏቴ

IN THE COUNTRY

ZONED OUT!

cool zone	deu·ga	ደጋ
hot zone	kol·la	ቆላ
temperate zone	way·na deu·ga	ወይና ደጋ

THE ENVIRONMENT

Does (this area) have a problem with ...?	(əz·zi a·ka·ba·bi) yeu ... chig·gər al·leu?	(እዚህ አካባቢ) የ ... ችግር አለ?
air pollution	ai·yeur meu·beu·keul	ያየር መበከል
deforestation	deun meu·meun·ţeur	ደን መመንጠር
drought	dərķ	ድርቅ
famine	reu·hab	ረሃብ
fertilisers	ma·da·beu·ri·ya	ማዳበሪያ
irrigation	meus·no	መስኖ
pesticides	yeu teu·bai meu·keu·la·keu·ya meud·ha·nit	የተባይ መከላከያ መድሃኒት
soil erosion	a·feur meu·sheur·sheur	አፈር መሸርሸር

See also Expressing Opinions, page 115.

IN THE COUNTRY

FAUNA   እንስሳት

What wildlife is there in this area?
əz·zi a·ka·ba·bi mən ai·neut yeu dur a·ra·wi·toch al·lu? — እዚህ አካባቢ ምን አይነት የዱር አራዊቶች አሉ?

What (animal) is that?
ya (ən·sə·sa) mən·dən nō? — ያ (እንስሳ) ምንድን ነው?

Is it native?
i·tə·yo·pi·ya bə·cha ye·mi·geuny nō? — ኢትዮጵያ ብቻ የሚገኝ ነው?

Are there any protected species?
yeu·mi·ţeu·beu·ķu ən·sə·soch al·lu? — የሚጠበቁ እንስሶች አሉ?

It's a mammal/reptile.
aţ·bi/teu·sa·bi nō — አጥቢ/ተሳቢ ነው

Domestic የቤት እንስሳት

With more livestock than virtually any other African country,
you'll see farm animals everywhere – on city streets, in back yards
and, of course, out in the field. A rooster is more likely to step
out of someone's front door than a dog!

camel	gə·meul	ግመል
cat	də·meut	ድመት
chicken	do·ro	ዶሮ
cow	lam	ላም
dog	wu·sha	ውሻ
donkey	a·hə·ya	አህያ
goat	fə·yeul	ፍየል
ox	beu·re	በሬ
rooster	ow·ra do·ro	አውራ ዶሮ
sheep	beug	በግ

Wildlife የዱር አራዊት

ape	ṭo·ṭa	ጦጣ
bat	yeu le·lit weuf	የሌሊት ወፍ
buffalo	gosh	ጎሽ
bush duiker	mi·da·kwa	ሚዳቋ
bushbuck	də·kwa·la	ድቋላ
chameleon	ə·səst	እስስት
Colobus monkey	gu·re·za	ጉሬዛ
crocodile	a·zo	አዞ
elephant	zə·hon	ዝሆን
Ethiopian	wa·li·ya ai·beks	ዋሊያ አይቤክስ
mountain goat		
fish	a·sa	አሳ
gazelle	a·ga·zeun	ኣጋዘን
Gelada baboon	chi·la·da	ጭላዳ
giraffe	keu·chə·ne	ቀጭኔ
hippopotamus	gum·mar·re	ጉማሬ
hyena	jib	ጅብ

jackal	ķeu·beu·ro	ቀበሮ
klipspringer	sass	ሳስ
leopard	neu·bər	ነብር
lion	an·beus·sa	አንበሳ
lizard	ən·shi·la·lit	እንሽላሊት
monkey	zən·jeu·ro	ዝንጀሮ
mouse	aiyṭ	አይጥ
panther	gə·sə·la	ግስላ
porcupine	jart	ጃርት
rabbit	ṭən·cheul	ጥንቸል
rhinoceros	ow·ra·ris	አውራሪስ
squirrel	shə·ko·ko	ሽኮኮ
snake	ə·bab	እባብ
large snake	zeun·do	ዘንዶ
toad	gurṭ	ጉርጥ
tortoise	e·li	ኤሊ
wildlife	yeu dur a·ra·wit	የዱር አራዊት
zebra	yeu me·da a·hə·ya	የሜዳ አህያ

Birds ወፎች

I'm looking for a ...
... ə·yeu·feul·leu·ku nō   ... እየፈለኩ ነው።
What do you call that bird?
ya·nən weuf mən   ያንን ወፍ ምን
tə·lu·tal·la·chu?   ትሉታላችሁ?

bird/birds	ər·gəb/ər·gə·boch	እርግብ/እርግቦች
bird of prey	a·mo·ra	አሞራ
crow/raven	ķu·ra	ቁራ
duck	da·kə·ye	ዳክዬ
eagle	nə·sər	ንስር
fowl	jəg·ra	ጅግራ
owl	gug·gut	ጉጉት
vulture (bearded)	chu·leu·le	ጩሌሌ
woodpecker	gən·deu ķor·ķur	ግንደ ቆርቆር

Insects

ተባይ

Is it poisonous?

meur·zeu·nya nō?   መርዘኛ ነው-?

ant	gun·dan	ጉንዳን
bedbug	tə·hwan	ትኋን
bee/bee hive	nəb; yeu nəb ķeu·fo	ንብ/የንብ ቀፎ
beetle	təl	ትል
butterfly	bi·ra·bi·ro	ቢራቢሮ
caterpillar	a·ba cheu·gwa·re	አባ ጨጓሬ
cockroach	beu·reur·ro	በረሮ
flea	ķu·nə·cha	ቁንጫ
fly	zəmb	ዝምብ
grasshopper	am·beu·ṭa	አምበጣ
insect	teu·bai	ተባይ
lice	ķə·mal	ቅማል
maggot	yeu sə·ga təl	የስጋ ትል
mosquito	bim·bi	ቢምቢ
scorpion	ginṭ	ጊንጥ
spider	sheu·reu·rit	ሸረሪት
wasp	teurb	ተርብ

FLORA & CROPS

ዕፅዋትና ሰብል

Ethiopia has a stunning range of native flora. Imports include the ubiquitous ba·hər zaf (eucalyptus tree, literally 'from over the sea'), imported by Emperor Menelik from Australia in the late 19th century. See Food, page 139, and On the Farm, page 162, for related words.

What (tree) is that?

ya mən ai·neut (zaf) nō?   ያ ምን አይነት (ዛፍ) ነው-?

What's it used for?

leu·mən
tə·ṭeu·ķeu·mu·beu·tal·la·chu?   ለምን ትጠቀሙብታላችሁ?

acacia tree	gə·rar	ግራር
bamboo	sheum·beu·ķo	ሽምበቆ
banana tree	yeu muz teu·kəl	የሙዝ ተክል
barley	geubs	ገብስ
branch	ķə·rən·chaf	ቅርንጫፍ
cactus	ķul·ķwal	ቀልቋል
cedar tree	zəg·ba	ዝግባ
chat (mira)	chat	ጫት
coffee plant	yeu bun·na teu·kəl	የቡና ተክል
corn plant	yeu beu·ķo·lo teu·kəl	የበቆሎ ተክል
cotton	ţəţ	ጥጥ
daisy	yeu meus·ķeul a·beu·ba	የመስቀል አበባ
eucalyptus tree	bahər zaf	ባህር ዛፍ
false banana tree	ko·ba	ኮባ
flower	a·beu·ba	አበባ
forest	cha·ka/deun	ጫካ/ደን
grass	sar	ሳር
juniper/cedar tree	ţəd	ጥድ
leaf	ķə·ţeul	ቅጠል
log	gənd	ግንድ
millet	ţef	ጤፍ
mushroom	ən·gu·dai	እንጉዳይ
palm tree	zeu·mə·ba·ba	ዘምባባ
to pick (coffee/fruit)	meul·ķeum	መልቀም
root	sər	ስር
seed	fə·re	ፍሬ
sorghum	ma·shə·la	ማሽላ
stalk	a·geu·da	አገዳ
tef	ţef	ጤፍ
thorn	ə·shoh	እሾህ
tree/trees	zaf/za·foch	ዛፍ/ዛፎች
wheat	sən·de	ስንዴ
wood	ən·cheut	እንጨት

IN THE COUNTRY

STAR GAZING

Where's a good place to see
the stars?
   ko·ko·bo·chən leu ma·yeut   ኮከቦችን ለማየት
   tə·ru bo·ta yeut no?   ጥሩ ቦታ የት ነው-?
Will it be cloudy tonight?
   za·re ma·ta deu·meu·na·ma   ዛሬ ማታ ደመናማ
   yi·ho·nal?   ይሆናል?
Look! A meteor!
   teu·meul·keut/teu·meul·keuch!   ተመልከት/ተመልከች!
   beu·ra·ri ko·keub! (m/f)   በራሪ ኮከብ!

(full) moon	(mu·lu) cheu·reu·ḳa	(ሙ-ሉ-) ጨረቃ
stars	ko·ko·boch	ኮከቦች
universe	a·leu·mat	አለማት

Toss around a kwass, 'ball', dabble in some da·ma, 'checkers', or take a tan·kwa, 'canoe', down the weunz, 'river'. With some of the world's top distance athletes, a great outdoors and a population keen on sports, Ethiopia's a great place for cheu·wa·ta, 'games'.

TYPES OF SPORT   የስፖርት አይነቶች

What sport do you play?
mən ai·neut sport	ምን አይነት ስፖርት
tə·cha·weu·tal·leuh/	ትጫወታለህ/
tə·cha·weu·chal·leush? (m/f)	ትጫወቻለሽ?

I play ...	... ə·cha·weu·tal·lō	... እጫወታለሁ
basketball	kər·chat kwass	ቅርጫት ኳስ
handball	əj kwass	እጅ ኳስ
hockey	geun·na	ገና
soccer (football)	ə·gər kwass	እግር ኳስ
table tennis	țe·bəl te·nis	ቴብል ቴኒስ
volleyball	meu·reub kwass	መረብ ኳስ

I like ...	... ə·weud·dal·lō	... እወዳለሁ
athletics	at·le·tiks	አትሌቲክስ
boxing	boks/bu·ți	ቦክስ/ቡጢ
cycling	bəs·klet meu·ga·leub	ብስክሌት መጋለብ
distance running	reu·jim ru·cha	ረጅም ሩጫ
	meu·roț	መሮጥ
weightlifting	kəb·deut man·sat	ክብደት ማንሳት
gymnastics	jəm·na·stik	ጂምናስቲክ
	meus·rat	መስራት
running	ru·cha	ሩጫ
swimming	wa·na	ዋና

TALKING ABOUT SPORT   ስለ ስፖርት ማውራት

People love chatting about Ethiopian distance-running champions
and major sporting events like the soccer finals.

Do you like to watch sport?
sport ma·yeut tə·weud·dal·leuh/	ስፖርት ማየት
tə·weu·jal·leush? (m/f)	ትወዳለህ/ትወጃለሽ?

Yes, very much.
ow beu·tam ə·weud·dal·lō	አዎ በጣም እወዳለሁ

No, not at all.
aiy al·weud·dəm	አይ አልወድም

What sports do you follow?
yeu·tə·nyow·ən sport	የትኛውን ስፖርት
tə·keu·ta·teu·lal·leuh/	ትከታተላለህ/
tə·keu·ta·teu·yal·leush? (m/f)	ትከታተያለሽ?

I follow ...
... ə·keu·ta·teu·lal·lō	... እከታተላለሁ

What team do you support?
yeu·tə·nya·wən bu·dən	የትኛውን ቡድን
tə·deu·gə·fal·leuh/	ትደግፋለህ/
tə·deu·gə·fi·yal·leush? (m/f)	ትደግፋያለሽ?

I support ...
... ə·deu·gə·fal·lō	... እደግፋለሁ

SOCCER   እግር ኳስ

English terms are often used for words like 'goal' and 'offside'.

Do you follow soccer?
ə·gər kwass	እግር ኳስ
tə·keu·ta·teu·lal·leuh/	ትከታተላለህ/
tə·keu·ta·teu·yal·leush? (m/f)	ትከታተያለሽ?

Who's the best team?
keu·hul·lu yeu·mi·beul·ţow	ከሁሉ የሚበልጠው
bu·dən man nō?	ቡድን ማን ነው?

My favourite player is ...
yeu·mə·weud·dō	የምወደው
teu·cha·wach ... nō	ተጫዋች ... ነው

ACTIVITIES

free kick	ri·go·ri	ሪጎሪ
match	gəṭ·mi·ya	ግጥሚያ
penalty	kə·ṭat	ቅጣት
player	teu·cha·wach	ተጫዋች
team	bu·dən	ቡድን

GOING TO A MATCH

ጨዋታ ለማየት መሄድ

Where can I see a (soccer) match?
yeu (ə·gər kwass) cheu·wa·ta
yeut yi·ta·yal?
የ (እግር ኳስ) ጨዋታ የት
ይታያል?

What time does it start?
beu sənt seu'at yi·jeu·mə·ral?
በስንት ሰዓት ይጀምራል?

Which team is winning/losing?
yeu·tə·nyow bu·dən
ə·ya·sheu·neu·feu/
ə·yeu·teu·sheu·neu·feu nō?
የትኛው ቡድን እያሸነፈ
እየተሸነፈ ነው?

What's the score?
sənt leu sənt na·chō?
ስንት ለስንት ናቸው?

That was a great game!
kon·jo cheu·wa·ta neub·beur!
ቆንጆ ጨዋታ ነበር!

ACTIVITIES

seat (place)	bo·ta	ቦታ
stadium	sta·di·yeum	ስታዲያም
ticket	ti·ket	ትኬት
ticket office	ti·ket meu·sheu·cha	ትኬት መሸጫ

JOINING IN   አብሮ መጫወት

In Ethiopia, all that's required for a great soccer game is space for playing, a ball (bound rags do the job) and a few willing players.

Can you play (soccer)?
  (ə·gər kwass) meu·cha·wot   (እግር ኳስ)መጫወት
  tə·cha·lal·leuh/   ትችላለህ/ትችያለሽ?
  tə·cha·yal·leush? (m/f)

I don't know how to play.
  meu·cha·wot al·chal·leum   መጫወት አልችልም

Shall we have a game of (basketball)?
  (kər·chat kwass) ə·nə·cha·weut?   (ቅርጫት ኳስ) እንጫወት?

Is there a ball?
  kwass al·leu?   ኳስ አለ?

Can I join in?
  keun·nan·teu gar meu·cha·wot   ከናንተ ጋር መጫወት
  ə·cha·lal·lō?   እችላለሁ?

Over here!
  weu·deu·zi!   ወደዚህ!

That was a great game!
  kon·jo cheu·wa·ta!   ቆንጆ ጨዋታ!

ball	kwass	ኳስ
boundary	meus·meur	መስመር
goal	gol	ጎል
goal post	yeu gol mə·seu·so	የጎል ምሶሶ
foul	fowl/tə·fat	ፋወል/ጥፋት
kick-off	cheu·wa·ta	ጨዋታ
	yeu·mi·jeu·meu·rə·beut	የሚጀመርበት
net	meu·reub	መረብ
referee	da·nya	ዳኛ

ACTIVITIES

KEEPING FIT
ስፖርት መስራት

Where's the nearest ...?	yeu·mi·keur·bō ... yeut nō?	የሚቀርበው ... የት ነው?
recreation centre	meuz·na·nya bo·ta	መዝናኛ ቦታ
swimming pool	meu·wa·nya bo·ta	መዋኛ ቦታ
tennis court	yeu me·da te·nis me·da	የሜዳ ቴኒስ ሜዳ

What's the charge per ...?	leu ... sant nō?	ለ ... ስንት ነው?
day	keun	ቀን
game	cheu·wa·ta	ጨዋታ
hour	seu'at	ስዓት

Can I hire ...?	... meu·keu·ra·yeut ə·cha·lal·lō?	... መከራየት እችላለሁ?
a bicycle	bəs·klet	ብስክሌት
a racquet	ra·ket	ራኬት
(two) racquet(s)	(hu·leutt) ra·ket	(ሁለት) ራኬትና
and a ball	ə·na kwass	ኳስ

Where's the best place to jog/
run around here?
əz·zi a·ka·ba·bi leu ru·cha
yeu·mi·hon tə·ru bo·ta yeut nō?

እዚህ አካባቢ ለሩጫ
የሚሆን ጥሩ ቦታ የት ነው?

Where are the changing rooms?
ləbs meu·keu·yeu·ri·yow
kə·fəl yeut nō?

ልብስ መቀየሪያው
ክፍል የት ነው?

Would you like to play tennis?
te·nis meu·cha·wot
tə·feul·lə·gal·leuh/
tə·feul·lə·gi·yal·leush? (m/f)

ቴኒስ መጫወት ትፈልጋለህ/
ትፈልጊያለሽ?

MUSIC MOVES

to clap	ma·cheub·cheub	ማጨብጨብ
to jump	meuz·leul	መዝለል
movement	shəb·sheu·ba	ሽብሸባ
shoulder dance	əs·kəs·ta	እስክስታ
ululation	ə·ləl·ta	እልልታ

bicycle	bəs·klet	ብስክሌት
jogging	ru·cha	ሩጫ
massage	meu·ta·sheut	መታሻት
racquet	ra·ket	ራኬት
shower	sha·weur	ሻወር
table tennis bat	yeu ṭeu·reu·pe·za	የጠረጴዛ
	te·nis ra·ket	ቴኒስ ራኬት
tournament	wə·də·dər	ውድድር
towel	fo·ṭa	ፎጣ
warm-up	sō·neu·tən	ሰውነትን ማማሟቅ
	ma·ma·mwaḳ	
weights	kəb·deut	ክብደት

OUTDOOR SPORTS   የውጭ ስፖርቶች

Activities like rafting and rock climbing are usually run by English-speaking guides for Western tourists. Ethiopians may call you deuf·far, 'adventurous'.

I love ...	... ə·weud·dal·lō	... እወዳለሁ
bird watching	yeu weuf	የወፍ
	ai·neu·to·chən	አይነቶችን ማየት
	ma·yeut	
canoeing/	beu jeul·ba	በጀልባ
rafting	ə·yeu·ḳeu·zeu·fu	እየቀዘፉ መንዞ
	meu·gwaz	
fishing	a·sa maṭ·meud	አሳ ማጥመድ
mountain/rock	teu·ra·ra/ḳwa·ṭəny	ተራራ/ቋጥኝ
climbing	mō·ṭat	መውጣት

Am I allowed to (fish) here?		
əz·zi (a·sa maṭ·meud)	እዚህ (አሳ ማጥመድ)	
yi·cha·lal?	ይቻላል?	
Is there a place I can rent (a canoe)?		
(tan·kwa) yeu·mi·ya·keu·rai	(ታንኳ) የሚያከራይ	
sō al·leu?	ሰው አለ?	

Can we stop here?

əz·zi ma·ķom ən·chə·lal·leun? እዚህ ማቆም እንችላለን?

That was great!

beu·ţam ķon·jo neub·beur! በጣም ቆንጆ ነበር!

I want to go again!

ən·deu·geu·na meu·hed እንደገና መሄድ
ə·feul·lə·gal·lō! እፈልጋለሁ!

bank/shore	yeu weunz dar	የወንዝ ዳር
big wave	ma'ə·beul	ማዕበል
boat	jeul·ba	ጀልባ
canoe	tan·kwa	ታንኳ
cliff	geu·deul	ገደል
creek	jə·reut	ጅረት
crocodile	a·zo	አዞ
deep	ţəlķ	ጥልቅ
downward slope	ķul·ķu·leut	ቁልቁለት
fish	a·sa	አሳ
fish hook	meun·ţeu·ko	መንጠቆ
fisherman	a·sa aţ·maj	አሳ አጥማጅ
fishing net	a·sa maţ·meu·ja	አሳ ማጥመጃ
	meu·reub	መረብ
motor	mo·teur	ሞተር
river	weunz	ወንዝ
rock	a·leut	አለት
rope	geu·meud	ገመድ
to row	meuķ·zeuf	መቅዘፍ
shallow (water)	ţəlķ yal·ho·neu	ጥልቅ ያልሆነ
	(wu·ha)	(ው·ሃ)
strong current	geus·gash wu·ha	ጐጋሽ ው·ሃ
upward slope	da·geut	ዳገት
waterfall	fwa·fwa·te	ፏፏቴ
waterproof	wu·ha yeu·mai·zeul·ķo	ው·ሃ የማይዘልቀው

ACTIVITIES

TRADITIONAL SPORTS   ባህላዊ ስፖርቶች

Almost every region of Ethiopia has a danger sport. Some famous
ones include:

geun·na   ገና

a type of hockey played in some regions at Christmas. Brandish-
ing sticks curved at the ends, two teams compete to whack an
i·rur (wooden ball) over their opponent's boundary line.

gugs   ጉግስ

a type of mock warfare on horseback played in some regions
at ṭəm·ḳeut, or the Epiphany. Riders in stunning traditional
costumes pursue each other with wooden sticks/clubs and round
hide shields.

don·ga   ዶንጋ

Surma/Mursi stick fighting

CYCLING   ብስክሌት መጋለብ

Cycle races are sometimes held in Ethiopian towns. For general
terminology on cycling, see page 64 in Getting Around.

Where does the race pass through?
  wə·də·də·ru beu·yeut   ወድድሩ በየት
  beu·kul yal·fal?   በኩል ያልፋል?
Who's winning?
  man ə·yeu·meu·ra nō?   ማን እየመራ ነው?
How many kilometres is
today's race?
  yeu za·re wə·də·dər sənt   የዛሬ ው·ድድር
  ki·lo me·tər nō?   ስንት ኪሎ ሜትር ነው?

Where does it finish?

meu·cheu·reu·show yeut nō? መጨረሻው የት ነው?

My favourite cyclist is ...

yeu·mə·weud·dō የምወደው

sai·kə·leu·nya ... nō ሳይክለኛ ... ነው

cycling	bəs·klet meu·ga·leub	ብስክሌት መጋለብ
cyclist	sai·kə·leu·nya	ሳይክለኛ
leg (of race)	zu·ri·ya	ዙሪያ
winner	a·sheu·na·fi	አሸናፊ

GAMES   ጨዋታዎች

Billiards and dominoes are popular games at coffee houses. Around
Ethiopia's streets, you might see people playing geu·beu·ṭa, a
traditional African game using a board and tiny balls.

Do you play ...?	... tə·cha·weu·tal·leuh/	ት-ጫወታለህ/
	tə·cha·weu·chal·leush? (m/f)	ት-ጫወቻለሽ?
billiards	bil·yard	ቢልያርድ
bingo	bin·go	ቢንጎ
cards	kar·ta	ካርታ
chess	chez	ቼዝ
checkers	da·ma	ዳማ

Shall we play ...?

... ə·nə·cha·weut? ... እንጫወት?

How do you play (checkers)?

(dama) ən·det nō (ዳማ) እንዴት ነው

yeum·tə·cha·weu·tut? የምትጫወቱት?

What are the rules?

hə·gu mən·dən nō? ሕጉ ምንድን ነው?

Whose turn is it?

yeu·man teu·ra nō? የማን ተራ ነው?

It's my turn.

yeu·ne teu·ra nō? የኔ ተራ ነው?

ACTIVITIES

I'm winning.	ə·ya·sheu·neuf·ku nō	እያሸነፍኩነው
I'm losing.	ə·yeu·teu·sheu·neuf·ku nō	እየተሸነፍኩ ነው
Well done!	gob·bez!	ጎበዝ!
No cheating!	ma·ta·leul ai·chal·ləm!	ማታለል አይቻልም!

Cards

ካርታ

Words like 'bridge' and 'poker' are similar to English.

Do you want to play cards?
kar·ta meu·cha·wot
tə·feul·lə·gal·leuh/
tə·feul·lə·gi·yal·leush? (m/f)

ካርታ መጫወት
ትፈልጋለህ/
ትፈልጊያለሽ?

I don't know how to play.
meu·cha·wot al·chəl·ləm

መጫወት አልችልም

I'll teach you.
a·sa·yi·hal·lō/a·sa·yi·shal·lō (m/f)

አሳይሃለሁ/አሳይሻለሁ

It's your turn to pick up a card.
kar·ta man·sat yan·teu/
yan·chi teu·ra nō (m/f)

ካርታ ማንሳት ያንተ/
ያንች ተራ ነው

የኔ ተራ ነው

ማታለል አይቻርም!

Chess

ቼዝ

Shall we play chess?
chez ə·nə·cha·weut?

ቼዝ እንጫወት?

White starts.
neuch yi·jeu·mə·ral

ነጭ ይጀምራል

It's my move.
yeu·ne teu·ra nō

የኔ ተራ ነው

bishop	pa·pas	ጳጳስ
black/white pieces	tə·ḳur/neuch	ጥቁር/ነጭ
	weu·ta·deur	ወታደር
castle/rook	ka·səl	ካስል
chessboard	seun·ṭeu·reuzh	ሰንጠረዥ
chess tournament	yeu chez wə·də·dər	የቼዝ ውድድር
king	nə·gus	ንጉስ
knight	feu·reus	ፈረስ
pawn(s)	mi·da·ḳwa	ሚዳቋ
queen	nə·gəst	ንግስት

WHAT ARE YOUR LEGS?

(Deratu Tulu) is amazing!	(deu·rar·tu tu·lu) beu·ṭam as·deu·na·ḳi neuch!	(ደራርቱ ቱሉ) በጣም አስደናቂ ነች!
Ethiopians are great ... runners!	i·tə·yo·pi·ya·noch beu ... ta·wa·ḳi rwa·choch na·chō!	ኢትዮጵያኖች በ ... ታዋቂ ሯጮች ናቸው·!
marathon	ma·ra·ton	ማራቶን
long distance	reu·jim rə·ḳeut	ረጂም ርቀት
altitude	keu·fə·ta	ከፍታ
bare feet	ba·do ə·ger	ባዶ እግር
endurance	tə·gəst	ትግስት
(gold) medal	(weurk) meu·da·li·ya	(ወርቅ) መዳሊያ
Olympic Games	yeu o·lom·pik cheu·wa·ta	የኦሎምፒክ ጨዋታ
hard training	keu·bad lə·mə·med	ከባድ ልምምድ
(Boston) marathon	yeu (bos·teun) ma·ra·ton	የ (ቦስተን) ማራቶን
5000 metres	a·məst shi me·tər	አምስት ሺ ሜትር
10,000 metres	a·sər shi me·tər	አስር ሺ ሜትር

ACTIVITIES

TV & VIDEO   ቴሌና ቪዲዮ

Most words related to TV and video, an·te·na for example, sound
like their English equivalents.

Where can we hire videos?
  yeu vi·di·yo kas·set yeut   የቪዲዮ ካሴት የት
  meu·keu·ra·yeut ən·chə·lal·leun?   መከራየት እንችላለን?
How long can I borrow this for?
  leu sənt gi·ze meu·keu·ra·yeut   ለስንት ጊዜ መከራየት
  ə·chə·lal·lō?   እችላለሁ?
Do you mind if I switch the
TV on/off?
  ti·vi·wən lək·feu·tō/   ቴሌውን ልክፈተው/
  laṭ·fow?   ላጥፈው?
Do you mind if I turn the
volume up/down?
  dəm·ṣun keu·fə/zəḳ lar·gō?   ድምፁን ከፍ/ዝቅ ላርገው?
Can I change the channel?
  chan·na·lun meu·ḳeu·yeur   ቻናሉን መቀየር
  ə·chə·lal·lō?   እችላለሁ?
The TV isn't working.
  ti·vi·yu ai·seu·ram   ቴሌው አይሰራም

I want to watch ...	... ma·yeut ə·feul·lə·gal·lō	... ማየት እፈልጋለሁ
a film	film	ፊልም
the news	ze·na	ዜና
a soap opera	teu·keu·ta·tai film	ተከታታይ ፊልም
sport	sport	ስፖርት

Make as·ə·leut, 'vow', at an island monastery. Smell the a·beu·ba, 'flowers', over Meskel. Whatever your religion, you'll find Ethiopia's traditions and festivals a fascinating blend.

RELIGION   ሃይማኖት

Religion plays a major role in Ethiopian social and cultural life, which includes Christian, Muslim, Jewish and pagan traditions.

Talking about Religion   ስለ ሃይማኖት ማውራት

It's considered normal to inquire about someone's religion, but strange for people to have no religion.

What's your religion?

hai·ma·no·təh mən·dən nō? (m)	ሃይማኖትህ ምንድን ነው?
hai·ma·no·təsh mən·dən nō? (f)	ሃይማኖትሽ ምንድን ነው?
hai·ma·no·to mən·dən nō? (pol)	ሃይማኖትዎ ምንድን ነው?

Catholic	ka·to·lik	ካቶሊክ
Christian	krəs·ti·yan	ክርስቲያን
Hindu	hin·du	ሂንዱ
Jewish	ai·hu·da·wi	አይሁዳዊ
Muslim	əs·lam	እስላም
Orthodox	or·to·doks	ኦርቶዶክስ
Protestant	pro·tes·tant	ፕሮቴስታንት

To avoid confusion with Amharic words with similar sounds, but different, offensive meanings, Buddhists are advised to use the term yeu əs·ya hai·ma·not, 'Eastern religion'. Shinto followers are advised to use the term yeu ja·pan hai·ma·not, 'Japanese religion'.

I'm not a strict follower.
    aṭ·ba·ḳi ai·deul·leu·hum   አጥባቂ አይደለሁ-ም
I believe in God/Allah.
    beu əg·zya·ber/al·lah   በእግዚ ሃብሔር/አላህ
    am·nal·lō   አምናለሁ-
I believe in destiny/fate.
    beu ə·dəl/a·ga·ṭa·mi am·nal·lō   በ እድል/በ እ ጋጣሚ አምናለሁ-
I'm interested in astrology/
philosophy.
    (ko·keub ḳo·ṭeu·ran;   (ኮኮብ ቆጠራ-ን/ፍልስፍና-ን)
    fəl·sə·fə·nan) leu ma·weuḳ   ለማወቅ ፍላጎት አለኝ
    fə·la·got al·leuny

At the Church &   ቤተ ክርስቲያን ና ደብር
Monastery

Dating back to the 4th century AD, the Ethiopian Orthodox
religion has influenced everything from Ethiopian eating habits
to everyday greetings. Many devoted followers visit churches
several times a week, bowing, touching the walls and ground, and
giving alms to the needy outside. The main church services are on
Sunday mornings from 6 am.

If you're visiting a church, try to do as the locals do – if shoes
are left outside, do the same. Women usually cover their heads in
neu·ṭeu·la, 'shawls'. Ask permission before entering monasteries.

Am I allowed to enter?
    meug·bat yi·cha·lal?   መግባት ይቻላል?
Can I pray here?
    əz·zi meu·ṣeu·lai yi·cha·lal?   እዚህ መፀለይ ይቻላል?
When does the next service begin?
    yeu·mi·ḳeu·ṭəl·lō ḳə·da·se   የሚ ቀጥለው- ቅዳሴ
    meu·che yi·jeu·mə·ral?   መቼ ይጀምራ-ል?
This is my contribution to
(the monastery).
    yi·he leu (deub·ru) ər·da·ta nō ይህ ለ (ደብሩ-) እርዳታ ነው-

angel	meul'ak	መልአክ
Bible	meu·ṣə·haf kə·dus	መጽሐፍ ቅዱስ
chanting/songs	ze·ma	ዜማ
church	be·teu krəs·ti·yan	ቤተ ክርስቲያን
church leader	a·bun	አቡን
clergy	deub·teu·ra	ደብተራ
cross	meus·keul	መስቀል
God	əg·zer	እግዜር
mass/service	kə·da·se	ቅዳሴ
monastery	deu·bər	ደብር
monastery head	ab·bat	አበት
monk	meu·neu·ku·se	መነኩሴ
nun	meu·neu·ku·se	መነኩሴ
prayer	ṣeu·lot	ጸሎት
prayer sticks	meu·kwa·mi·ya	መቋሚያ
priest	kess	ቄስ
sistrum	ṣeu·na·ṣəl	ጸናጽል
(jangling rattles)		
turban	təm·təm	ጥምጥም
Ark of the Covenant	ta·bot	ታቦት
(including replicas)		

At the Mosque   መስጊድ

Islam has a strong following in eastern and southern Ethiopia. It is said that during the time of the Prophet Mohammed, an Ethiopian named Bilal was the first muz·zin to call the faithful to prayer. Universal Muslim words like i·mam are used in Amharic, as are relevant words in local languages like Harari (Harar is one of the principle holy cities of Islam). Always ask permission before entering mosques.

giving alms	za·kat	ዛካት
Koran	ku·ran	ቄርኣን
mosque	meus·gid	መስጊድ
obligatory prayer	sa·lat	ሳላት
profession of faith	sha·ha·da	ሻሃዳ

At the Synagogue   ም`ኩራ·ብ
People often prefer to use be·teu əs·ra·el instead of feu·la·sha to refer to Ethiopia's unique Jewish community. Special Jewish celebrations include Rosh Hashanah (Jewish New Year).

| holy book | to·rah | ቶራ |
| priest | ka·hən | ካህን |

Pagan Worship   ጣኦት ማምለክ
The celestial deity *Wak* (waḳ) remains popular with groups in the south, especially in relation to farming and weather. Trees, springs, mountains and other objects of nature are considered to hold strong spiritual qualities. Local languages are used.

ancestor	ḳə·də·meu a·yat	ቅድመ አያት
paganism	ṭa'ot mam·leuk	ጣኦት ማምለክ
sacred place	yeu·teu·ḳeu·deu·seu bo·ta	የተቀደስ ቦታ

SUPERSTITIONS   አምልኮ
Superstitions play a powerful role in Ethiopian life, crossing all religious boundaries. People read fortunes in coffee sediment and even animal entrails. It's said that if someone gives you bu·da (the evil eye), you'll suffer grave harm. Health is also believed to be affected by strange forces.

Where can I find protection from bu·da?
  yeu bu·da meud·ha·nit yeut   የቡ·ዳ መድሃኒት የት
  yi·geu·nyal?   ይገኛል?
He/She is possessed by bu·da.
  bu·da beu·low/beu·lat   ቡ·ዳ በላው·/በላት

curse	ər·gə·man	እርግማን
guardian spirit	ad·bar	አድባር
the evil eye	bu·da	ቡ·ዳ
protection from bu·da	yeu bu·da meud·ha·nit	የቡ·ዳ መድሃኒት
spirit (benevolent or evil)	zar	ዛር
type of fortune teller	ko·keub ḳo·ṭa·ri	ኮክብ ቆጣሪ
witch doctor/sorcerer	ṭeun·ḳwai	ጠንቋይ

FESTIVALS &   በዓላትና የእረፍት
HOLIDAYS   ጊዜዎች

Dates listed here are for the Gregorian calendar; they may vary.

What time does the parade/
celebration start?
    seul·fu/beu'a·lu beu sənt seu'at   ሰልፉ/በዓሉ በስንት ሰዓት
    yi·jeu·mə·ral?   ይጀምራል?
What's the purpose of this occasion?
    yi·he a·meut be'al leu mən·dən   ይህ ዓመት በዓል
    nō yeu·mi·keu·beu·rō?   ለምንድነው· የሚከበረው·?
Can I watch?
    ma·yeut yi·cha·lal?   ማየት ይቻላል?

bell	deu·weul	ደወል
ceremony	sə·neu sə·reu'at	ሥነ ሥርዓት
drum	keu·beu·ro	ከበሮ
fasting	şom	ፆም
festival/holiday	a·meut be'al	ዓመት በዓል
festival banquet	də·gəs	ድግስ
incense granules	ə·tan	ዕጣን
incense stick	neud	ነድ
Muslim pilgrimage	ha·ji	ሃጅ
parade	seu·ləf	ሰልፍ
(to go on a) pilgrimage	meu·sa·leum	መሳለም
tent (large)	dass	ዳስ

Secular Holidays   በሕዝብ የሚከበሩ ቀኖች

yeu seu·ra·teu·nyoch ķeun   የሠራተኞች ቀን
    1 May – International Labour Day

yeu ad·wa dəl meu·ta·seu·bi·ya   የአድዋ ድል መታሰቢያ
    2 March – Victory of Adwa. Celebrating Menelik II's famous
    defeat of Italian colonial forces at the Battle of Adwa in 1896,
    thus maintaining Ethiopia's independence from European rule.

yeu ar·beu·nyoch meu·ta·seu·bi·ya   የአርበኞች መታሰቢያ
    April or May – Patriots' Victory Day (Liberation Day). Ethio-
    pia's ar·beu·nya (patriots) are honoured in the anniversary of
    Italy's defeat in WWII.

RELIGION & HOLIDAYS

Christian Festivals & Holy Days

የክርስቲያን በዓላትና የተቀደሱ ቀኖች

Bright processions, traditional costumes, and colourful dances are the hallmark of most Ethiopian Orthodox festivals, which include:

geun·na/lə·det   ገና/ልደት

6 or 7 January – Ethiopian Christmas. People attend all-night church services from Christmas eve onwards. Some communities play geun·na, a traditional sport (see page 186). This is a smaller celebration than fa·si·ka (Easter).

ṭəm·ķeut   ጥምቀት

19 January – Feast of Epiphany, celebrating Christ's Baptism. Three days of bright and colourful celebrations, including a procession where church *tabots* (see page 197) are taken to a body of water. Priests bless the water and pass the blessing to onlookers by sprinkling holy water on them. Dancing and singing follows. The final day is the feast of St Michael the Archangel.

fa·si·ka   ፋሲካ

April or May – Ethiopian Orthodox Easter Sunday. Family members gather to feast and celebrate, following overnight mass. Spicy meat dishes are eaten with gusto, ending the long Lent fast. See Food, page 144 for fasting terms.

eun·ķu·ṭa·ṭash   እንቁጣጣሽ

11 September – Ethiopian New Year and feast of St John the Baptist. Families and friends gather together for a springtime celebration of renewed life and the beginning of a new year on the Ethiopian calendar.

meus·ķeul   መስቀል

27 or 28 September – Celebrates the finding of Christ's cross by Empress Helena in the 4th century AD. People stack poles topped with yeu meus·ķeul a·beu·ba (daisies) to form a pyramid around a cross known as deu·meu·ra. This is later fanned by chi·bo (torches of eucalyptus twigs). Dancing and feasting follow.

Although not public holidays, the following are popular with children and young adults: bu·he (12 July in the north-east, 21 August elsewhere), where children carry bread and torches in memory of young shepherds following Christ and the disciples up Mount Tabor. On fɔl·seu·ta (24 August) young girls celebrate the Ascension of Mary.

Happy ...!	
ən·kwan leu ...	እንኳን ለ ... አደረሰህ!
a·deu·reu·seuh! (m)	
ən·kwan leu ...	እንኳን ለ ... አደረሰሽ!
a·deu·reu·seush! (f)	
ən·kwan leu ...	እንኳን ለ ... አደረሰዎት!
a·deu·reu·sot! (pol)	
Merry Christmas!	
ən·kwan leu geun·na	እንኳን ለገና አደረስዎት!
a·deu·reu·sot!	

Saints' Days   የቅዱሳን ቀኖች

Saints remain popular throughout Ethiopia. Each church holds an annual ceremony for their specific saint, with feasting and celebrations in the local community. Families celebrate particular saints' days by inviting priests and visitors and giving alms. Though not national holidays, the following are popular occasions:

a·bu·neu man·feus kə·dus   አቡነ መንፈስ ቅዱስ
    mid-March – Pilgrims climb a rocky, extinct volcano on Mount Zuqualla in Ethiopia's south to celebrate Abune Manfes Kedus, an Ethiopian saint

ma·ri·yam ṣi·yon   ማርያም ፅዮን
    late November – Festival in Aksum at St Mariam of Zion church, in which the church's *tabot*, believed to be the original Ark of the Covenant, is carried out

ḳul·lə·bi   ቁልቢ
    late December – Feast of St Gabriel, the saint who protects homes. The feast includes a pilgrimage to the church in Kullibi in Eastern Ethiopia.

RELIGION & HOLIDAYS

Several days of the month are named after saints and holy figures.
Farmers often use these instead of numeric dates.

lə·deu·ta	1st (Birth of Mary)	ልደታ
ba·ta	3rd (St Mary)	ባታ
ab·bo	5th (St Gebre Manfes Kedus)	አቦ
sə·las·se	7th (Trinity)	ስላሴ
mi·ka·el	12th (St Michael)	ሚካኤል
ki·da·neu mə·reut	16th (Covenant of Mercy)	ኪዳነ ምሕረት
gab·re'el	19th (St Gabriel)	ገብርኤል
ma·ri·yam	21st (St Mary)	ማርያም
gi·yor·gis	23rd (St George)	ጊዮርጊስ
teuk·leu hai·ma·not	24th (legendary Ethiopian saint)	ተክለ ሃይማኖት
meud·ha·ne a·leum	27th (Saviour of the World)	መድኃኔ አለም
beu'al weuld	29th (Festival of the Son)	በአለ ወልድ

Muslim Festivals & Holy Days

የእስላም ዓመት በዓልና
የተቀደሱ ቀኖች

Universal Muslim festivals and occasions are respected and
celebrated by Ethiopian Muslims. Don't forget that dates vary
from year to year.

Idd Al Fiṭr   ኢድ አልፈጥር
  November or December – End of month-long Ramadan
  fasting. Great feasting and celebrations, particularly in Harar and
  other Muslim centres; it usually lasts three days. Another
  important date during Ramadan is Lailat al Qadr, in which
  Muslims pray for Allah to grant them a good destiny.

Mau·lid   መውሊድ
  (May or April) Birth of the Prophet Mohammed

Idd Al Adha   ኢድ አል አድሃ
  (February or January) The culmination of the Hajj, the holy
  pilgrimage to Mecca (one of the five pillars of Islam)

WEDDINGS   ሠርግ

You can use the general term 'Congratulations' at weddings, christenings and other social occasions.

> Congratulations!
> ən·kwan deus al·leuh/   እንኳን ደስ አለህ/
> al·leush! (m/f)   አለሽ!

You'll probably come across a few Ethiopian weddings in your travels. In urban areas, many people choose their own partners and have ceremonies similar to Western weddings – with the added spice of joyful singing, dancing and ululations.

engagement	meu·ta·cheut	መታጨት
(to get engaged)		
honeymoon	yeu cha·gu·la gi·ze	የጫጉላ ጊዜ
wedding	seurg	ሠርግ
wedding cake	yeu seurg kek	የሠርግ ኬክ
wedding present	yeu seurg sə·to·ta	የሠርግ ስጦታ

MUSLIM PIGRIMAGE

A famous event on the Ethiopian Muslim calendar is the pilgrimage to the shrine of Sheikh Hussein, a 13th-century mystic prophet. Thousands of pilgrims travel for weeks or months to reach the sacred site near Goba in the south. Celebrations occur twice a year, on the anniversaries of the birth and death of the Prophet Mohammed.

RELIGION & HOLIDAYS

TOASTS & CONDOLENCES

የደስታና የሀዘን መግለጫ

Ethiopians are quick to offer congratulations and encouragement, but birthdays are only celebrated in childhood, and even then, usually only by city children.

Good luck!
  meul·kam ə·dəl!

መልካም ዕድል!

Hope it goes well!
  cheur yig·ṭeu·məh/
  yig·ṭeu·məsh! (m/f)

ቸር ይግጠምህ/
ይግጠምሽ!

Chin up/Be strong!
  ai·zoh/ai·zosh! (m/f)

አይዞህ/አይዞሽ!

Ethiopians go out of their way to express condolences to people suffering from illness or the loss of a loved one. At funerals, you will hear mu·sho (mournful chants) and leuḳ·so (wailing).

May God bring your health back.
  əg·zer yi·ma·rəh/
  yi·ma·rəsh (m/f)

እግዜር ይማርህ/
ይማርሽ

My deepest sympathy.
  neubs yi·mar
  (lit: may the soul be forgiven)

ነብስ ይማር

RELIGION & HOLIDAYS

HEALTH

Most urban medical professionals speak fluent English. In more isolated areas, it's best to carry a first-aid kit.

I'm sick.
  a·mo·nyal   አሞኛል
My (male) friend is sick.
  gwa·deu·nya·yen a·meum·mō   ጓደኛዬን አመመዉ
My (female) friend is sick.
  gwa·deu·nya·yen a·meum·mat   ጓደኛዬን አመማት
He/She needs medical treatment.
  hə·kə·mə·na yas·feul·lə·geu·wal/   ሕክምና ያስፈልገዋል/
  yas·feul·lə·ga·tal   ያስፈ..ጋታል
I need medical treatment.
  hə·kə·mə·na yas·feu·lə·geu·nyal   ሕክምና ያስፈልገኛል
I need a doctor (immediately).
  ha·kim (bas·cheu·kwai)   ሐኪም (ባስቸኳይ)
  ə·feul·lə·gal·lō   እፈል.ጋለሁ
I'm hurt/injured.
  teu·go·də·chal·lō   ተጎድቻለሁ
I've been bitten by a (dog).
  (wu·sha) neu·keu·seuny   (ዉሻ) ነከሰኝ
It's an emergency!
  as·cheu·kwai nō!   አስቸኳይ ነዉ!

Where can I find a (good) ...?	(tə·ru) ... yeut yi·geu·nyal?	(ጥሩ) ... የት ይገኛል?
dentist	yeu tərs ha·kim	የጥርስ ሐኪም
doctor	ha·kim	ሐኪም
hospital	hos·pi·tal	ሆስፒታል
medical centre	yeu hə·kə·mə·na ta·bi·ya	የህክምና ጣቢያ
nurse	neurs	ነርስ
pharmacy	far·ma·si	ፋርማሲ

HEALTH

I need ...	... ə·feul·lə·gal·lō	... እፈልጋለሁ ...
My (male) friend needs ...	gwa·deu·nya·ye ... yas·feul·lə·geu·wal	ጓደኛዬ ... የስፈልገዋል
My (female) friend needs ...	gwa·deu·nya·ye ... yas·feul·lə·ga·tal	ጓደኛዬ ... የስፈልጋታል
an ambulance	am·bu·lans	አምቡላንስ
transport to the hospital	weu·deu hos·pi·tal meu·ki·na	ወደ ሆስፒታል መኪና
an examination/ a check-up	hə·kə·mə·na/ mər·meu·ra	ሕክምና/ ምርመራ
first aid	yeu meu·jeu·meu·ri·ya ər·da·ta	የመጀመሪያ እርዳታ
medicine/ tablets	meud·ha·nit/ kə·nin	መድሃኒት/ ክኒን
urgent treatment	as·cheu·kwai hə·kə·mə·na	አስቸኳይ ሕክምና

AT THE DOCTOR   ሐኪም ቤት

(Please) Help me.
  (ə·ba·kon) yir·duny   (እባክዎን) ይርዱኝ
I have a pain here.
  əz·zi ga ya·meu·nyal   እዚህ ጋ ያመኛል
That hurts!
  ya·mal!   ያማል!
I'm feeling better.
  teu·shə·lo·nyal   ተሻሉኛል
I'm feeling worse.
  bə·so·bə·nyal   ብሶብኛል
I'm on medication for ...
  leu ... meud·ha·nit   ለ ... መድሃኒት
  ə·yeu·weu·seud·ku nō   እየወሰድኩ ነው
Where's the toilet?
  shənt be·tu yeut nō?   ሽንት ቤቱ የት ነው?

HEALTH

THE DOCTOR MAY SAY ...

mən ho·nu?   ምን ሆኑ?
  What's the problem?

yeut lai ya·mə·hal/   የት ላይ ያምሃል/
ya·mə·shal? (m/f)   ያምሻል?
  Where does it hurt?

yeu weur a·beu·ba lai neush?   የወር አበባ ላይ ነሽ?
  Are you menstruating?

tə·ku·sat al·leuh/al·leush?   ትኩሳት አለህ/አለሽ?
  Do you have a temperature?

keu·jeu·meu·reuh/   ከጆ መረህ/ከጆ መረሽ
keu·jeu·meu·reush   ስንት ጊዜ ሆነ?
sənt gi·ze ho·neu? (m/f)
  How long have you been like this?

keuz·zi beu·fit yi·he chig·gər   ከዚህ በፊት ይሄ ችግር
neub·beu·reu·bəh/   ነበረብህ/ነበረብሽ?
neub·beu·reu·bəsh? (m/f)
  Have you had this before?

meud·ha·nit tə·weus·dal·leuh/   መድኃኒት ትወስዳለህ/
tə·weus·jal·leush? (m/f)   ትወስጃለሽ?
  Are you on medication?

ta·cheu·sal·leuh? (m)   ታጨሳለህ?
ta·cheu·shal·leush? (f)   ታጨሻለሽ?
  Do you smoke?

meu·teut tə·teu·tal·leuh/   መጠጥ ትጠጣለህ/
tə·teu·chal·leush? (m/f)   ትጠጫለሽ?
  Do you drink?

drag tə·weus·dal·leuh/   ድራግ ትወስዳለህ/
tə·weus·jal·leush? (m/f)   ትወስጃለሽ?
  Do you take drugs?

yeu·mais·ma·mah/   የማይስማማህ/
yeu·mais·ma·mash   የማይስማማሽ
neu·geur al·leu? (m/f)   ነገር አለ?
  Are you allergic to anything?

ər·guz neush?   እርጉዝ ነሽ?
  Are you pregnant?

AILMENTS

ሕመሞች

I'm ill.
a·mo·nyal አሞኛል

I've been vomiting.
yas·meul·lə·seu·nyal ያስመልሰኛል

I feel tired.
deu·kə·mo·nyal ደክሞኛል

I can't sleep.
ən·kəlf əm·bi al·leuny እንቅልፍ እምቢ አለኝ

I feel ...
dizzy ra·sen a·zo·reuny ራሴን አዞረኝ
shivery yan·keu·teu·kə·teu·nyal ያንቀጠቀጠኛል

Different verbs are used depending on what the ailment is.

I have ... ... al·leu·bəny ... አለብኝ
anaemia deum ma·neus ደም ማነስ
asthma as·ma አስማ
diabetes sə·kwar beu·shə·ta ስኳር በሽታ
high blood deum bə·zat ደም ብዛት
  pressure

I have (a) ... ... yi·zo·nyal ... ይዞኛል
cold gun·fan ጉንፋን
malaria yeu weu·ba beu·shə·ta የወባ በሽታ
dysentery yeu teuk·mat የተቅማጥ በሽታ
  beu·shə·ta
rabies yeu wu·sha beu·shə·ta የውሻ በሽታ
venereal disease yeu a·ba·leu zeur የአባለዘር በሽታ
  beu·shə·ta
skin disease yeu ko·da beu·shə·ta የቆዳ በሽታ

I have a ... ... ya·meu·nyal ... ያመኛል
backache weu·geu·ben ወገቤን
headache ra·sen ራሴን
sore throat gu·ro·ro·yen ጉሮሮዬን
stomachache ho·den ሆዴን
toothache tər·sen ጥርሴን

I have (a/an) ...

bite (insect)	teu·neu·deuf·ku	ተነደፍኩ
breathing problems	meu·teun·feus yas·cheu·gə·reu·nyal	መተንፈስ ያስቸግረኛል
broken (leg)	(əg·re) teu·seub·rwal	(እግሬ) ተሰብሯል
burn (from fire)	ə·sat a·ḳa·ṭeu·leuny	እሳት አቃጠለኝ
constipation	hod dər·ḳeut al·leuny	ሆድ ድርቀት አለኝ
diarrhoea	yas·ḳeu·mə·ṭeu·nyal	ያስቀማጠናል
fever	tə·ku·sat al·leuny	ትኩሳት አለኝ
fleas	ku·nə·cha beu·lany	ቁንጫ በላኝ
food poisoning	yeu mə·gəb meu·beu·keul nō ya·sa·meu·meuny	የምግብ መበከል ነው· ያሰመመኝ
heat exhaustion	bə·zu ṣeu·hai meu·tany	ብዙ ፀሐይ መታኝ
indigestion	ya·ḳə·reu·nyal	ያቅረኛል
itch	ya·sa·kə·keu·nyal	ያሳክከኛል
sunburn	bə·zu ṣeu·hai meu·tany	ብዙ ፀሃይ መታኝ
sunstroke	məch meu·tany	ምች መታኝ
wound	ḳo·sə·yal·lō	ቆስያለሁ·

I've been vaccinated.
teu·keu·tə·bi·yal·lō   ተከትቤአለሁ·

I have my own syringe.
yeu·ra·se sə·rinj al·leuny   የራሴ ስሪንጅ አለኝ

This is my usual medicine.
bə·zu gi·ze yi·he·nən   ብዙ ጊዜ ይሃንን መድሃኒት
meud·ha·nit nō yeu·mə·weus·dō   ነው· የምወስደው·

If you can't find something you need in the following list, try using the English word for it.

HEALTH

accident	a·deu·ga	አደጋ
addiction	sus	ሱስ
bite (dog)	nə·kə·sha	ንክሻ
blood group	yeu deum ai·neut	የደም አይነት
blood pressure	yeu deum gə·fit	የደም ግፊት
blood test	yeu deum mər·meu·ra	የደም ምርመራ
contagious	teu·la·la·fi	ተላላፊ
emergency	as·cheu·kwai	አስቸኳይ
faeces/stools	ai·neu mə·dər	አይነ ምድር
inhaler	ai·yeur weu·deu wəsţ meu·sab	አየር ወደ ውስጥ መሳብ
to have an injection	meur·fe meu·weu·gat	መርፌ መወጋት
malnutrition	yeu mə·gəb ma·neus	የምግብ ማነስ
medicine	meud·ha·nit	መድኃኒት
patient	beu·sha·teu·nya	በሽተኛ
poison	meurz	መርዝ
pus	meu·gəl	መግል
splinter	chi·reut	ጭረት
syringe	sə·rinj	ስሪንጅ
urine	shənt	ሽንት
vitamin	vi·ta·min	ቪታሚን

SOUNDING OFF

Excuse me!	yi·kər·ta!	ይቅርታ!
Bless you!	yi·ma·rəh! (m)	ይማርህ!
(sneezing)	yi·ma·rəsh! (f)	ይማርሽ!
to sneeze	mas·neu·ţeus	ማስነጠስ
cough	sal	ሳል
hiccup	sə·kə·ta	ስቅታ
fart	feuss	ፈስ

PARTS OF THE BODY

የሰውነት ክፍሎች

I have a pain in my ...	... ya·meu·nyal	... ይመኛል
I can't move my ...	... man·keu·sa·keus al·chəl·ləm	... ማንቀሳቀስ አልችልም

HEALTH

ankle	kur·chəm·chə·mit	ቁርጭምጭሚት
appendix	tərf an·jeut	ትርፍ አንጀት
arm	kənd	ክንድ
back	weu·geub	ወገብ
bone	a·tənt	አጥንት
chest	deu·reut	ደረት
ears	jo·ro	ጆሮ
eyes	ain	አይን
face	fit	ፊት
finger	ṭat	ጣት
foot	ə·gər	እግር
hand	əj	እጅ
head	rass	ራስ
heart	ləb	ልብ
kidney	ku·la·lit	ኩላሊት
knee	gul·beut	ጉልበት
leg	ə·gər	እግር
liver	gu·beut	ጉበት
lung	sam·ba	ሳምባ
mouth	aff	አፍ
muscle	ṭun·cha	ጡንቻ
neck	an·geut	አንገት
nose	a·fən·cha	አፍንጫ
shoulder	tə·kə·sha	ትክሻ
skin	ko·da	ቆዳ
spine	yeu jeur·ba a·tənt	የጀርባ አጥንት
stomach	hod	ሆድ
teeth	ṭərs	ጥርስ
throat	gu·ro·ro	ጉሮሮ
tongue	mə·las	ምላስ
tonsils	ən·ṭəl	እንጥል
vein	yeu deum sər	የደም ስር

HEALTH

WOMEN'S HEALTH

የሴቶች ጤና

Could I see a female doctor?
   yeu set dok·teur ma·yeut
   ə·chə·lal·lō?

የሴት ዶክተር
ማየት እችላለሁ-?

I'm pregnant.
   ər·guz neuny

እርጉዝ ነኝ

I think I'm pregnant.
   ya·reu·geuz·ku yə·meu·sə·leu·nyal

ያረገዝኩ ይመስለኛል

I'm on the Pill.
   yeu weu·lid meu·keu·la·keu·ya
   meud·ha·nit ə·yeu·weu·seud·ku nō

የወሊድ መከላከያ
መድሃኒት እየወሰድኩ ነው-

I haven't had my period for ... weeks.
   yeu weur a·beu·ba·ye leu ...
   sam·mənt al·meu·ṭam

የወር አበባዬ ... ሳምንት
አልመጣም

I'd like to use (contraceptive pills).
   (yeu ṣəns meu·keu·la·keu·ya
   meud·ha·nit) mō·seud
   ə·feul·lə·gal·lō

(የፅንስ መከላከያ
መድሃኒት) መውሰድ
እፈልጋለሁ-

I'd like to have a pregnancy test.
   yeu ər·gə·zə·na mər·meu·ra
   ə·feul·lə·gal·lō

የእርግዝና ምርመራ
እፈልጋለሁ-

abortion	ṣən·ṣən mas·weu·reud	ፅንስን ማስወረድ
cystitis	yeu shənt fi·nya beu·shə·ta	የሽንት ፊኛ በሽታ
diaphragm	di·yaf·ram	ዲያፍራም
female circumcision	yeu set gə·rə·zat	የሴት ግርዛት
menstruation	yeu weur a·beu·ba	የወር አበባ
to have a miscarriage	as·weu·reu·dat	አስወረዳት
period pain	beu·weur a·beu·ba gi·ze yeu·mi·seu·ma hə·meum	በወር አበባ ጊዜ የሚሰማ ሕመም
venereal disease	yeu a·ba·leu zeur beu·shə·ta	የአባለ ዘር በሽታ

SPECIAL HEALTH NEEDS

ልዩ የጤና ፍላጎቶች

I have diabetes/epilepsy.

(sə·kwar beu·shə·ta; yeu·mi·țəl
beu·shə·ta) al·leu·bəny

(ስኳር በሽታ/የሚጥል
በሽታ) አለብኝ

I'm anaemic.

deum ma·neus al·leu·bəny

ደም ማነስ አለብኝ

HEALTH

I'm allergic to ...	... ais·ma·ma·nyəm	... አይስማማኝም
My (male) friend	gwa·deu·nya·ye ...	ጓደኛዬ ...
is allergic to ...	ais·ma·ma·wəm	አይስማማው·ም
My (female) friend	gwa·deu·nya·ye ...	ጓደኛዬ ...
is allergic to ...	ais·ma·ma·təm	አይስማማትም
codeine	ko·din	ኮዲን
penicillin	pe·ni·si·lin	ፔኒሲሊን
pollen	bə·nany	ብናኝ
bees	nəb	ንብ

ምን ሆነ?

ቂንጪ በላኝ

I have a skin allergy.

yeu ķo·da meu·ķo al·leu·bəny

የቆዳ መቆ አለብኝ

I have high/low blood pressure.

deum bə·zat/ma·neus
al·leu·bəny

ደም ብዛት/ማነስ አለብኝ

I have a weak heart.

lə·be deu·ka·ma nō

ልቤ ደካማ ነው.

I'm on a special diet.

beu ha·kim yeu·ta·zeu·zeu
mə·gəb ə·weus·dal·lō

በሐኪም የታዘዘ ምግብ
እወስዳለሁ.

HEALTH

AT THE CHEMIST   መድሃኒት ቤት

It's better to use English when referring to medicines, but you can use Amharic for purchasing general pharmaceutical items.

Where's a chemist?
meud·ha·nit bet yeut nō?   መድሃኒት ቤት የት ነው?

I want medicine for ...
leu ... meud·ha·nit ə·feul·lə·gal·lō   ለ ... መድሃኒት እፈልጋለሁ

How many times a day?
beu keun sənt gi·ze?   በቀን ስንት ጊዜ?

Can I drive on this medication?
yi·hen meud·ha·nit   ይሄን መድሃኒት ከወሰድኩ
keu·weu·seud·ku bo·hal·la   በኋላ መንዳት እችላለሁ?
meun·dat ə·chə·lal·lō?

antibiotics	an·ti·bai·yo·tik	አንቲ ባዮቲክ
antiseptic	an·ti·sep·tik	አንቲሴፕቲክ
aspirin	as·prin	አስፐሪን
bandage	fa·sha	ፋሻ
Band-Aid (plaster)	yeu ku·səl plas·teur	የቁስል ፕላስተር
condoms	kon·dom	ኮንዶም
contraceptive	yeu səns	የፆንስ
pill	meu·keu·la·keu·ya	መከላከያ
	meud·ha·nit	መድሃኒት
cough medicine	yeu sal meud·ha·nit	የሳል መድሃኒት
cream (ointment)	krem/ka·bat	ክሬም/ቅባት
gauze	shash	ሻሽ
laxatives	yeu·mi·yas·keu·maṭ	የሚያስቀምጥ
	meud·ha·nit	መድሃኒት
painkillers	hə·meum	ህመም
	yeu·mi·yas·ta·gəs	የሚያስታግስ
	meud·ha·nit	መድሃኒት
sleeping pills	yeu·mi·yas·teu·nya	የሚያስተኛ
	kə·nin	ክኒን

See Toiletries on page 132 for related words.

ALTERNATIVE TREATMENTS

ሴላ የሕክምና አይነቶች

Traditional medicine is popular in Ethiopia. See also Superstition on page 194.

chiropractor	kai·ro·prak·tor	ካይሮፕራክተር
healer	yeu ba·həl	የባህል መድኃኒተኛ
	meud·ha·ni·teu·nya	
herbs	kə·teu·la kə·teul	ቅጠላ ቅጠል
homeopathy	ho·mi·yo·pa·ti	ሆሚዮፓቲ
massage	meu·ta·sheut	መታሸት

HEALTH

AT THE DENTIST

የጥርስ ሐኪም

Where's a dentist?
yeu tərs ha·kim
yeut yi·geu·nyal?

የጥርስ ሐኪም የት ይገኛል?

I have a toothache.
tər·sen ya·meu·nyal

ጥርሴን ያመኛል

I don't want it extracted.
ən·di·neu·keul al·feul·lə·gəm

እንዲነቀል አልፈልግም

I want an anaesthetic.
ma·deun·zeu·zha meur·fe
ə·feul·lə·gal·lō

ማደንዘዣ መርፌ
እፈልጋለሁ

I need a filling.
tər·sen mas·mo·lat
ə·feul·lə·gal·lō

ጥርሴን ማስሞላት
እፈልጋለሁ

My tooth is broken.
tər·se te·seb·rwal

ጥርሴ ተሰብሯል

My gums hurt.
də·den ya·meu·nyal

ድዴን ያመኛል

Ouch!	wəy!	ው·ይ!

HEALTH

AT THE OPTOMETRIST

የዓይን ሐኪም

Where's an optometrist?
yeu ain ha·kim yeut yi·geu·nyal?

የዓይን ሐኪም የት ይገኛል?

I'd like my eyes checked.
ai·nen meu·meur·meur
ə·feul·lə·gal·lō

ዓይኔን መመርመር
እፈልጋለሁ፡፡

I'm long/short sighted.
kərb/ruk ma·yeut
yas·cheu·gə·reu·nyal

ቅርብ/ሩቅ ማየት
ያስቸግረኛል

Could you fix my glasses?
meu·neu·şa·ren sə·ra·liny?

መነፅሬን ስራልኝ?

I need new (glasses/contact lenses).
ad·dis (meu·neu·şər; kon·takt
lens) ə·feul·lə·gal·lō

አዲስ (መነፅር/ኮንታክት
ሌንስ) እፈልጋለሁ፡፡

DISABLED TRAVELLERS

What services do you have for disabled people?
a·ka·la·chō leu teu·go·da sō·woch mən a·geul·glot al·la·chu?

አካላቸው ለተጎዳ ሰዎች ምን አገልግሎት አላችሁ?

Is there wheelchair access?
leu wil·cher meug·bi·ya meun·geud al·leu?

ለዊል ቸር መግቢያ መንገድ አለ?

Speak more loudly, please.
ə·ba·kon chok yi·beu·lu

እባክዎን ጮክ ይበሉ

Are guide dogs permitted?
ai·neu sə·wə·rən yeu·mi·meu·ra wə·sha tə·feuk̄·dal·la·chu?

አይነ ስውርን የሚመራ ውሻ ትፈቅዳላችሁ?

Can you please assist?
ə·ba·ka·chu ər·duny?

እባካችሁ እርዱኝ?

Braille library	yeu bə·ran·na be·teu meu·ṣə·haf	የብራና ቤተ መጽሃፍ
disabled person	a·ka·lu yeu·teu·go·da sō	አካሉ የተጎዳ ሰው·
guide dog	ai·neu sə·wə·rən yeu·mi·meu·ra wə·sha	አይነ ስውርን የሚመራ ውሻ
walking stick	mər·kuz	ምርኩዝ
wheelchair	teush·keur·ka·ri weun·beur; wil·cher	ተሽከርካሪ ወንበር/ ዊል ቸር

TRAVELLING WITH THE FAMILY   ከቤተሰብ ጋር መንዝ

You may like to specify a·lə·cha mə·gəb (food that's not too hot or spicy) for children at restaurants.

Are there facilities for babies?
  leu hə·șan lə·joch mən   ለህፃን ልጆች ምን
  a·geul·glot al·la·chu?   አገልግሎት አላችሁ?
Do you have a child-minding service?
  yeu meu·wa·leu hə·șa·nat   የመዋል ህፃናት አገልግሎት
  a·geul·glot al·la·chu?   አላችሁ?
Where can I find a/an
(English-speaking) babysitter?
  (ən·gli·zə·nya yeu·mət·chəl)   (እንግሊዝኛ የምትችል)
  yeu lə·joch mog·zit yeut   የልጆች ሞግዚት
  a·geu·nyal·lō?   የት አገኛለሁ?
Do you have a cradle/cot?
  yeu hə·șan al·ga al·la·chu?   የሕፃን አልጋ አላችሁ?
Is there a family discount?
  leu be·teu·seub kə·nash al·leu?   ለቤተሰብ ቅናሽ አለ?
Do you charge extra for children?
  leu lə·joch teu·cheu·ma·ri   ለልጆች ተጨማሪ
  kə·fə·ya al·leu?   ክፍያ አለ?
Do you have food for children?
  leu lə·joch mə·gəb al·la·chu?   ለልጆች ምግብ አላችሁ?
Are there any places for
children to play?
  leu lə·joch meu·cha·weu·cha   ለልጆች መጫወቻ
  bo·ta al·leu?   ቦታ አለ?
Is it nearby?
  əz·zi a·ka·ba·bi nō?   እዚህ አካባቢ ነው?

babysitter	mog·zit	ሞግዚት
cradle/cot	yeu hə·șan al·ga	የሕፃን አልጋ
nursery	meu·wa·leu hə·șa·nat	መዋል ህፃናት

LOOKING FOR A JOB   ሥራ መፈለግ

Foreigners on tourist visas are generally not allowed to seek or accept work in Ethiopia. Apply to the appropriate consulates and ministries for work and residence permits.

Do I need a work permit?
    yeu sə·ra feu·kad yas·feul·lə·gal?   የስራ ፈቃድ ያስፈልጋል?
I've had experience.
    yeu sə·ra ləmd al·leuny   የስራ ልምድ አለኝ

casual	gi·ze'a·wi	ጊዜአዊ
employee	seu·ra·teu·nya	ሰራተኛ
employer	keu·ṭa·ri	ቀጣሪ
full time	kwa·mi	ቋሚ
job	sə·ra	ስራ
job advertisement	yeu sə·ra	የስራ
	mas·ta·weu·ki·ya	ማስታወቂያ
traineeship	səl·ṭeu·na	ስልጠና
wage	deu·moz	ደሞዝ
voluntary	feu·ka·deu·nya	ፈቃደኛ

SPECIFIC NEEDS

ON BUSINESS   ንግድና ሥራ

See Social Issues, page 115, and In the Country, page 161, for additional words related to overseas aid and development.

We're attending a ...	yeu ... teu·sa·ta·fi·woch neun	የ ... ተሳታፊዎች ነን
conference	gu·ba'e	ጉባኤ
meeting	səb·seu·ba	ስብሰባ
trade fair	nəgd ba·zar	ንግድ ባዛር

I'm on a course.
  kors lai neuny
  ኮርስ ላይ ነኝ

I have an appointment with ...
  keu ... gar keu·teu·ro al·leuny
  ከ ... ጋር ቀጠሮ አለኝ

Here's my business card.
  kar·den lə·stəh/lə·stəsh (m/f)
  ካርዴን ልስጠህ/ልስጠሽ

I need an interpreter.
  as·teur·gwa·mi ə·feul·lə·gal·lō
  አስተርጓሚ እፈልጋለሁ

I'd like to use a computer.
  kom·pyu·teur meu·teu·keum
  ə·feul·lə·gal·lō
  ኮምፒውተር መጠቀም
  እፈልጋለሁ

I'd like to send a fax/an email.
  faks/i·mel meu·lak
  ə·feul·lə·gal·lō
  ፋክስ/ኢሜል መላክ
  እፈልጋለሁ

  እባክዎን ጮኽ ይበሉ-

  ከ ጓደኛዬ ጋር ቀጠሮ አለኝ

aid organisation	ər·da·ta də·rə·jət	እርዳታ ድርጅት
aid worker	yeu ər·da·ta də·rə·jət seu·ra·teu·nya	የእርዳታ ድርጅት ሠራተኛ
client	deun·beu·nya	ደንበኛ
colleague	yeu sə·ra bal·deu·reu·ba	የስራ ባልደረባ
distributor	a·keu·fa·fai	አከፋፋይ
exhibition	eg·zi·bi·shən	ኤግዚቢሽን
investment	meu·wa·leu nwai	መዋለ ንዋይ
labour	yeu gul·beut wa·ga	የጉልበት ዋጋ
manager	sə·ra as·ki·yaj	ስራ አስኪያጅ
permit	feu·kad	ፈቃድ
profit	tərf	ትርፍ
proposal	ha·sab	ሃሳብ
report	ri·port	ሪፖርት
sample	na·mu·na	ናሙና

FILM, TV & JOURNALISM

ፊልም ቲቪና ጋዜጠኝነት

May we film (here)?
(əz·zi) film man·sat
yi·cha·lal?

(እዚህ) ፊልም ማንሳት
ይቻላል?

We have a permit.
feu·ḳad al·leun

ፈቃድ አለን

We'd like to come (next Wednesday).
(yeu·mi·meu·ṭow rob)
meum·ṭat
ən·feul·lə·gal·leun

(የሚመጣው ሮብ)
መምጣት
እንፈልጋለን

Please speak to our boss.
a·leu·ḳa·chən
ya·neu·ga·gə·ru

አለቃችን ያነጋግሩ

We're filming here.
əz·zi film ə·ya·neu·san nō

እዚህ ፊልም እያነሳን ነው

We're shooting a ...
film
documentary
TV program

... ə·ya·neu·san nō
film
təm·hər·ta·wi film
yeu ti·vi pro·gram

... እያነሳን ነው
ፊልም
ትምህርታዊ ፊልም
የቲቪ ፕሮግራም

I'm writing about ...
sə·leu ... ə·yeu·ṣaf·ku nō

ስለ ... እየፃፍኩ ነው

I would like to speak to
you (tomorrow).
(neu·geu) la·neu·ga·gə·rot
ə·feul·lə·gal·lō

(ነገ) ላነጋግርዎት
እፈልጋለሁ

I'll bring a translator.
as·teur·gwa·mi a·meu·ṭal·lō

አስተርጓሚ አመጣለሁ

SPECIFIC NEEDS

SPECIFIC NEEDS

ADOPTION & TRACING ROOTS

ዘመዶችን መፈለግና ጉድፈቻ

(I think) My ancestors came from this area.

| kəd·meu a·ya·to·che keuz·zi a·ka·ba·bi yeu meu·ţu (yə·meus·leu·nyal) | ቅድመ አያቶቼ ከዚህ አካባቢ የመጡ (ይመስለኛል) |

I'm looking for my relatives.

| zeu·meu·do·chen ə·yeu·feul·leu·ku nō | ዘመዶቼን እየፈለኩ ነው |

Is there anyone here by the name of ...?

| ... yeu·mi·ba·lu sō əz·zi a·ka·ba·bi yi·no·ral·lu? | ... የሚባሉ ሰው እዚህ አካባቢ ይኖራሉ? |

adoption	gud·feu·cha	ጉድፈቻ
adopted children	yeu gud·feu·cha lə·joch	የጉድፈቻ ልጆች
adoption contract	yeu gud·feu·cha wul	የጉድፈቻ ውል
contract	wul	ውል
court	fərd bet	ፍርድ ቤት
date of birth	yeu tu·ləd keun	የትውልድ ቀን
family	be·teu·seub	ቤተሰብ
lawyer	ţeu·beu·ķa	ጠበቃ
orphaned	a·sa·da·gi	አሳዳጊ
	yeu·le·lō ləj	የሌለው ልጅ
representative	teu·weu·kai	ተወካይ
witness	mə·sə·kər	ምስክር

TELLING THE TIME ሰዓቱን ማወቅ

Ethiopia is three hours ahead of GMT/UTC time.

The Ethiopian method of marking time is quite different to the way it's done in most Western countries. The Ethiopian clock starts when the sun comes up, so don't be surprised if you're asked to breakfast at 2 o'clock in the morning! To avoid confusion when checking the time, always ask:

Is that Ethiopian/foreign time?
beu ha·beu·sha/feu·reunj በሀበሻ/በፈረንጅ
a·ko·ta·teur nō? አቆጣጠር ነው?
What time is it?
sənt seu·at nō? ስንት ሰዓት ነው?

It's ...	... nō	... ነው
(one) o'clock	(and) seu·at	(አንድ) ሰዓት
quarter past (one)	(and) seu·at keu·rub	(አንድ) ሰዓት ከሩብ
half past (one)	(and) seu·at teu·kul	(አንድ) ሰዓት ተኩል
(ten) past (one)	(and) seu·at keu (as·sər)	(አንድ) ሰዓት ከ (አስር)
quarter to (one)	leu (and) seu·at rub gu·dai	ለ (አንድ) ሰዓት ሩብ ጉዳይ
(five) minutes to (one)	leu (and) seu·at (a·məst) gu·dai	ለ (አንድ) ሰዓት (አምስት) ጉዳይ

The Amharic equivalent to 'am' and 'pm' is expressed through phrases like 'in the morning', 'in the evening' or 'at night'.

It's (three) o'clock ...	keu ... (sost) seu·at nō	ከ ... (ሶስት) ሰዓት ነው
in the morning	teu·wa·tu	ጠዋቱ
in the evening	mə·sha·tu	ምሽቱ
at night	le·li·tu	ሌሊቱ

When/What time ...?	meu·che/beu sənt seu·at ...?	መቼ/በስንት ሰዓት ...?
does it start	yi·jeu·mə·ral	ይጀምራል
does it finish	yal·kal	ያልቃል
does it open	yi·keu·feu·tal	ይከፈታል
does it close	yiz·zeu·gal	ይዘጋል

DAYS OF THE WEEK   የሳምንቱ ቀኖች
Monday	seu·nyo	ሰኞ
Tuesday	mak·seu·nyo	ማክሰኞ
Wednesday	rob	ሮብ
Thursday	ha·mus	ሃሙስ
Friday	arb	አርብ
Saturday	kə·da·me	ቅዳሜ
Sunday	ə·hud	እሁድ

ETHIOPIAN CALENDAR   የኢትዮጵያ ቀን መቁጠሪያ

The Ethiopian calendar is made up of 12 months of 30 days each and a 13th month of five days (six in a leap year). The Ethiopian New Year commences on 11 September by the Gregorian calendar. Although most calendars and public facilities in Ethiopia carry both Ethiopian and Gregorian dates, it's worth becoming acquainted with Ethiopian dates, as they're still in common use.

Months   ወሮች

The Ethiopian months do not exactly correspond to the Gregorian calendar months. To refer to Western dates, the English word for the particular month will be understood.

September/October	meus·keu·reum	መስከረም
October/November	tə·kəmt	ጥቅምት
November/December	hə·dar	ኅዳር
December/January	ta·hə·sas	ታህሳስ
January/February	tər	ጥር
February/March	yeu·ka·tit	የካቲት
March/April	meu·ga·bit	መጋቢት
April/May	mi·ya·zi·ya	ሚያዚያ
May/June	gən·bot	ግንቦት
June/July	seu·ne	ሰኔ
July/August	ham·le	ሐምሌ
August/September	neu·ha·se	ነሐሴ
September (five or six days)	pa·gu·me	ጳጉሜ

TIME & DATES

DATES
ቀኖች

What day is it (today)?

    (za·re) ķeu·nu mən·dən nō?   (ዛሬ) ቀኑ ምንድን ነው-?

What is the date (today)?

    (za·re) ķeu·nu sənt nō?   (ዛሬ) ቀኑ ስንት ነው-?

It's the 1st/20th of (March).

    (March) and/ha·ya nō   (ማርች) አንድ/ሃያ ነው-

Is that the Ethiopian/Gregorian
calendar date?

    beu ha·beu·sha/feu·reunj   በሃበሻ /በፈረንጅ
    zeu·meun a·ko·ta·teur nō?   ዘመን አቆጣጠር ነው-?

PRESENT
የአሁን ጊዜ

immediately	weu·di·yow·nu	ወዲያውኑ
now	a·hun	አሁን
this afternoon	za·re keu·seu'at	ዛሬ ከሰአት
this evening	za·re mə·shət	ዛሬ ምሽት
this month	beuz·zi weur	በዚህ ወር
this morning	za·re teu·wat	ዛሬ ጠዋት
this week	beuz·zi sam·mənt	በዚህ ሳምንት
this year	beuz·zi a·meut	በዚህ ዓመት
today	za·re	ዛሬ
tonight	za·re ma·ta	ዛሬ ማታ

PAST
ያለፈው ጊዜ

day before yesterday	keu tə·nan·tə·na weu·di·ya	ከትናንትና ወዲያ
(three) days ago	keu (sost) ķeun beu·fit	ከ (ሶስት) ቀን በፊት
last night	tə·nan·tə·na ma·ta	ትናንትና ማታ
last week	ya·leu·fō sam·mənt	ያለፈው ሳምንት
last year	ya·leu·fō a·meut	ያለፈው ዓመት
yesterday	tə·nan·tə·na	ትናንትና
yesterday afternoon	tə·nan·tə·na keu·seu'at	ትናንትና ከሰዓት
yesterday morning	tə·nan·tə·na teu·wat	ትናንትና ጠዋት

FUTURE   የወደፊት

after (three) days	keu (sost) ķeun bo·hal·la	ከ (ሶስት) ቀን ቡኋላ
day after tomorrow	keu neu·geu weu·di·ya	ከነገ ወዲያ
next week	yeu·mi·meu·ţow sam·mənt	የሚመጣው ሳምንት
next month	yeu·mi·meu·ţow weur	የሚመጣው ወር
next year	yeu·mi·meu·ţow a·meut	የሚመጣው ዓመት
tomorrow	neu·geu	ነገ
tomorrow afternoon	neu·geu keu·seu'at	ነገ ከሰዓት
tomorrow morning	neu·geu ţeu·wat	ነገ ጠዋት
tomorrow night	neu·geu ma·ta	ነገ ማታ
within (three) days	beu (sost) ķeun wəsţ	በ (ሶስት) ቀን ውስጥ

DURING THE DAY   በቀን ውስጥ

afternoon	keu·seu'at	ከሰዓት
evening	mə·shət	ምሽት
midnight	ə·ku·leu le·lit	እኩለ ሌሊት
midday/noon	ə·ku·leu ķeun	እኩለ ቀን
morning	ţeu·wat	ጠዋት
night	ma·ta	ማታ
sunrise	yeu şeu·hai mō·ţat	የፀሀይ መውጣት
sunset	yeu şeu·hai meug·bat	የፀሀይ መግባት

TIME & DATES

NUMBERS & AMOUNTS

Arabic numerals are commonly used to write numbers throughout Ethiopia.

CARDINAL NUMBERS

ተራ ቁጥሮች

1	and	አንድ
2	hu·leutt	ሁለት
3	sost	ሶስት
4	a·rat	አራት
5	a·məst	አምስት
6	sə·dəst	ስድስት
7	seu·bat	ሰባት
8	sə·mənt	ስምንት
9	zeu·ṭeuny	ዘጠኝ
10	as·sər	አስር
11	as·sra and	አስራ አንድ
12	as·sra hu·leutt	አስራ ሁለት
13	as·sra sost	አስራ ሶስት
14	as·sra a·rat	አስራ አራት
15	as·sra a·məst	አስራ አምስት
16	as·sra sə·dəst	አስራ ስድስት
17	as·sra seu·bat	አስራ ሰባት
18	as·sra sə·mənt	አስራ ስምንት
19	as·sra zeu·ṭeuny	አስራ ዘጠኝ
20	ha·ya	ሃያ
21	ha·ya and	ሃያ አንድ
22	ha·ya hu·leutt	ሃያ ሁለት
30	seu·las·sa	ሰላሳ
31	seu·las·sa and	ሰላሳ አንድ
40	ar·ba	አርባ
50	ham·sa	አምሳ
60	səl·sa	ስልሳ
70	seu·ba	ሰባ

80	seu·man·ya	ሰማንያ
90	zeu·ṭeu·na	ዘጠና
100	meu·to	መቶ
101	meu·to and	መቶ አንድ
200	hu·leutt meu·to	ሁለት መቶ
300	sost meu·to	ሶስት መቶ
400	a·rat meu·to	አራት መቶ
500	a·məst meu·to	አምስት መቶ
1000	and shi	አንድ ሺ
2000	hu·leutt shi	ሁለት ሺ
100,000	meu·to shi	መቶ ሺ
1,000,000	and mil·li·yon	አንድ ሚሊዮን

I want (three) ...
   (sost) ... ə·feul·lə·gal·lō   (ሶስት) ... እፈልጋለሁ·
(One) tea.
   (and) shai   (አንድ) ሻይ
I only asked for (one).
   (and) bə·cha nō ya·zeuz·kut   (አንድ) ብቻ ነው· የጠዠኩት

ORDINAL NUMBERS   መደበኛ ቁጥሮች

1st	an·deu·nya	አንደኛ
2nd	hu·leu·teu·nya	ሁለተኛ
3rd	sos·teu·nya	ሶስተኛ
4th	a·ra·teu·nya	አራተኛ
5th	a·məs·teu·nya	አምስተኛ
6th	sə·dəs·teu·nya	ስድስተኛ
7th	seu·ba·teu·nya	ሰባተኛ
8th	sə·mən·teu·nya	ስምንተኛ
9th	zeu·ṭeu·neu·nya	ዘጠነኛ
10th	as·sə·reu·nya	አሰረኛ

FRACTIONS

ክፍልፋይ

1/4	and a·ra·teu·nya; rub	አንድ አራተኛ/ሩብ
1/2	gə·mash	ግማሽ
1/3	and sos·teu·nya	አንድ ሶስተኛ
3/4	sost a·ra·teu·nya	ሶስት አራተኛ
1 ½	and mu·lu and hu·leut·teu·nya	አንድ ሙሉ አንድ ሁለተኛ

ETHIOPIC NUMBERS

Ethiopic numbers are not widely used in writing, largely due to the lack of 'zero'.

፩	፪	፫	፬	፭	፮	፯	፰	፱	፲
1	2	3	4	5	6	7	8	9	10

USEFUL WORDS

ጠቃሚ ቃሎች

about	ya·həl	ያህል
amount	meu·teun/bə·zat	መጠን/ብዛት
change	meuls	መልስ
coin	san·tim	ሳንቲም
count	meu·ku·teur	መቁጠር
(a) dozen	deur·zeun	ደርዘን
enough	beu·ki	በቂ
Ethiopian birr	bərr	ብር
a few	tən·nish	ትንሽ
last	meu·cheu·reu·sha	መጨረሻ
less	yan·neu·seu	ያነሰ
a lot/many	bə·zu	ብዙ
more	teu·cheu·ma·ri	ተጨማሪ
once	and gi·ze	አንድ ጊዜ
percent	meu·to·nya	መቶኛ
single	and	አንድ

NUMBERS & AMOUNTS

size	lək	ልክ
some	an·dand	አንዳንድ
too little	beu·tam tən·nish	በጣም ትንሽ
too much	beu·tam bə·zu	በጣም ብዙ
total	ṭeuk̩·lal·la	ጠቅላላ
twice	hu·leutt gi·ze	ሁለት ጊዜ
weight	kəb·deut	ክብደት
the whole amount	beu·mu·lu	በሙሉ

NUMBERS & AMOUNTS

EMERGENCIES

Additional emergency medical phrases can be found in the Health chapter, page 201.

Danger!	a·deu·geu·nya!	አደገኛ!
Fire!	ə·sat!	እሳት!
Help!	ər·duny!	እርዱኝ!
It's an emergency!	as·cheu·kwai nō!	አስቸኳይ ነው!
Stop!	kum!	ቁም!
Thief!	le·ba!	ሌባ!
Catch him!	ya·zō!	ያዘው!
Watch out!	teu·teun·keuk!	ተጠንቀቅ!
Go away!/	teu·meul·leuss!	ተመለስ!
Go back!		

There's (a/an) ...	... al·leu	... አለ
There's been (a/an) ...	... neub·beur	... ነበር
(car) accident	(yeu meu·ki·na)	የ (መኪና)
	a·deu·ga	አደጋ
fighting	wə·gi·ya	ውጊያ
fire	yeu ə·sat ka·teu·lo	የእሳት ቃጠሎ
flood	yeu wu·ha mu·lat	የውሃ ሙላት
robbery	zər·fi·ya	ዝርፊያ
rockfall	na·da	ናዳ

Somebody help me, please.
 ə·ba·ka·chu ər·duny   እባካችሁ እርዱኝ

I'm lost.
 meun·geud teuf·to·bə·nyal   መንገድ ጠፍቶብኛል

Is there a telephone around here?
 əz·zi a·ka·ba·bi səlk al·leu?   እዚህ አካባቢ ስልክ አለ?

I'd like to make a call.
 səlk meu·deu·weul ə·feul·lə·gal·lō   ስልክ መደወል እፈልጋለሁ

It's urgent!
 as·cheu·kwai nō!   አስቸኳይ ነው!

227

EMERGENCIES

POLICE   ፖሊስ

Call the police!
| po·lis ţə·ra! (m) | ፖሊስ ጥራ! |
| po·lis ţə·ri! (f) | ፖሊስ ጥሪ! |

Where's the nearest police station?
| yeu·mi·ķeur·bō po·lis ţa·bi·ya | የሚቀርበው ፖሊስ ጣቢያ |
| yeut nō? | የት ነው-? |

I've been ...
attacked	teu·meu·tow	ተመታሁ
hurt	teu·go·də·chal·lō	ተጎድቻለሁ
raped	teu·deu·feur·ku	ተደፈርኩ
robbed	teu·zeu·reuf·ku	ተዘረፍኩ

ሰላም ደህና ነህ?

ደህና ነኝ

They've stolen my watch/money.
| seu·a·ten/geun·zeu·ben | ሰአቴን/ገንዘቤን |
| seu·reu·ķuny | ሰረቀኝ |

I've lost my bag/passport.
| shan·ţa·ye/pas·por·te | ሻንጣዬ/ፓስፖርቴ |
| ţeuf·to·bə·nyal | ጠፍቶብብኛል |

I don't speak Amharic.
| a·ma·rə·nya al·chəl·ləm | አማርኛ አልችልም |

I don't understand.
| al·geu·ba·nyəm | አልገባኝም |

I'm sorry, I didn't realise I was
doing anything wrong.
| yi·ķər·ta a·la·weu·kum | ይቅርታ አላወኩም |

I'm sorry/I apologise.
| yi·ķər·ta beu·ţam az·nal·lō | ይቅርታ በጣም አዝናለሁ |

I didn't do it.
| ə·ne a·la·deu·reu·kum | እኔ አላደረኩም |

EMERGENCIES

What am I accused of?
   beu mən·dən nō   በምንድነው የተከሰስኩት?
   yeu·teu·keu·seus·kut?

You'll be charged ...   yi·keu·seu·sal·lu   ... ይከሰሳሉ
with ...
You're charged ...   teu·keu·seu·wal   ... ተከሰዋል
with ...

anti-government activity	şeu·reu meun·gəst beu·ho·nu teu·gə·ba·roch	ፀረ መንግስት በሆነ ተግባሮች
assault	keu sō gar beu·meu·ţa·lat	ከሰው ጋር በመጣላት
disturbing the peace	hu·keut beu meuf·ţeur	ሁከት በ መፍጠር
illegal entry	hə·geu weuţ beu·ho·neu meun·geud a·geur wəşţ beu·meug·bat	ሕጋ ወጥ በሆነ መንገድ አገር ውስጥ በመግባት
murder	beu neufs gə·də·ya weun·jeul	በነፍስ ግድያ ወንጀል
not having a visa	ya·leu vi·za beu·meu·zeu·wa·weur	ያለ ቪዛ በመዘዋወር
overstaying your visa	beu vi·za keu·teu·feu·keu·dō gi·ze beu·lai beu·meu·ko·yeut	በቪዛ ከተፈቀደው ጊዜ በላይ በመቆየት
possession (of illegal substances)	beu həg yeu teu·keu·leu·keu·leu ə·şə beu·meu·yaz	በሕግ የተከለከለ እጽ በመያዝ
rape	sō·wən a·sə·geu·də·do beu meud·feur	ሰውን አስገድዶ በመድፈር
robbery/theft	beu zər·fi·ya	በዝርፊያ
traffic violation	yeu tra·fik həg beu·meu·ţas	የትራፊክ ሕግ በመጣስ
working without a permit	ya·leu sə·ra feu·ḳad beu meus·rat	ያለ ስራ ፈቃድ በመስራት

EMERGENCIES

I want to contact my embassy.
em·ba·si·yen ma·neu·ga·geur
ə·feul·lə·gal·lō

ኤምባሲዬን ማነጋገር
እፈልጋለሁ

I know my rights.
meub·ten ow·kal·lō

መብቴን አው.ቃለሁ

Can I make a phone call?
səlk meu·deu·weul ə·chə·lal·lō?

ስልክ መደወል እችላለሁ?

I want a lawyer who speaks English.
ən·gli·zə·nya yeu·mi·chəl
ţeu·beu·ka ə·feul·lə·gal·lō

እንግሊዝኛ የሚችል ጠበቃ
እፈልጋለሁ

to be arrested	meu·ta·seur	መታሰር
cell	ma·reu·fi·ya bet	ማረፊያ ቤት
consulate	kon·sə·la	ቆንስላ
fine (payment)	meu·keu·cha	መቀጫ
guilty	ţə·fa·teu·nya	ጥፋተኛ
lawyer	ţeu·beu·ka	ጠበቃ
not guilty	keu weun·jeul neu·sa	ከወንጅል ነፃ
	meu·hon	መሆን
police officer	yeu po·lis bal·deu·reu·ba	የፖሊስ ባልደረባ
police station	po·lis ţa·bi·ya	ፖሊስ ጣቢያ
prison	ə·sər bet	እስር ቤት
prosecutor	a·ka·be həg	ዐቃቤ ሕግ
trial	fərd	ፍርድ

A

to be able/can	meu·chal	መቻል

Can I take your photo?
fo·to la·neu·sah ə·cha·lal·lõ? (m) — ፎቶ ላነሳህ እችላለሁ-?
fo·to la·neu·sash ə·cha·lal·lõ? (f) — ፎቶ ላነሳሽ እችላለሁ-?
fo·to la·neu·sa·chu ə·cha·lal·lõ? (pl) — ፎቶ ላነሳችሁ- እችላለሁ-?

above ...	keu ... lai	ከ ... ላይ
to accept	meu·keu·beul	መቀበል
accident	a·deu·ga	አደጋ
across ...	keu ... ma·do	ከ ... ማዶ
addiction	sus	ሱስ
address	ad·ra·sha	አድራሻ
to admit	ma·meun	ማመን
adult	awa·ki	አዋቂ
advice	mə·ker	ምክር
aeroplane	ai·ro·plan	አይሮፕላን
to be afraid of	meuf·rat	መፍራት
after	bo·hal·la	በኋላ
in the afternoon	keu·seu'at bo·hal·la	ከስዓት በኋላ
this afternoon	za·re keu·seu'at	ዛሬ ከሰዓት
again	ən·deu·geu·na	እንደገና
age	əd·may	እድሜ
(three days) ago	keu (sost keun) beu·fit	ከ (ሶስት ቀን) በፊት
to agree	meus·ma·mat	መስማማት

I don't agree.
als·ma·mam — አልስማማም

We've agreed!
teus·mam·teu·nal! — ተስማምተናል!

agriculture	gə·brən·na	ግብርና
ahead	weu·deu·fit	ወደፊት
aid (organisation)	(ər·da·ta) də·rə·jet	(እርዳታ) ድርጅት
AIDS	edz	ኤድስ
air	ai·yeur	አየር
air-conditioner	yeu ai·yeur ma·keuz·keu·zha	የአየር ማቀዝቀዣ
airmail	yeu ai·yeur meul'əkt	የአየር መልዕክት
airport	ai·ro·plan ma·reu·fi·ya	አይሮፕላን ማረፊያ
alarm clock	yeu·mi·deu·wəl seu'at	የሚደውል ሰዓት
all	hul·lu	ሁሉ

I'm allergic to ...
... ais·ma·ma·nyem — ... አይስማማኝም

to allow	meuf·keud	መፍቀድ

It's allowed.
teu·feuk·dwal — ተፈቅድዋል

It's not allowed.
al·teu·feu·keu·deum — አልተፈቀደም

alone	bə·cha	ብቻ
already	as·keu·də·mo	አስቀድሞ
also	deg·mo • deu·mo	ደግሞ • ደም
altitude	keu·fə·ta	ከፍታ
always	hul·gi·ze	ሁልጊዜ
amputate	meu·ku·reut	መቁረጥ
ancient	yeu du·ro	የዱሮ
and	ə·na • -na	እና • -ና
angry	yeu·teu·na·deu·deu	የተናደደ
animals	ən·sə·sa	እንስሳ
animals (domestic)	yeu bet ən·sə·sa	የቤት እንስሳ
annual	a·meu·ta·wi	ዓመታዊ
ant	gun·dan	ጉንዳን
antibiotics	an·ti·bai·yo·tik	አንቲባዮቲክ
antiseptic	an·ti·sep·tik	አንቲሴፕቲክ
any	ma·nəm	ማንም
appointment	keu·teu·ro	ቀጠሮ
architecture	yeu hən·ṣa a·seu·rar	የሕንፃ አሰራር
to argue	meu·cheu·ka·cheuḳ	መጨቃጨቅ
arm	kənd	ክንድ
art	ki·neu ṭə·beub	ኪነ ጥበብ
art gallery	yeu ki·neu·zeu·ker	የስዕል መክበር
artist	yeu ki·neu ṭə·beub sö	የኪነ ጥበብ ሰው
to ask	meu·ṭeu·yeuḳ	መጠየቅ
aspirin	as·prin	አስፐሪን
asthma	as·ma	አስማ
aunt	a·kəst	አክስት

B

baby	hə·ṣan	ሕፃን
baby food	yeu hə·ṣan mə·gəb	የሕፃን ምግብ
babysitter	mog·zit	ሞግዚት
back (body)	jeur·ba	ጀርባ
backpack	shan·ṭa	ሻንጣ
bad	meuṭ·fo	መጥፎ
bag	shan·ṭa	ሻንጣ
baggage	gwaz	ጓዝ
balcony	beu·reun·da	በረንዳ
ball	kwass	ኳስ
bandage	fa·sha	ፋሻ
bank	bank	ባንክ
bar	bun·na bet	ቡና ቤት
basket	kər·chat	ቅርጫት
bath	yeu geu·la meu·ta·ṭeu·bi·ya	የነ መታጠቢያ
bathing suit	yeu wa·na ləbs	የዋና ልብስ
battery	bat·ri	ባትሪ
to be	meu·hon	መሆን
beautiful	ḳon·jo	ቆንጆ

because	mək·ni·ya·tum	ምክኒያቱም
bed	al·ga	አልጋ
bedroom	meu·nyi·ta bet	መኝታ ቤት
before (time)	keu ... beu·fit	ከ ... በፊት
beggar	məs·kin • leu·many	ምስኪን • ለማኝ
to begin	meu·jeu·meur	መጀመር
below ...	keu ... beu·tach	ከ ... በታች
beside ...	keu ... gon	ከ ... ጎን
bet	wə·rə·rəd	ወ-ርርድ
better	yeu·teu·shal·leu	የተሻለ
between	beu ... meu·ha·keul	በ ... መሃከል
Bible	meu·sə·haf ḳə·dus	መጽሐፍ ቅዱስ
bicycle	bəs·klet	ብስክሌት
big	təl·ləḳ	ትልቅ
bill	hi·sab	ሂሣብ
biography	yeu hi·wot ta·rik	የሕይወት ታሪክ
bird	weuf	ወፍ
bite (animal)	nə·kə·sha	ንክሻ
to be bitten (insect)	meu·neu·deuf	መነደፍ
blanket	bərd ləbs	ብርድ ልብስ
to bleed	meud·mat	መድማት
to bless	meu·ba·reuk	መባረክ
blood	deum	ደም
blood group	yeu deum ai·neut	የደም አይነት
blue	seu·ma·ya·wi	ሰማያዊ
boat	jeul·ba	ጀልባ
body	sō·neut	ሰውነት

| Bon appetit! | | |
| meul·kam mə·gəb! | | መልካም ምግብ! |

bone	a·ṭənt	አጥንት
book	meu·sə·haf	መጽሐፍ
to book	beu·ḳəd·mi·ya	በቅድሚያ ቦታ
	bo·ta mas·meuz·geub	ማስመዝገብ
bookshop	meu·sə·haf bet	መጽሐፍ ቤት
border	dən·beur	ድንበር
boring	deu·ba·ri	ደባሪ
to borrow	meu·was	መዋስ
both	hu·leut·tu	ሁለቱ
bottle	ṭeur·mus	ጠርሙስ
bottle opener	yeu ṭeur·mus meuk·feu·cha	የጠርሙስ መክፈቻ
box	sa·ṭən	ሣጥን
boy	weund ləj	ወንድ ልጅ
brave	deuf·far • jeug·na	ደፋር • ጀግና
bread	dab·bo	ዳቦ
to break	meus·beur	መስበር
broken	yeu·teu·seu·beu·reu	የተሰበረ
breakfast	ḳurs	ቁርስ
breasts	ṭut	ጡት

to breathe	meu·teun·feus	መተንፈስ
bribe	gub·bo	ጉቦ
bridge	dəl·dəy	ድልድይ
to bring	mam·tat	ማምጣት
brother	weun·dəm	ወንድም
brown	bun·na ai·neut	ቡና አይነት
bruise	seun·beur	ሰንበር
to build	meus·rat	መስራት
building	hən·ṣa	ሕንፃ
bus	ow·to·bəs	አው-ቶብስ
bus station	ow·to·bəs ṭa·bi·ya	አው-ቶብስ ጣቢያ
business	nəgd	ንግድ
business person	neu·ga·de	ነጋዴ
busy	sə·ra yeu·mi·beu·za·beut	ስራ የሚበዛበት
but	gən • neu·geur gən	ግን • ነገር ግን
to buy	meug·zat	መግዛት

I'd like to buy ...
... meug·zat ə·feul·lə·gal·lō   ... መግዛት እፈልጋለሁ-

Where can I buy a ticket?
ti·ket yeut meug·zat ə·chə·lal·lō?   ትኬት የት መግዛት እችላለሁ-?

café	bun·na bet	ቡና ቤት
calendar	keun meu·ku·ṭeu·ri·ya	ቀን መቁጠሪያ
camera	ka·me·ra • fo·to man·sha	ካሜራ • ፎቶ ማንሻ
to camp	dən·kwan meut·keul	ድንኳን መትከል
camp site	dən·kwan meut·keu·ya bo·ta	ድንኳን መትከያ ቦታ
can (to be able)	meu·chal	መቻል

We can.
ən·cha·lal·leun   እንችላለን

I can't.
al·chəl·ləm   አልችልም

can (tin)	ḳor·ḳo·ro	ቆርቆሮ
can opener	yeu ḳor·ḳo·ro meuk·feu·cha	የቆርቆሮ መክፈቻ
to cancel	meu·seu·reuz	መሰረዝ
candle	sha·ma	ሻማ
car	meu·ki·na	መኪና
to carry	meu·sheu·keum	መሸከም
castle	a·bə·ya·teu meun·gəst • gəmb	አብያተ መንግስት • ግምብ
cat	də·meut	ድመት
cave	wa·sha	ዋሻ
centimetre	sen·ti me·tər	ሴንቲ ሜትር
celebration	beu·al	በዓል
chair	weun·beur	ወንበር
chance	a·ga·ṭa·mi	ኢጋጣሚ

change (coins)	zər·zər	ዝርዝር
to change	meu·keu·yeur	መቀየር
changing rooms	ləbs meu·keu·yeu·ri·ya	ልብስ መቀየሪያ
	ke·fə·loch	ክፍሎች
charming	deus yeu·mil	ደስ የሚል
cheap	rə·kash	ርካሽ
cheat	a·tal·lai	አታላይ

Cheat!
weus·lat·ta! — ወስላታ!

to check (examine)	meu·meur·meur	መመርመር
checkpoint	ke·la	ኬላ
chemist	meud·ha·nit bet	መድሃኒት ቤት
chest	deu·reut	ደረት
chicken	do·ro	ዶሮ
child	ləj	ልጅ
children	lə·joch	ልጆች
chocolate	cheu·ko·let	ቸኮሌት
to choose	meu·mə·reuṭ	መምረጥ
church	be·teu kə·rəs·ti·yan	ቤተ ክርስቲያን
cigarettes	si·ga·ra	ሲጋራ
cinema	si·ni·ma bet	ሲኒማ ቤት
circus	seur·keus	ሰርከስ
city	keu·teu·ma	ከተማ
city centre	meu·hal keu·teu·ma	መሃል ከተማ
clean	nə·suh	ንጹህ
to climb	mō·tat	መወጣት
clock	yeu ṭeu·reu·peza seu'at	የጠረጴዛ ሰዓት
to close	meuz·gat	መዝጋት
closed	teu·zeug·twal	ተዘግቷል
clothing	lə·bsoch	ልብሶች
cloud	deu·meu·na	ደመና
cloudy	deu·meu·na·ma	ደመናማ
coat hanger	yeu kot meus·keu·ya	የኮት መስቀያ
coin	san·tim	ሳንቲም
coins	san·ti·moch	ሳንቲሞች
cold (adj)	keuz·kaz·za	ቀዝቃዛ

It's cold.
keuz·kaz·za nō — ቀዝቃዛ ነው

I have a cold.
gun·fan yi·zo·nyal — ጉንፋን ይዞኛል

cold water	keuz·kaz·za wu·ha	ቀዝቃዛ ውሃ
colour	keu·leur • keu·leum	ከለር • ቀለም
to come	meum·ṭat	መምጣት
comedy	yeu·mi·ya·sek	የሚያስቅ
companion	gwa·deu·nya	ጓደኛ
compass	kom·pass	ኮምፓስ

to confirm (a booking)	ma·reu·ga·geuṭ	ማረጋገጥ

Congratulations! ən·kwan deus al·leuh/ al·leush! (m/f)		እንኳን ደስ አለህ/ አለሽ!

constipation	hod dər·ḳeuṭ	ሆድ ድርቀት
consulate	ḳon·sa·la	ቆንስላ
contact lenses	kon·takt lens	ኮንታክት ሌንስ
contraception	yeu ṣəns meu·keu·la·keu·ya meud·ha·nit	የጽንስ መከላከያ መድሃኒት
contract	wul	ውል
convent	yeu se·toch geu·dam	የሴቶች ገዳም
to cook	mə·gəb meus·rat	ምግብ መስራት
cool (colloquial)	a·rif	አሪፍ
corner	ma'ə·zeun	ማእዘን
corruption	mu·sə·na	ሙስና
cotton	ṭəṭ	ጥጥ
country	a·geur	አገር
countryside	geu·teur	ገጠር
cough	sal	ሳል
to count	meu·ḳu·teur	መቁጠር
crafts	ṭə·beub	ጥበብ
credit card	kre·dit kard	ክሬዲት ካርድ

Can I pay by credit card? beu kre·dit kard meuk·feul yi·cha·lal?		በክሬዲት ካርድ መከፈል ይቻላል?

cup (drink)	ku·ba·ya	ኩባያ
cupboard	kum sa·ṭən	ቁም ሳጥን
current affairs	yeu seu·mo·nu weu·re	የሰሞኑ ወሬ
customs	gəm·ruk	ግምሩክ
to cut	meu·ḳu·reuṭ	መቁረጥ
cycling	bəsk·let meu·ga·leub	ብስክሌት መጋለብ
cyclist	sai·kə·leu·nya	ሳይክለኛ

D

dad	a·ba·ye	አባዬ
daily	beu·yeu·ḳeu·nu	በየቀኑ
dairy products	weu·teut neuk yeu mə·gəb wə·ṭe·toch	ወተት ነክ የምግብ ውጤቶች
to dance	meu·da·neus • meu·cheuf·feur	መደነስ • መጨፈር
dangerous	a·deu·geu·nya	አደገኛ
date (appointment)	ḳeu·ṭeu·ro	ቀጠሮ
date (time)	ḳeun	ቀን
to date (someone)	meuḳ·ṭeur	መቅጠር
date of birth	yeu tu·ləd ḳeun	የትውልድ ቀን
daughter	set ləj	ሴት ልጅ

dawn	nə·gat	ንጋት
day	ķeun	ቀን
dead	mut	ሙት
deaf	deun·ķo·ro	ደንቆሮ
death	mot	ሞት
to decide	meu·weu·seun	መወሰን
deep	təlķ	ጥልቅ
deforestation	yeu deun meu·meun·ţeur	የደን መመንጠር

It's delayed
zeu·ġəy·twal   ዘግይቷል

dentist	yeu ţərs ha·kim	የጥርስ ሃኪም
to deny	meu·kad	መካድ
to depart (leave)	leu meu·hed meu·neu·sat	ለመሄድ መነሳት
desert	beu·reu·ha	በረሃ
destination	meu·dreu·sha	መድረሻ
detail	zər·zər	ዝርዝር
diabetic	sə·ķwar beu·sha·ta ya·leu·beut	ስኳር በሽታ ያለበት
diarrhoea	ķə·zeun	ትዝን
dictionary	meuz·geu·beu ķa·lat	መዝገበ ቃላት
to die	meu·mot	መሞት
different	le·la	ሌላ
difficult	as·cheu·ga·ri	አስቸጋሪ
dinner	ə·rat	እራት
dirty	ķo·sha·sha	ቆሻሻ
disabled	a·ka·leu sən·kul	አካለ ስንኩል
discount	ķə·nash	ቅናሽ
to discover	mag·nyeut • meuf·ţeur	ማግኘት • መፍጠር
disease	beu·sha·ta	በሽታ
distributor (person)	a·keu·fa·fai	አከፋፋይ
to do	mad·reug	ማድረግ

What are you doing?
mən ta·deur·gal·leuh? (m)   ምን ታደርጋለህ?
mən ta·deur·gi·yal·leush? (f)   ምን ታደርጊያለሽ?

I didn't do it.
ə·ne a·la·deu·reu·kum   እኔ አላደረኩም

doctor	ha·kim	ሐኪም
dog	wu·sha	ውሻ
doll	a·shan·gu·lit	አሻንጉሊት
door	beur	በር
double	hu·leutt	ሁለት
double bed	and al·ga leu hu·leutt sõ	አንድ አልጋ ለሁለት ሰው
to dream	həlm mal·leum	ሕልም ማለም
dress	ķeu·miss	ቀሚስ
drink	meu·ţeuţ	መጠጥ
to drink	meu·ţeu·ţat	መጠጣት

to drive	meun·dat	መንዳት
drivers licence	meun·ja feu·kad	መንጃ ፈቃድ
drug (medicine)	meud·ha·nit	መድሃኒት
drum	keu·beu·ro	ከበሮ
to be drunk	meus·keur	መስከር
to dry (clothes)	meud·reuk	መድረቅ

E

each	ə·yan·dan·du	እያንዳንዱ
ear(s)	jo·ro	ጆሮ
early	keu·deum bə·lo	ቀደም ብሎ
early (morning)	ma·leu·da	ማለዳ
earth (soil)	a·feur	አፈር
earthquake	yeu meu·ret meun·keut·keut	የመሬት መንቀጥቀጥ
east	məs·rak	ምስራቅ
easy	keul·lal	ቀላል
to eat	meub·lat	መብላት
economy	e·ko·no·mi	ኢኮኖሚ
editor	a·zeu·gaj	አዘጋጅ
education	təm·hərt	ትምህርት
election	mər·cha	ምርጫ
electricity	e·le·trik	ኤሌትሪክ
embarrassment	a·sa·fa·ri	አሳፋሪ
embassy	em·bas·si	ኤምባሲ
emergency	as·cheu·kwai	አስቸኳይ
employer	keu·ta·ri	ቀጣሪ
empty	ba·do	ባዶ
end	meu·cheu·reu·sha	መጨረሻ
engagement	meu·ta·cheut	መታጨት
engine	mo·teur	ሞተር
English	ən·gli·zə·nya	እንግሊዝኛ
to enjoy (oneself)	meu·deu·seut	መደሰት
enough	beu·ki	በቂ

| Enough!
beu·ka! | | በቃ! |

to enter	meug·bat	መግባት
envelope	en·veu·lop	ኤንቨሎ፡ፕ
environment (area)	a·ka·ba·bi	አካባቢ
epilepsy	yeu·mi·təl beu·sha·ta	የሚጥል በሽታ
equality	e·ku·la·neut	እኩልነት
equipment	ə·ka	እቃ
evening	ma·shat	ምሽት
every day	beu·yeu·keu·nu	በየቀኑ
example	ma·sa·le	ምሳሌ

| For example ...
leu ma·sa·le ... | | ለምሳሌ ... |

| to exchange | meu·leu·wa·weut | መለዋወጥ |
| exchange rate | yeu mə·nə·za·ri wa·ga | የምነዛሪ ዋጋ |

| Excuse me. yi·ḳər·ta | | ይቅርታ |

exit	meu·wə·cha	መውጫ
expensive	wədd	ውድ
express	feu·ṭan	ፈጣን
eye	ain	አይን

F

face	fit	ፊት
factory	fab·ri·ka	ፋብሪካ
family	be·teu·seub	ቤተሰብ
famous	zə·neu·nya	ዝነኛ
fans (of a team)	deu·ga·fi	ደጋፊ
far	ruḳ	ሩቅ
farm	ər·sha	እርሻ
farmer	geu·beu·re	ገበሬ
fast (speed)	feu·ṭan	ፈጣን
fat	weu·fram	ወፍራም
father	ab·bat	አባት
father-in-law	a·mat	አማት
fault (someone's)	ṭə·fat	ጥፋት
fear	fər·hat	ፍርሃት
feelings	sə·met	ስሜት
fence	a·ṭər	አጥር
festival	beu·al	በዓል
fever (temperature)	ta·ku·sat	ትኩሳት
few	tən·nish	ትንሽ
to have a fight	meu·ṭa·lat	መጣላት
to fill	meu·mu·lat	መሙላት
film	film • si·ni·ma	ፊልም • ሲኒማ
to find	mag·nyeut	ማግኘት
finger	ṭat	ጣት
to finish	meu·cheu·reus	መጨረስ
fire	ə'sat	እሳት
firewood	yeu ma·geu·do ən·cheut	የማገዶ እንጨት
first (name)	yeu meu·jeu·meu·ri·ya (səm)	የመጀመሪያ (ስም)
first-aid kit	yeu meu·jeu·meu·ri·ya ər·da·ta sa·ṭən	የመጀመሪያ እርዳታ ሳጥን
fish	a·sa	ዓሳ
flag	ban·di·ra	ባንዲራ
flashlight	yeu əj ba·tri	የእጅ ባትሪ
flea	ḳu·na·cha	ቁንጪ
floor	weu·leul	ወለል
floor (storey)	foḳ	ፎቅ
flour	du·ḳet	ዱቄት

flower	a·beu·ba	አበባ
flower seller	a·beu·ba shach	አበባ ሻጭ
fly	zəmb	ዝምብ
to follow	meu·keu·teul	መከተል
food	ma·gəb	ምግብ
foot	ə·gər	እግር
football (soccer)	ə·gər kwass	እግር ኳስ
foreign	ba·əd	ባዕድ
foreigner	yeu wə·ch a·geur sō	የውጭ አገር ሰው
forest	cha·ka	ጫካ
forever	leu·zeu·la·leum	ለዘላለም
to forget	meur·sat	መርሳት

> **I forget.**
> reu·sow   ረሳሁ

to forgive	yi·kər ma·leut	ይቅር ማለት
friend	gwa·deu·nya	ጓደኛ
full	mul·lu	ሙሉ
to have fun	meu·cha·wot	መጫወት
to make fun of/mock	ma·shof	ማሾፍ
funeral	keu·bər	ቀብር
future	weu·deu fit	ወደ ፊት

G

garage	ga·raj	ጋራጅ
garden	yat·kəlt bota	ያትክልት ቦታ
gate (entrance)	meug·bi·ya	መግቢያ
generally	ab·za·nya·wən gi·ze	አብዛኛውን ጊዜ
gift	sə·to·ta	ስጦታ
girl (child)	set ləj	ሴት ልጅ
to give	meus·teut	መስጠት

> **Could you give me ...?**
> ə·ba·kəsh ... sə·teuny? (m)   እባክህ ... ስጠኝ?
> ə·ba·kəsh ... sə·chəny? (f)   እባክሽ ... ስጭኝ?

glass (drinking)	bər·cha·ko	ብርጭቆ
glass (material)	meus·ta·wot	መስታወት
to go	meu·hed	መሄድ

> **Let's go.**
> ən·hid   እንሂድ

> **We'd like to go to ...**
> weu·deu ... meu·hed   ወደ ... መሄድ እንፈልጋለን
> ən·feul·lə·gal·leun

> **Go straight ahead.**
> beu keu·ţa·ta hid/hij/hi·du (m/f/pl)   በቀጥታ ሂድ/ሂጂ/ሂዱ

God (Christian)	əg·zya·ber • əg·zer	እግዚአብሔር • እግዜር
God (Muslim)	al·lah	አላህ

| good | tə·ru | ጥሩ |
| good hotel | tə·ru ho·tel | ጥሩ ሆቴል |

| Good afternoon.
ən·deu·mən walk/walsh (m/f) | | እንደምን ዋልክ/ዋልሽ |

| Good evening/night.
ən·deu·man a·meu·sheuh/
a·meu·sheush (m/f) | | እንደምን አመሸህ/አመሸሽ |

| Good health/Cheers!
leu·te·na·chən! | | ለጤናችን! |

| Good luck!
meul·kam ə·dəl! | | መልካም እድል! |

| Good morning.
ən·deu·mən ad·deurk/
ad·deursh (m/f) | | እንደምን አደርክ/
አደርሽ |

| Goodbye.
deu·na hun/hu·nyi/
hu·nu (m/f/pl) | | ደህና ሁን/ሁኚ/ሁኑ |

government	meun·gəst	መንግስት
grandchild	yeu ləj ləj	የልጅ ልጅ
grandfather	weund a·yat	ወንድ አያት
grandmother	set a·yat	ሴት አያት
grass	sar	ሣር
great	təl·ləķ • ta·laķ	ትልቅ • ታላቅ

| Great!
beu·tam tə·ru! | | በጣም ጥሩ! |

green	a·reun·gwa·de	አረንጓዴ
to grow	ma·deug	ማደግ
to guess	meu·geu·meut	መገመት
guide (person)	meu·ri	መሪ
guide dog	meu·ri wə·sha	መሪ ውሻ
guitar	gi·tar	ጊታር

H

hair	şeu·gur	ፀጉር
half	ga·mash	ግማሽ
hand	əj	እጅ
handbag	yeu əj por·sa	የእጅ ፖርሳ
handicrafts	yeu əj sə·ra·woch	የእጅ ስራዎች
handsome	meul·keu meul·kam	መልከ መልካም
happy	deu·sə·teu·nya	ደስተኛ

| Happy birthday!
meul·kam lə·deut! | | መልካም ልደት! |

| hard (substance) | ţeun·ka·ra | ጠንካራ |

hard (difficult)	keu·bad	ከባድ
to harass	mas·cheu·neuķ	ማስጨነቅ

Do you have ...?
... al·leuh? (m)　　　　　　... አለህ?
... al·leush? (f)　　　　　　... አለሽ?
... al·la·chu? (pl)　　　　　... አላችሁ?

I have ...
... al·leuny　　　　　　　　... አለኝ

I don't have ...
... yeul·leu·nyam　　　　　... የለኝም

he	əs·su	እሱ
head	rass	ራስ
health	ṭe·na	ጤና
to hear	meus·mat	መስማት
heat	mu·ķeut	ሙቀት
heavy	keu·bad	ከባድ

Hello.
ṭe·na yis·ṭəl·ləny　　　　ጤና ይስጥልኝ

Hello. (answering telephone)
al·lo　　　　　　　　　　　አሉ

helmet	hel·met	ሄልሜት
help (n)	ər·da·ta	እርዳታ
here	əz·zi	እዚህ
high school	hu·leut·teu·nya deu·reu·ja	ሁለተኛ ደረጃ
	təm·hərt bet	ትምህርት ቤት
hiking	yeu·gər gu·zo	የግር ጉዞ
hill	ko·reub·ta	ኮረብታ
to hire	meu·ķeu·ra·yeut	መከራየት
HIV	ech ai vi	ኤች አይ ቪ
holiday(s) (vacation)	yeu ə·reuft gi·ze	የዕረፍት ጊዜ
holiday(s)	beu'al • beu'a·loch	በዓል • በዓሎች
honey	mar	ማር
honeymoon	yeu cha·gu·la gi·ze	የጫጉላ ጊዜ
horrible	ya·mi·ya·seu·ķaķ	የሚያስፈራ
horse	feu·reus	ፈረስ
horse racing	ye feu·reus gəl·bi·ya	የፈረስ ግልቢያ
	wə·də·dər	ወድድር
hospital	hos·pi·tal	ሆስፒታል
hot	muķ	ሙቅ

I'm hot
mo·ķeuny　　　　　　　　ሞቀኝ

house	bet	ቤት
housework	yeu bet sə·ra	የቤት ስራ

ENGLISH – ETHIOPIAN AMHARIC

how	ən·det	እንዴት

How? ən·det?		እንዴት?
How much is it? sənt nõ?		ስንት ነው-?
How do I get to ...? weu·deu ... ən·det ə·he·dal·lõ?		ወደ ... እንዴት እሄዳለሁ-?
How do you say ...? ... ən·det nõ yeu·mi·bal·lõ?		... እንዴት ነው- የሚባለው-?

human rights	yeu sõ·woch neu·ṣa·neut	የሰዎች ነፃነት
hundred (one)	meu·to (and)	መቶ (አንድ)
to be hungry	meur·rab	መራብ
husband	bal	ባል

I

ice	beu·reu·do	በረዶ

I'm ill. a·mo·nyal		አሞኛል

immigration	i·mi·gə·re·shin	ኢምግሬሽን
important	as·feu·la·gi	አስፈላጊ

It's important. as·feu·la·gi nõ		አስፈላጊ ነው-
It's not important. as·feu·la·gi ai·deul·leum		አስፈላጊ አይደለም

in front of	fit leu fit	ፊት ለፊት
industry	in·dus·tri	ኢንዱስትሪ
inequality	meu·beu·la·leuṭ	መበላለጥ
to give an injection	meur·fe mõ·gat	መርፈ- መው-ጋት
injury	gu·dat	ጉዳት
insect	beu·reur·ro	በረሮ
inside	wəṣt	ው-ስጥ
insurance	was·tə·na	ዋስትና
interesting	yeu·mi·yas·deu·sət	የሚያስደስት
international	a·leum a·keuf	ዓለም አቀፍ
interview	ḳa·leu meu·ṭeu·yiḳ	ቃለ መጠይቅ
island	deu·set	ደሴት
itch	ə·keuk	እከክ
itinerary	yeu gu·zo pro·gram	የጉዞ ፕሮግራም

J

jealous	ḳeu·na·teu·nya	ቀናተኛ
jewellery	ge·ṭa geṭ	ጌጣ ጌጥ
job	sə·ra	ስራ

joke	ķeuld	ቀልድ
to joke	meu·ķeu·leud	መቀለድ
journalist	ga·ze·țeu·nya	ጋዜጠኛ
journey	gu·zo	ጉዞ
juice	cha·ma·ķi	ጭማቂ
to jump	meuz·leul	መዝለል
jumper (sweater)	shu·rab	ሹ·ራ·ብ
justice	fa·tah	ፍትህ

K

key	meuk·feu·cha • ķulf	መከፈቻ • ቁልፍ
to kill	meug·deul	መግደል
kilometre	ki·lo me·tar	ኪሎ ሜትር
kind	deug	ደግ
kindergarten	meu·wa·leu ha·șa·nat	መዋለ ሕፃናት
king	na·gus	ንጉስ
to kiss	meu·sam	መሳም
kitchen	weuț bet	ወጥ ቤት
knife	bi·la·wa	ቢላዋ
to know	ma·weuķ	ማወቅ

I know.
ow·ķal·lō — አው·ቃለ·

I don't know.
a·la·wa·ķam — አላው·ቅም

L

lake	haiķ	ሃይቅ
land	meu·ret	መሬት
last	meu·cheu·reu·sha	መጨረሻ
last month	ya·leu·fō weur	ያለፈው ወር
last night	ta·nan·ta·na ma·ta	ትናንትና ማታ
last week	ya·leu·fō sam·mant	ያለፈው ሳምንት
last year	ya·leu·fō a·meut	ያለፈው ዓመት

It's late.
reu·feu·deu — ረፈደ

to laugh	meu·saķ	መሳቅ
launderette	lown·deu·ri	ላውንደሪ
law	hag	ሕግ
lazy	seu·neuf	ሰነፍ
to learn	meu·mar	መማር
leather	ko·da	ቆዳ
left (not right)	ga·ra	ግራ
leg	a·ger	እግር
legal	ha·ga·wi	ሕጋዊ
lens	lens	ሌንስ

less	ya·neu·seu	ያነሰ
letter	deub·dab·be	ደብዳቤ
liar	wu·sheu·tam	ውሸታም
library	be·teu meu·ṣa·haf	ቤተ መጻሕፍ
to lie	meu·wa·sheut	መዋሸት
life	hi·wot	ሕይወት
light (weight)	ḳeul·lal	ቀላል
light (sun/lamp)	bər·han	ብርሃን
light bulb	am·pul	አምፑል
lighter	lai·teur • ma·ḳeu·ṭa·ṭeu·ya	ላይተር • ማቀጣጠያ
to like	meuw·deud	መው·ደድ
line	meus·meur	መስመር
lips	keun·feur	ከንፈር
to listen	ma·da·meuṭ	ማዳመጥ
little (small)	tən·nish	ትንሽ
a little (amount)	tən·nish	ትንሽ
to live (reside)	meu·nor	መኖር

Long live ...!
... leu·zeu·la·leum yi·nur! ... ለዘላለም ይኑር!

local	a·ka·ba·bi	አካባቢ
location	sə·fə·ra	ስፍራ
to lock	meu·ḳo·leuf	መቆለፍ
long	reu·jim	ረጅም
long distance	reu·jim rə·ḳeut	ረጅም ርቀት
to look	ma·yeut	ማየት
to look for	meu·feul·leug	መፈለግ
to lose	ma·ṭat	ማጣት
lost property	yeu·ṭeu·fa ə·ḳa	የጠፋ ዕቃ
to love	maf·keur	ማፍቀር
lover	fək·reu·nya	ፍቅረኛ
low (position)	zə·ḳə·teu·nya	ዝቅተኛ
luck	ə·dəl	እድል
lucky	ə·da·leu·nya	እድለኛ
lunch	mə·sa	ምሳ
lunchtime	yeu mə·sa seu'at	የምሳ ሰዓት

M

made (of)	yeu·teu·seu·row	የተሰራው
magazine	meu·ṣa·het	መጽሔት
mail	pos·ta	ፖስታ
mailbox	yeu pos·ta sa·ṭən	የፖስታ ሳጥን
to make	meus·rat	መስራት
make-up (cosmetics)	meu·kwa·kwa·ya	መኳኳያ
man	sō	ሰው
manager	sə·ra as·ki·yaj	ስራ አስኪያጅ
many	bə·zu	ብዙ

map	kar·ta	ካርታ

Can you show me on the map?
kar·tow lai ya·sa·yu·nyal? — ካርታው· ላይ ያሳይኛል?

marijuana	ma·ri·wa·na	ሚሪዋና
market	geu·bi·ya	ገቢያ
marriage	ga·be·cha	ጋብቻ
to marry	mag·bat	ማግባት
mass (church)	ke·da·se	ቅዳሴ
massage	meu·ta·sheut	መታሸት
mat	man·taf	ምንጣፍ
match(es)	ke·brit	ክብሪት

It doesn't matter.
ged yeul·leum — ግድ የለም

maybe	me·nal·bat	ምናልባት
medicine	meud·ha·nit	መድሃኒት
to meet	meu·geu·na·nyeut	መገናኘት
men	sō·woch	ሰዎች
menstruation	yeu weur a·beu·ba	የወር አበባ
menu	yeu me·geb zer·zer • me·nu	የምግብ ዝርዝር • ሜኑ
message	meul'əkt	መልእክት
metal	be·reut	ብረት
metre	me·ter	ሜትር
midnight	e·ku·leu le·lit	እኩለ ሌሊት
milk	weu·teut	ወተት
mind	a'ma·ro	አእምሮ
minute	deu·ki·ka	ደቂቃ

Just a minute.
and gi·ze — አንድ ጊዜ

mirror	meus·ta·weut	መስታወት
to miss	meu·na·feuk	መናፈቅ

I miss you.
e·na·fe·ke·hal·lō (m) — እናፍቅሃለሁ·
e·na·fe·ke·shal·lō (f) — እናፍቅሻለሁ·

mistake	se·ha·teut	ስህተት
to mix	meu·deu·ba·leuk	መደባለቅ
monastery	deu·ber	ደብር
money	geun·zeub	ገንዘብ
monk	meu·neu·ku·se	መነኩሴ
month	weur	ወር
in this month	beuz·zi weur	በዚህ ወር
monument	ha·welt	ሐወልት
moon	cheu·reu·ka	ጨረቃ
more (adj)	yi·beult	ይበልጥ
morning	teu·wat	ጠዋት
mosque	meus·gid	መስጊድ

mosquito net	yeu bim·bi meu·reub	የቢዛቢ መረብ
mother	ən·nat	እናት
mother-in-law	a·mat	አማት
motorcycle	mo·teur sai·kəl	ሞተር ሳይክል
mountain	teu·ra·ra	ተራራ
mouth	aff	አፍ
mud	chə·ka	ጭቃ
mum	ə·ma·ye	እማዬ
muscle	ṭun·cha	ጡንቻ
museum	be·teu meu·zeu·kər	ቤተ መዘክር
music	mu·zi·ka	ሙዚቃ
musician	mu·zi·keu·nya	ሙዚቀኛ
Muslim	əs·lam	እስላም

N

name	səm	ስም
national park	bə·he·ra·wi park	ብሔራዊ ፓርክ
nationality (citizen)	ze·gə·neut	ዜግነት
nature	teu·feu·tro	ተፈጥሮ
near	a·teu·geub	አጠገብ
necessary	as·feu·la·gi	አስፈላጊ
necklace	ha·bəl • yan·geut geṭ	ሐብል • ያንገት ጌጥ
needle and thread	meur·fe·na kər	መርፌና ክር
to need	meu·feul·leug	መፈለግ
net	meu·reub	መረብ
never	beu·chə·rash	በጭራሽ
new	ad·dis	አዲስ
news	ze·na	ዜና
newspaper	ga·ze·ṭa	ጋዜጣ
New Year	ad·dis a·meut	አዲስ ዓመት
next (adv)	keu·ṭə·lõ	ቀጥሎ
next month	yeu·mi·meu·ṭow weur	የሚመጣው· ወር
next to ...	keu ... a·teu·geub	ከ ... አጠገብ
next week	yeu·mi·meu·ṭow sam·mənt	የሚመጣው· ሳምንት
next year	yeu·mi·meu·ṭow a·meut	የሚመጣው· ዓመት
nice	ṭə·ru	ጥሩ
night	ma·ṭa	ማታ
no (it's not there)	yeul·leum	የለም
no (it isn't)	ai·deul·leum	አይደለም
noisy	cha·cha·ta	ጫጫታ
none	ma·nəm	ማንም
north	seu·men	ሰሜን
nose	a·fən·cha	አፍንጫ
notebook	deub·teur	ደብተር
nothing	mə·nəm	ምንም
not yet	geu·na nõ	ገና ነው·
now	a·hun	አሁን
nuclear bomb	yeu nyu·kə·ler bom	የኑ·ክለር ቦምብ

nuclear energy	yeu nyu·ko·ler hail	የኒዩ-ክሌር ሃይል
nun	meu·neu·ku·sit	መነኩሲት
nurse	neurs	ነርስ

O

obvious	gəlş	ግልፅ
ocean	wuk·ya·nos	ውቅያኖስ
office	bi·ro	ቢሮ
often	bə·zu gi·ze	ብዙ ጊዜ
oil (cooking)	zayt	ዘይት
oil (crude)	yal·teu·ţa·ra·zayt	ያልተጣራ ዘይት
OK	ə·shi	እሺ
on	lai	ላይ
old	a·ro·ge	አሮጌ
on time	beu seu'at	በሰዓት
one-way (ticket)	meu·he·ja bə·cha (ti·ket)	መሄጃ ብቻ (ትኬት)
only	bə·cha	ብቻ
open	kəft	ክፍት

It's open.		
kəft nō.		ክፍት ነው.

to open	meuk·feut	መክፈት
operator	o·pə·re·teur	ኦፐሬተር
opinion	ha·sab	ሃሳብ
opposite (opinion)	teu·ka·ra·ni	ተቃራኒ
opposite (prep)	fit leu fit	ፊት ለፊት
or	waym	ወይም
oral (medicine)	yeu·mi·waţ	የሚዋጥ
to order	ma·zeuz	ማዘዝ
ordinary	teu·ra	ተራ
to organise	ma·zeu·ga·jeut	ማደራጀት
organisation	ma·hə·beur	ማኅበር
original	wan·na	ዋና
original (adj)	yeu meu·jeu·meu·ri·ya	የመጀመሪያ
orphan	a·sa·da·gi yeu·le·lō ləj	አሳዳጊ የሌለው ልጅ
other	le·la	ሌላ
outside	wəch	ውጭ
over ...	beu ... lai	በ ... ላይ
owner	ba·leu·bet	ባለቤት

P

packet	pa·ko	ፓኮ
padlock	meu·ko·leu·fi·ya gan	መቆለፊያ ጋን
pagan	a·reu·ma·wi	አረማዊ
page	geuş	ገፅ
pain	wu·gat	ውጋት

painkillers	hə·meum yeu·mi·yas·ta·gəs	ህመም የሚያስታግስ
	meud·ha·nit	መድሃኒት
to paint	meu·keu·bat	መቀባት
painter (art)	seu·a·li	ሰዓሊ
painting (art)	sə·əl	ስዕል
palace	be·teu meun·gəst	ቤተ መንግስት
pan	meut·beu·sha	መጥበሻ
paper	weu·reu·keut	ወረቀት
parcel	tə·kəll	ጥቅል
parents	weu·la·joch	ወላጆች
park	meu·na·feu·sha bo·ta	መናፈሻ ቦታ
to park	ma·kom	ማቆም
party (fiesta)	gəb·zha	ግብዣ
passenger	meun·geu·deu·nya	መንገደኛ
passport	pass·port	ፓስፖርት
past	ya·leu·feu	ያለፈ
path	yeu·gər meun·geud	የጎር መንገድ
patient (adj)	te·gas·teu·nya	ትዕግስተኛ
to pay	meuk·feul	መክፈል
payment	kə·fə·ya	ክፍያ
peace	seu·lam	ሰላም
peak (mountain)	chaf	ጫፍ
pen (ballpoint)	əs·krip·to	እስክሪፕቶ
pencil	ər·sass	እርሳስ
penknife	seun·ti	ሰንጢ
pensioner	tu·reu·teu·nya	ጡረተኛ
people	sö·woch	ሰዎች
per cent	keu·meu·to	ከመቶ
performance	cheu·wa·ta	ጨዋታ
permanent	kwa·mi	ቋሚ
permission	feu·kad	ፈቃድ
person	sö	ሰው
personality	ba·hə·ri	ባህሪ
to perspire/sweat	ma·lab	ማላብ
petrol	ben·zin	ቤንዚን
pharmacy	far·ma·si • meud·ha·nit bet	ፋርማሲ • መድሃኒት ቤት
phone book	yeu səlk mow·cha	የስልክ ማውጫ
photo	fo·to	ፎቶ

May I take a photo?
fo·to man·sat yi·cha·lal?   ፎቶ ማንሳት ይቻላል?

to pick up	man·sat	ማንሳት
piece (bread)	ku·rash	ቁራሽ
pig	a·sa·ma	አሳማ
pillow	ta·rass	ትራስ
place	bo·ta	ቦታ
place of birth	yeu·tu·ləd bo·ta	የተወ-ልድ ቦታ
plain	leut ya·leu meu·ret	ለጥ ያለ መሬት
planet	a·leum	ዓለም

plant	teu·kəl	ተክል
to plant	meut·keul	መትከል
plate	sa·hən	ሳህን
plateau	am·ba	አምባ
platform	meud·reuk	መድረክ
play (theatre)	çheu·wa·ta • dra·ma	ጨዋታ • ድራማ
to play (a game)	meu·cha·wot	መጫወት
to play music	mu·zi·ka meu·cha·wot	ሙዚቃ መጫወት
to play cards	kar·ta meu·cha·wot	ካርታ መጫወት
plug (bath)	meud·feu·nya	መድፈኛ
to point	ma·meul·keut	ማመልከት
police	po·lis	ፖሊስ
politics	po·leu·ti·ka	ፖለቲካ
politician	po·leu·ti·keu·nya	ፖለቲከኛ
pollen	bə·nany	ብናኝ
poor	deu·ha	ደሃ
popular	həzb yeu·mi·weu·dō	ሕዝብ የሚወደው
possibly	mə·nal·bat	ምንልባት

It's (not) possible.
li·hon (ai·chəl·ləm)   ሊሆን (አይችልም)

postcard	post kard	ፖስት ካርድ
postage	tem·bər	ቴምብር
post office	pos·ta bet	ፖስታ ቤት
pottery	sheuk·la	ሽክላ
poverty	də·hə·neut	ድህነት
power	hail	ኃይል
power cut	yeu e·le·trik meu·kwa·reuṭ	የኤሌትሪክ መቋረጥ
prayer	ṣeu·lot	ፀሎት
prayer book	yeu ṣeu·lot meu·ṣə·haf	የፀሎት መጽሐፍ
to prefer	meu·mə·reuṭ	መምረጥ
to prepare	ma·zeu·ga·jeut	ማዘጋጀት
presenter (TV etc)	a·kə·ra·bi	አቅራቢ
president	prez·dant	ፕሬዝዳንት
pretty	kon·jo • wub	ቆንጆ • ውብ
price	wa·ga	ዋጋ
pride	ku·rat	ኩራት
priest	kess	ቄስ
prime minister	ṭeuk·lai mi·nis·tər	ጠቅላይ ሚኒስትር
prison	ə·sər bet	እስር ቤት
prisoner	əs·reu·nya	እስረኛ
private	yeu·gəl	የግል
promise	kal ki·dan	ቃል ኪዳን
proposal	ha·sab	ሐሳብ
prostitute	set a·da·ri	ሴት አዳሪ
to protect	meu·keu·la·keul	መከላከል
protest	teu·kow·mo	ተቃውሞ
to pull	meu·sab	መሳብ
to punish	meuk·tat	መቅጣት

pure	nə·suh	ንጹህ
to push	meug·fat	መግፋት
to put	mas·keu·meut	ማስቀመጥ

Q

qualifications	chə·lo·ta	ችሎታ
quality	ai·neut	አይነት
quarter	rub	ሩብ
queen	nə·gəst	ንግስት
question	tə·ya·ke	ጥያቄ
to question	meu·teu·yeuk	መጠየቅ
queue	teu·ra • seulf	ተራ • ሰልፍ
quick	keul·ţa·fa	ቀልጣፋ
quiet	şeuţ ya·leu	ጸጥ ያለ
to quit	meul·keuk	መልቀቅ

R

race (sport)	wə·də·dər	ውድድር
racism	zeu·reu·nyə·neut	ዘረኝነት
railway	yeu ha·did meun·geud	የሃዲድ መንገድ
railway station	ba·bur ţa·bi·ya	ባቡር ጣቢያ
rain	zə·nab	ዝናብ

| It's raining. | | |
| ə·yeu·zeu·neu·beu nō | እየዘነበ ነው· | |

rape	yeu weu·sib də·fə·reut	የወሲብ ድፍረት
rare	bərk	ብርቅ
rat	aiyţ	አይጥ
raw	ţə·re	ጥሬ
razor	yeu şim mə·laçh	የሺም ምላጭ
razor blades	mə·laçh	ምላጩ
to read	man·beub	ማንበብ
ready	zə·gə·ju	ዝግጁ
reason	mək·ni·yat	ምክንያት
receipt	deu·reu·seuny	ደረሰኝ
to receive	meu·keu·beul	መቀበል
recently	seu·mo·nun	ሰሞኑን
red	kai	ቀይ
Red Cross	kai meus·keul	ቀይ መስቀል
refrigerator	fri·ji • ma·keuz·keu·zha	ፍሪጅ • ማቀዝቀዣ
refugee	sə·deu·teu·nya	ስደተኛ
refund (money)	teu·meu·lash geun·zeub	ተመላሽ ገንዘብ
to refuse	əm·bi ma·leut	እምቢ ማለት
registered mail	ya·deu·ra deub·dab·be	ያደራ ደብዳቤ
to regret	meu·ko·çheut	መቆጨት
relationship (love)	yeu fə·kər gə·nu·nyə·neut	የፍቅር ግኑኝነት

relatives	zeu·meu·doch	ዘመዶች
religion	hai·ma·not	ሃይማኖት
to remember	mas·ta·weus	ማስታወስ
to rent	meu·keu·ra·yeut	መከራየት
to repair	meu·teu·geun	መጠገን
to repeat	meud·geum	መድገም
reservation	beu·kəd·mi·ya bo·ta	በቅድሚያ ቦታ
	mas·meuz·geub	ማስመዝገብ
respect	ak·bə·rot	አክብሮት
rest (relaxation)	ə·reuft	እረፍት
to rest	ma·reuf	ማረፍ
restaurant	ma·gəb bet	ምግብ ቤት
to retire	ţu·reu·ta mō·ţat	ጡረታ መውጣት
to return	meu·meul·leus	መመለስ
rice	ruz	ሩዝ
rich (wealthy)	hab·tam	ሃብታም
to ride (a horse)	meu·ga·leub	መጋለብ
right (correct)	tə·kə·kəl	ትክክል

You're right.
tə·kə·kəl neuh/neush (m/f)   ትክክል ነህ/ነሽ

right (not left)	keuny	ቀኝ
ring (on finger)	keu·leu·beut	ቀለበት
ring (of phone)	deu·weul	ደወል

I'll ring you.
ə·deu·wə·lal·lō   እደውላለሁ-

river	weunz	ወንዝ
road (main)	(wan·na) meun·geud	(ዋና) መንገድ
road map	yeu meun·geud kar·ta	የመንገድ ካርታ
to rob	meuz·reuf	መዝረፍ
rock	kwa·ţeny	ቋጥኝ
romance	fə·kər	ፍቅር
room	kə·fəl	ክፍል
room number	yeu kə·fəl ku·ţər	የክፍል ቁጥር
rope	geu·meud	ገመድ
round (adj)	kəb	ክብ
rubbish	wu·da·ķi/ķo·sha·sha	ዉዳቄ/ቆሻሻ
rug	yeu·gər mən·taf	የግር ምንጣፍ
ruins	fə·rash	ፍራሽ
rules	hə·goch	ሕጎች
to run	meu·roţ	መሮጥ

S

to be sad	ma·zeun	ማዘን
saint	ķə·dus	ቅዱስ
salary	deu·moz	ደሞዝ
salt	chō	ጨው-

same	and aiy·neut	አንድ አይነት
sand	a·sheu·wa	አሸዋ
sap	mu·cha	ሙጫ
to save (someone)	ma·dan	ማዳን
to say	ma·leut	ማለት
school	təm·hərt bet	ትምህርት ቤት
science	sə·neu fə·treut	ስነ ፍጥረት
scenery	yeu meu·ret a·keu·ma·meuṭ	የመሬት አቀማመጥ
scissors	meu·keuss	መቀስ
sea	ba·hər	ባሕር
seat	meu·keu·meu·cha	መቀመጫ
to see	ma·yeut	ማየት

We'll see!
ə·na·yal·leun!   እናያለን!

See you tomorrow.
neu·geu ə·nə·geu·na·nyal·leun   ነገ እንገናኛለን

selfish	ra·sun weu·dad	ራሱን ወዳድ
to sell	meu·sheuṭ	መሸጥ
to send	meu·lak	መላክ
sentence (words)	a·reuf·teu neu·geur	ዓረፍተ ነገር
to separate	meu·leu·yeut	መለየት
serious	a·sa·sa·bi	አሳሳቢ
service	a·geul·glot	አገልግሎት
several	an·dand	አንዳንድ
to sew	meus·fat	መስፋት
sex	yeu gə·breu sə·ga	የግብረ ስጋ
	gə·nu·nya·neut	ግኑኝነት
to have sex	yeu gə·breu sə·ga	የግብረ ስጋ
	gə·nu·nya·neut mad·reug	ግኑኝነት ማድረግ
safe sex	beu ṭan·ka·ḳe yeu·mi·deurg	በጥንቃቄ የሚደረግ
	yeu gə·breu sə·ga	የግብረ ስጋ ግኑኝነት
	gə·nu·nya·neut	
sexism	yeu ṣo·ta lə·yu·neut	የፆታ ልዩነት
shade	ṭə·la	ጥላ
shadow	ṭə·la	ጥላ
shape	kərṣ	ቅርጽ
to share (with)	meu·ka·feul	መካፈል
to shave	meu·la·cheut	መላጨት
she	əs·swa	እሷ
sheep	beug	በግ
sheet (bed)	yeu al·ga ləbs	ያልጋ ልብስ
shell	kər·fit	ቅርፊት
shelves	meu·deur·deu·ri·ya	መደርደሪያ
ship	meur·keub	መርከብ
to ship	beu meur·keub meu·lak	በመርከብ መላክ
shirt	sheu·miz	ሸሚዝ
shoes	cham·ma	ጫማ

to shoot	meu·teu·kos	መተኮስ
shop	suk	ሱቅ
to go shopping	suk meu·hed	ሱቅ መሄድ
short (length)	a·chər	አጭር
shorts	kum·ta	ቁምጣ
shoulders	tə·ke·sha	ትከሻ
to shout	meu·choh	መጮህ
show	zə·gə·jət	ዝግጅት
to show	ma·sa·yeut	ማሳየት

Can you show me on the map?
kar·tow lai ta·sa·yeu·nyal·leuh? (m) ካርታው ላይ ታሳየኛለህ?
kar·tow lai ta·sa·yi·nyal·leush? (f) ካርታው ላይ ታሳይኛለሽ?

shower	sha·weur • yeu kum	ሻወር • የቂም
	meu·ta·teu·bi·ya	መታጠቢያ
to shut	meuz·gat	መዝጋት
shy	ai·neu a·far	አይን አፋር
sick	beu·sha·teu·nya	በሽተኛ
sickness	hə·meum	ሕመም
side	gon	ጎን
sign	ma·lə·kət	ምልክት
to sign	meu·feu·reum	መፈረም
silk	harr	ሃር
similar	teu·meu·sa·sai	ተመሳሳይ
simple	keul·lal	ቀላል
since (May)	keu (may) weu·dih	ከ (ሜይ) ወዲህ
to sing	meuz·feun	መዝፈን
singer	zeu·fany	ዘፋኝ
single (unmarried	weun·deu la·te (m)	ወንደ ላጤ
person)	se·teu la·te (f)	ሴት ላጤ
sister	ə·hot	እህት
to sit	meu·keu·meut	መቀመጥ
size (room)	sə·fat	ስፋት
size (clothes/shoes)	lək	ልክ
skin	ko·da	ቆዳ
sky	seu·mai	ሰማይ
to sleep	meu·teu·nyat	መተኛት
slow/slowly	beu keu·sə·ta	በቀስታ
small	tən·nish	ትንሽ
smell	sha·ta	ሽታ
to smell	mash·teut	ማሽተት
to smile	feu·geug ma·leut	ፈገግ ማለት
to smoke	ma·cheus	ማጨስ
snow	beu·reu·do	በረዶ
soap	sa·mu·na	ሳሙና
soldier	weu·ta·deur	ወታደር
some	an·dand	አንዳንድ
someone	and·sõ	አንድ ሰው
something	and neu·geur	አንድ ነገር

sometimes	an·dand gi·ze	እንዳንድ ጊዜ
son	weund ləj	ወንድ ልጅ
soon	beu·ḵər·bu	በቅርቡ

I'm sorry.
az·nal·lō. አዝናለሁ·

south	deu·bub	ደቡብ
souvenir	mas·ta·weu·sha	ማስታወሻ
to speak	meu·na·geur	መናገር
special	lə·yu	ልዩ
specialist	ba·leu mu·ya	ባለ ሙ·ያ
speed	fəṭ·neut	ፍጥነት
speed limit	yeu fəṭ·neut weu·seun	የፍጥነት ወሰን
spicy (hot)	beur·beu·re yeu·beu·za·beut	በርበሬ የበዛበት
sport	sport	ስፖርት
stage	meud·reuk	መድረክ
stamps	tem·bər	ቴምብር
standard (usual)	yeu·teu·leu·meu·deu	የተለመደ
standard of living	yeu·nu·ro deu·reu·ja	የኑሮ ደረጃ
stars	ko·keu·boch	ኮከቦች
to start	meu·jeu·meur	መጀመር
station	ṭa·bi·ya	ጣቢያ
to stay (remain)	meu·ḵo·yeut	መቆየት
to steal	meus·reuḵ	መስረቅ
stomach	hod	ሆድ
stomachache	hod ḵur·ṭeut	ሆድ ቁርጠት
stone	dən·gai	ድንጋይ
stoned (drugged)	beu drag	በድራግ የደነዘዘ
	yeu·deu·neu·zeu·zeu	
to stop	ma·ḵom	ማቆም

Stop!
ḵum! ቁም!

storm	ow·lo neu·fass	አውሎ ነፋስ
story	ta·rik	ታሪክ
stove	mə·də·ja	ምድጃ
strange	yal·teu·leu·meu·deu	ያልተለመደ
stranger	ən·gə·da	እንግዳ
street	meun·geud	መንገድ
strength	hail	ኃይል
string	si·ba·go	ሲባጎ
strong	ṭeun·ka·ra	ጠንካራ
student	teu·ma·ri	ተማሪ
suburb	seu·feur	ሰፈር
success	yeu sə·ra meu·sa·kat	የስራ መሳካት
to suffer	meu·seu·ḵa·yeut	መሰቃየት
sugar	sək·war	ስኳር
sun	ṣeu·hai	ፀሐይ
sunset	yeu ṣeu·hai meug·bat	የፀሐይ መግባት

sunrise	yeu şeu·hai mō·tat	የፀሃይ መውጣት
sunglasses	yeu şeu·hai meu·neu·şər	የፀሃይ መነፅር
sure	ər·gə·teu·nya	እርግጠኛ
surname	yeu meu·cheu·reu·sha səm	የመጨረሻ ስም
sweet	ţa·faç	ጣፋጭ
to swim	meu·wa·nyeut	መዋኘት
swimming pool	meu·wa·nya	መዋኛ
syringe	sə·rinj	ስሪንጅ

T

table	ţeu·reu·pe·za	ጠረጴዛ
to take	mō·seud	መውሰድ
to talk	mow·rat	ማውራት
tall	reu·jim	ረጅም
tasty	ţə·ru ţa'əm ya·lō	ጥሩ ጣዕም ያለው
tax	keu·reut	ቀረጥ
taxi stand	tak·si ma·ko·mi·ya	ታክስ ማቆሚያ
teacher	as·teu·ma·ri	አስተማሪ
teeth	ţərs	ጥርስ
telephone	səlk	ስልክ
to telephone	səlk meu·deu·weul	ስልክ መደወል
to tell	meun·geur	መንገር
tent pegs	meu·kon·ţeu·cha	መቆንጠጫ
test	mu·keu·ra	ሙከራ
to thank	ma·meus·geun	ማመስገን

| Thank you. | |
| a·meu·seu·gə·nal·lō | አመሰግናለሁ· |

they	ən·neus·su	እነሱ
thin	keu·çhon	ቀጭን
to think	ma·seub	ማሰብ
third	sos·teu·nya	ሶስተኛ
thought	ha·sab	ሃሳብ
throat	gu·ro·ro	ጉሮሮ
ticket	ti·ket	ትኬት
ticket office	yeu ti·ket bi·ro	የትኬት ቢሮ
tide	mo·geud	ሞገድ
tight (shoes/clothes)	ţeu·bab	ጠባብ
time	gi·ze	ጊዜ
timetable	yeu gi·ze seu·le·da	የጊዜ ሰሌዳ
tip (money)	gur·sha	ጉርሻ
tired	deu·ka·ma	ደካማ
today	za·re	ዛሬ
together	and lai	አንድ ላይ
toilet paper	soft	ሶፍት
toilet	shənt bet	ሽንት ቤት
tomorrow	neu·geu	ነገ
tonight	za·re ma·ta	ዛሬ ሌሊት

ENGLISH – ETHIOPIAN AMHARIC

too (as well) (use as suffix attached to subject)	-m	-ም

(She) too.
(əs·swa)m   እሷም

toothbrush	yeu ters bu·resh	የጥርስ ብርሽ
torch	yeu əj ba·tri	የእጅ ባትሪ
to touch	meun·kat	መንካት
tourist information office	yeu tu·rist bi·ro	የቱሪስት ቢሮ
towel	fo·ta	ፎጣ
track (path)	yeu·gər meun·geud	የእግር መንገድ
traffic	tra·fik	ትራፊክ
traffic lights	yeu tra·fik meub·rat	የትራፊክ መብራት
train	ba·bur	ባቡር
train station	ba·bur ta·bi·ya	ባቡር ጣቢያ
to translate	meu·teur·gom	መተርጎም
to travel	meu·gwaz	መንዛ
tree	ba·hər zaf	ባህር ዛፍ
trousers	su·ri	ሱሪ

It's true.
əw·neut nō   እውነት ነው።

to trust	ma·meun	ማመን
truth	hak	ሐቅ
to try	meu·mo·keur	መሞከር

Turn left.
weu·deu gra ta·teuf/   ወደ ግራ ታጠፍ/
ta·teu·fi (m/f)   ታጠፊ

Turn right.
weu·deu keuny ta·teuf/   ወደ ቀኝ ታጠፍ/
ta·teu·fi (m/f)   ታጠፊ

TV	ti·vi	ቲቪ
twice	hu·leutt gi·ze	ሁለት ጊዜ
typical	ai·neu·teu·nya	አይነተኛ
tyre	gom·ma	ጎማ

U

umbrella	jan·tə·la	ጃንጥላ

Do you understand?
geub·bah? (m)   ገባህ?
geub·bash? (f)   ገባሽ?

I understand.
geu·bany   ገባኝ

I don't understand.
al·geu·ba·nyəm   አልገባኝም

unemployed	sə·ra feut	ስራ ፈት
unemployment	sə·ra a·tə·neut	ስራ አጥነት
union	ma·hə·beur	ማኅበር
university	yu·ni·vers·ti	ዩኒቨርስቲ
unsafe	a·deu·geu·nya	አደገኛ
until (June)	əs·keu (jun) də·reus	እስከ (ጁን) ድረስ
uphill	a·ķeu·beut	አቀበት
urgent	as·cheu·kwai	አስቸኳይ
useful	ţeu·ķa·mi	ጠቃሚ

V

vaccination	kə·tə·bat	ክትባት
valuable	keuf ya·leu wa·ga yal·lō	ከፍ ያለ ዋጋ ያለው
vegetable	at·ķəlt	አትክልት
vegetarian	at·ķəlt bə·cha yeu·mi·beu·la	አትክልት ብቻ የሚበላ

I'm vegetarian.
sə·ga al·beu·lam   ስጋ አልበላም

very	beu·tam	በጣም
village	meun·deur	መንደር
virus	vai·reus	ቫይረስ
visa	vi·za	ቪዛ
to visit	meu·go·bə·nyeut	መጎብኘት
voice	dəmş	ድምፅ
to vote	yeu mər·cha dəmş meus·ţeut	የምርጫ ድምፅ መስጠት

W

Wait!
ķoyl/ķo·yi! (m/f)   ቆይ/ቆዪ!

waiter	a·sa·la·fi	አሳላፊ
waiting room	ma·reu·fi·ya kə·fəl	ማረፊያ ክፍል
to walk	beu·gər meu·hed	በግር መሄድ
wall	gəd·gəd·da	ግድግዳ
to want	meu·feul·leug	መፈለግ
war	ţor·neut	ጦርነት
to wash (something)	ma·ţeub	ማጠብ
to wash (oneself)	geu·la meu·ţa·ţeub	ገላ መታጠብ
watch (wrist)	yeu əj seu'at	የእጅ ሰዓት
to watch	meu·meul·keut	መመልከት
water	wu·ha	ውሃ
water bottle	yeu wu·ha ţeur·mus	የውሃ ጠርሙስ
waterfall	fwa·fwa·te	ፏፏቴ
way	meun·geud	መንገድ

Which way?
beu·yeut beu·kul?   በየት በኩል?

| we | ə·nya | እኛ |

to wear	meul·beus	መልበስ
wedding	seurg	ሠርግ
week	sam·mənt	ሳምንት
this week	beuz·zi sam·mənt	በዚህ ሳምንት
weekend	kə·da·me na əhud	ቅዳሜና እሁድ
to weigh	meu·meu·zeun	መመዘን
weight	kəb·deut	ክብደት
welcome	ən·kwan deu·na meu·tu	እንኳን ደህና መጡ
well	yeu wu·ha gud·gwad	የውሃ ጉድጓድ
west	me'ə·rab	ምዕራብ
wet	ər·ṭəb	እርጥብ
what	mən	ምን

What's he saying?
mən·dən nō yeu·mil·lō?   ምንድነው· የሚለው-?

What time is it?
sənt seu'at nō?   ስንት ሰዓት ነው-?

| when | meu·che | መቼ |

When does it leave?
meu·che yi·neu·sal?   መቼ ይነሳል?

| where | yeut | የት |

Where's the bank?
ban·ku yeut nō?   ባንኩ የት ነው-?

| white | neuch | ነጭ |
| who | man | ማን |

Who is it?
man nō?   ማን ነው-?

Who are they?
ə·neu·man na·chō?   እነማን ናቸው-?

whole (n)	mu·lu	ሙሉ
why	leu·mən	ለምን
wide	seuf·fi	ሰፊ
wife	mist	ሚስት
to win	ma·sheu·neuf	ማሸነፍ
wind	neu·fass	ነፋስ
window	meus·kot	መስኮት
wire	shi·bo	ሽቦ
to wish	meu·meu·nyeut	መመኘት
with	keu … gar	ከ … ጋር
with my friend	keu gwa·deu·nya·ye gar	ከጓደኛዬ ጋር
within	beu … wəṣṭ	በ … ውስጥ
within (an hour)	beu (and seu'at) wəṣṭ	በ (አንድ ሰዓት) ውስጥ

I'll return within (one year).
beu (and a·meut) wəṣṭ   በ (አንድ አመት)
ə·meul·leu·sal·lō   ውስጥ እመለሳለሁ-

without	ya·leu	ያለ
woman	set	ሴት
women	se·toch	ሴቶች
wood	ən·cheut	እንጨት
word	kal	ቃል
to work	meus·rat	መስራት
world	a·leum	ዓለም
World Cup	yeu a·leum wan·cha	የዓለም ዋንጫ
to worry	mas·seub	ማሰብ
worship	mam·leuk	ማምለክ
worth	te·kəm	ጥቅም
wound	ku·səl	ቁስል
to write	meu·saf	መጻፍ
writer	şeu·ha·fi	ፀሃፊ
wrong	sə·hə·teut	ስህተት

Y

year	a·meut	ዓመት
this year	beuz·zi a·meut	በዚህ ዓመት
yes	ow	አዎ
yesterday	te·nan·te·na	ትናንትና
yet	geu·na	ገና
you (m/f)	an·teu • an·chi	አንተ • አንቺ
you (pol)	ər·swo	እርስዎ
young	weu·tat	ወጣት

Z

zebra	yeu me·da a·hə·ya	የሜዳ አህያ

INDEX

263

SUSTAINABLE TRAVEL

As the climate change debate heats up, the matter of sustainability becomes an important part of the travel vernacular. In practical terms, this means assessing our impact on the environment and local cultures and economies – and acting to make that impact as positive as possible. Here are some basic phrases to get you on your way …

COMMUNICATION & CULTURAL DIFFERENCES

I'd like to learn some of your local dialects.

yeu·nan·teun ha·geur	የናንተን ሃገር
ku·wan·ku·wa·woch	ቋንቋዎች
meu·mar 'ə·feu·lə·ga·leu·hu	መማር እፈልጋለሁ

Would you like me to teach you some English?

tə·nəsh 'ən·gli·zeu·nya	ተንሽ እንግሊዘኛ
'ən·das·teum·rəh	እንዳስተምርህ
tə·feu·lə·ga·leuh?	ትፈልጋለህ?

Is this a local or national custom?

yəh yeu·ha·geu·ru	ይህ የሃገሩ
ba·həl neuw?	ባህል ነው?

I respect your customs.

ba·hə·lach·hun	ባህላችሁን
'a·keub·ra·leu·hu	አከብራለሁ

COMMUNITY BENEFIT & INVOLVEMENT

What sorts of issues is this community facing?

yeu·zih həb·reu·teu·seub	የዚህ ህብረተሰብ
chəg·roch mən·dən	ችግሮች ምንድን
na·cheuw?	ናቸው?

border conflict	yeu·dən·beur	የድንበር
	gə·chat	ግጭት
illiteracy	dən·kur·na	ድንቁርና
media control	yeu·mi·di·ya	የሚዲያ
	weu·geun·teu·nya·neut	ወገንተኛነት

political unrest	yeu·po·leu·ti·ka	የፖለቲካ
	keu·was	ቀውስ
poverty	də·hə·neut	ድህነት
religious conflict	yeu·hai·ma·not	የሃይማኖት
	gə·chət	ግጭት

I'd like to volunteer my skills to this community.

ya·hən hab·reu·teu·seub	ይህን ህብረተሰብ
beu·'əw·keu·te	በእውቀቴ
ma·geul·geul	ማገልገል
'ə·feu·lə·ga·leu·hu	እፈልጋለሁ

Are there any volunteer programs available in the area?

beu·zih hab·reu·teu·seub	በዚህ ህብረተሰብ
wəst yeu·beu·go	ውስጥ የበጎ
feu·ka·deuny·neut	ፈቃደኝነት
ma·hə·beu·rat 'al·lu?	ማህበራት አለ?

ENVIRONMENT

Where can I recycle this?

| yah·nən yeut ri·sai·kəl | ይህንን የት ሪሳይክል |
| ma·də·reug 'əch·la·leu·hu? | ማድረግ እችላለሁ? |

TRANSPORT

Can we get there by public transport?

| 'ə·zi·ya beu·ow·to·bis | እዚያ በአውቶቢስ |
| meu·hed 'ən·cha·la·leun? | መሄድ እንችላለን? |

Can we get there by bicycle?

| 'ə·zi·ya beu·bəs·kə·let | እዚያ በብስክሌት |
| meu·hed 'in·cha·la·leun? | መሄድ እንችላለን? |

I'd prefer to walk there.

| beu·'ə·gər meu·gu·waz | በእግር መንዝ |
| 'ə·meur·ta·leu·hu | እመርጣለሁ |

ACCOMMODATION

I'd like to stay at a locally run hotel.

beu·'a·ka·ba·biw	በአካባቢ·ው
yeu·mi·teu·da·deur ho·tel	የሚተዳደር ሆቴል
meu·kə·reum	መክረም
'ə·feu·lə·ga·leu·hu	እፈልጋለሁ

Can I turn the air conditioning off and open the window?

'a·yeur ma·keuz·keu·zhown	አየር ማቀዝቀዣውን
'a·tə·fə·che meus·ko·tun	አጥፍቼ መስኮቱን
meuk·feut 'əch·la·leu·hu?	መክፈት እችላለሁ?

Are there any ecolodges here?

'e·ko·ko·te·joch	ኤኮ·ኮቴጆች
'al·lu?	አሉ?

There's no need to change my sheets.

yeu·nen kə·fəl	የኔን ክፍል
'an·so·la·woch	አንሶላዎች
meu·keu·yeur	መቀየር
'a·yas·feu·lə·gəm	አያስፈልግም

SHOPPING

Where can I buy locally produced goods/souvenirs?

yeu·'a·ka·ba·bi·wən	የአካባቢ·ውን
yeu·ba·həl 'ə·ka yeut	የባህል እቃ የት
'a·geu·nya·leu·hu?	አገኛለሁ?

Is this made from animal skin?

yəh keu·'ən·seu·sa ko·da	ይህ ከእንስሳ ቆዳ
yeu·teu·seu·ra neuw?	የተሰራ ነው?

Which forest is this sourced from?

keu·yeut·nyow	ከየትኛው
deun neuw	ደን ነው
yeu·mi·meu·neu·cheuw?	የሚመነጨው?

SUSTAINABLE TRAVEL

FOOD

Do you sell ...?	... tə·sheu·ṭa·la·chə·hu?	... ትሸጣላችሁ?
locally produced food	beu·'a·ka·ba·bi·wə yeu·teu·zeu·ga·jeu mə·gəb neuw	በአካባቢ·ው የተዘጋጀ ምግብ ነው
organic produce	'or·ga·nik mə·rət neuw	ኦርጋኒክ ምርት ነው

Can you tell me what traditional foods I should try?

yeu·tə·nyo·chun	የትኞቹን
yeu·ba·həl mə·gə·boch	የባሀል ምግቦች
'ənd·ḳeum·sa·cheuw	እንድቀምሳቸው
tə·meu·kə·reu·nya·leuh?	ትመክረኛለህ?

SIGHTSEEING

Does your company ...?	yeu·nan·teu də·rə·jət ...?	የናንተ ድርጅት ...?
donate money to charity	leu·beu·go 'ad·ra·got geun·zeub yə·cheu·ral	ለበጎ አድራጎት ገንዘብ ይቸራል
hire local guides	teu·weu·laj gai·do·chən yə·ḳeu·ṭə·ral	ተወላጅ ጋይዶችን ይቀጥራል
visit local businesses	'a·ka·ba·bi beu·ḳeul yeu·go·jo 'in·dus·tə·ri·wo·chən yə·go·beu·nyal	አካባቢ· በቀል የነጆ ኢንዱስትሪ ዎችን ይነበኛል

Are cultural tours available?

| ba·həl neuk gu·bəny·toch 'al·lu? | ባህል-ነክ ጉብኝቶች አሉ? |

NOTES

don't just stand there, say something!

o see the full range of our language products, go to:

lonelyplanet.com

What kind of traveller are you?

A. You're eating chicken for dinner *again* because it's the only word you know.

B. When no one understands what you say, you step closer and shout louder.

C. When the barman doesn't understand your order, you point frantically at the beer.

D. You're surrounded by locals, swapping jokes, email addresses and experiences
– other travellers want to borrow your phrasebook or audio guide.

If you answered A, B, or C, you NEED Lonely Planet's language products ...

- **Lonely Planet Phrasebooks** – for every phrase you need in every language
you want

- **Lonely Planet Language & Culture** – get behind the scenes of English as it's
spoken around the world – learn and laugh

- **Lonely Planet Fast Talk & Fast Talk Audio** – essential phrases for short trips and
weekends away – read, listen and talk like a local

- **Lonely Planet Small Talk** – 10 essential languages for city breaks

- **Lonely Planet Real Talk** – downloadable language audio guides from
lonelyplanet.com to your MP3 player

... and this is why

- **Talk to everyone everywhere**
Over 120 languages, more than any other publisher

- **The right words at the right time**
Quick-reference colour sections, two-way dictionary, easy pronunciation,
every possible subject – and audio to support it

Lonely Planet Offices

Australia
90 Maribyrnong St, Footscray,
Victoria 3011
☎ 03 8379 8000
fax 03 8379 8111
✉ talk2us@lonelyplanet.com.au

USA
150 Linden St, Oakland,
CA 94607
☎ 510 250 6400
fax 510 893 8572
✉ info@lonelyplanet.com

UK
2nd floor, 186 City Rd
London EC1V 2NT
☎ 020 7106 2100
fax 020 7106 2101
✉ go@lonelyplanet.co.uk

lonelyplanet.com